Physical Education Instructional Techniques

PHYSICAL EDUCATION INSTRUCTIONAL TECHNIQUES

An Individualized Humanistic Approach

HELEN M. HEITMANN
University of Illinois, Chicago Circle

MARIAN E. KNEER
University of Illinois, Chicago Circle

PRENTICE-HALL, INC.
Englewood Cliffs, New Jersey

Library of Congress Cataloging in Publication Data

HEITMANN, HELEN M
Physical education instructional techniques.

Includes bibliographies and index.
1. Physical education and training.   I. Kneer,
Marian E., joint author.   II. Title.
GV341.H543   613.7   75-22475
ISBN 0-13-668251-0

10 9 8 7 6 5 4 3 2

PRENTICE-HALL INTERNATIONAL, INC., *London*
PRENTICE-HALL OF AUSTRALIA, PTY. LTD., *Sydney*
PRENTICE-HALL OF CANADA, LTD., *Toronto*
PRENTICE-HALL OF INDIA PRIVATE LIMITED, *New Delhi*
PRENTICE-HALL OF JAPAN, INC., *Tokyo*
PRENTICE-HALL OF SOUTHEAST ASIA (PTE.) LTD., *Singapore*

TO THE 10,000 STUDENTS
WHO TAUGHT US

Contents

Preface

The authors have spent twenty years instructing high school students in physical education. The schools differed in size, community setting, and facilities. During this time we became interested in the phenomena that caused some students to learn while others, experiencing the same environment, became discipline problems and unintentional or intentional nonlearners. We also had an opportunity to observe many physical education teachers and noted their successes and failures with various classes or students.

Each teacher and student brought into the gymnasium a variety of characteristics. Some found congruence, and learning took place; others were in disharmony, contributing to negative or nonproductive experiences. The seemingly common environment provided by a common lesson was external only. The internal environment experienced by each student was different. For some, the common lesson was boring; for others, stimulating; for still others, perhaps, threatening.

In order to reduce the disharmony between the diverse needs of students and the lessons offered them, we experimented with a variety of patterns for teaching and learning. At times homogeneous groups were formed by administrative arrangement, other times flexible groups within heterogeneous classes were constructed. Opportunities to select activities and levels of achievement were tried. Also teaching patterns were varied. Each of these experiments had successes and failures. The problem then reduced itself to: how could each student be free of the needs of other students in a class and receive instruction that would be productive for that student? Individualized instruction seemed to be the answer.

We note the same problems when trying to teach a class by a single common method in the university professional preparation program. Hence, individualized instruction seems here, too, to be the answer. Over the past several years a variety of ways of individualizing instruction have been tried. These have ranged from the contract systems and competency-based instruction to allowing the student complete freedom to design his own program. The system that has evolved is the one presented in this book. It has been field-tested in college activity courses for the general university student and physical education majors, with co-ed and single-sex classes, in theory courses, and with many high school and elementary classes in suburban, urban, inner city, and rural settings. The teaching has been done both by the authors and by other teachers, who through our graduate courses or our workshops, became interested in the system and successfully implemented it in their own classes.

Formal evaluation of the learning product and of student satisfaction has yielded high acceptance. Student achievement gain is equivalent to that of class-directed, teacher-controlled instruction. But the significant achievement is its ability to improve student satisfaction and the student's ability to learn how to learn.

Individualized instruction, simply stated, is choosing and making available whatever the student needs to pursue learning in a relevant and productive manner. For some it may be a very structured and other-directed environment. For others it may be only to point the way so the student can be self-directed. Hence, the environment is student-centered rather than class-centered.

Techniques suggested herein are being used in subjects other than physical education in some schools. We believe that through individualized learning the student will find more relevance, motivation, and success in education. As success is achieved, the student's self-esteem is improved. The goal of education is directed toward increasing the student's self-actualization. The teacher utilizing the humanistic approach works with each student as an individual bringing out the unique talents of that student.

The format of this book also uses the components of the individualized approach. Each reader brings a unique background to this moment when this book is being studied. The input material is broad. The readers will find that they can delete or augment reading or involvement tasks according to their need.

The diagnosis exercises will give some direction to the areas in which the reader may wish to concentrate. It should be remembered, however, that diagnostic tools are not infallible and some compensation should be made by the reader's good judgment. It is assumed that the burden of learning falls to both the student *and* the teacher. The student has the responsibility of seriously following the tenets of involvement. The teacher must set the learning environment that will be conducive to the student's mode of learning.

Learning necessitates involvement; so we suggest activities that will expand on the written words and/or clarify the points made. Furthermore, involvement allows the learner to experience knowledge firsthand. The reader should select those activities most helpful in learning the material. Since the conference stage is part of the individualized approach, students are encouraged to confer with their teachers.

The behavioral objectives identified are but minimum standards of performance. The global or behavioral objectives for any teacher is to cause learning to occur. This learning should be maximized to the student's potential. Often we underteach; or, by setting a specific goal, we cause students to assume that goal to be the ultimate and so they do not seek higher levels of competency.

It is hoped that this teaching model will help teachers bridge the gap between theory and practice. Not everything a student of teaching needs to know is contained herein. Each chapter suggests additional reading to broaden competency in understanding the process and the basic theory. The student of teaching must know all the components inherent in learning. Much of this can be read, but the teacher must be able to put it into practice. It is hoped that the reader will practice teaching—shifting styles, observing students, and evaluating the product and process in regard to individual students—in order to become an effective facilitator of learning for all pupils.

We are most grateful to our many teacher-students who have helped by questioning and trying the process and by encouraging us to continue to seek the answers with them. Also, to our many student teachers who encouraged us to seek more relevant ways to help them prepare themselves to bring more stimulating education to their future students, we express our gratitude. We also appreciate the encouragement and latitude given us by our administrators and colleagues to pursue our own ideas. Specific acknowledgment and appreciation is given to Eleanor Blyden for her faithful and untiring typing of the manuscript.

Helen M. Heitmann

Marian E. Kneer

Physical Education Instructional Techniques

PART I

WHAT'S INVOLVED

1

Rationale for Individualized Humanistic Instruction

INSTRUCTIONAL UNIT FOR CHAPTER 1
Learner's Diagnosis

Directions: Read the questions below. Write out, discuss, or mentally review the answers. If you believe that you know the information, check the "yes" column. If you are not sure of the answer, check the "no" column. After reading the questions and deciding your knowledge, check the accuracy of your answers by reading the summary at the end of this chapter. If you answered a question incorrectly, change your answer to the appropriate column.

Can you

Yes	No	Questions
		1. Identify the characteristics of class-oriented instrucstruction versus individualized instruction?
		2. Define individuation?
		3. Differentiate between an individualized approach and an individualized humanistic approach?
		4. Explain the goals of humanistic instruction?
		5. See reasons why learning how to learn is an important goal of education?
		6. Identify various philosophies and objectives of education and physical education that have prevailed through the century?
		7. Identify differences in teaching approaches that fostered the prevailing objectives of education and physical education?
		8. State the current philosophy and objectives of education and their implication for physical education instruction?

Yes	No	Questions
		9. State the differences in the roles of students and teachers between a class-oriented and an individual-oriented approach?
		10. Recite the goals of physical education as stated by the American Alliance for Health, Physical Education, and Recreation and explain their implications for instruction?
		11. Identify factors contributing to the student's learning some knowledge and skill, yet learning more not to like the activity?
		12. Explain the premises upon which the authors base the individualized humanistic approach to teaching physical education?

Suggested Prescription

Directions: Count the number of checks you have placed in the "yes" column. When the percentages are determined, you may increase your knowledge and skill by using the suggested Learning Program activities recommended in the Input and Practice columns. Input and practices not listed offer additional learning options.

Results	Input	Practice
More than 80%	#1, 4	#2, 3, 5
60% to 80%	#1, 2, 3 or 4	#1, 3, 5
40% to 60%	#1, 2, 3 or 4, 5	#1, 2, 3, 5
Less than 40%	#1, 2, 3 or 4, 5, 8	#1, 2, 3, 4, 5

Learning Program

Directions: The conclusions and implementation processes suggested by the authors have arisen from a specific philosophical rationale. It is important for the reader to understand this rationale and its implications for organizing learning environments. To facilitate this understanding, this learning program provides *input* and *practice* experiences. The reader may do any or all of the Input or Practice suggestions or devise others depending upon previous knowledge of the philosophical bases of this teaching approach.

Proposed Learning Objective: The learner will be able to discuss student-oriented education (individualized humanistic instruction) versus "class" or group-oriented education relative to the premise, outcomes, and the implications for the teacher and student roles and the process of instruction.

Input:

*1. Read Chapter 1 of this book.
   2. Read selected references from the bibliography at the end of this chapter.
   3. Observe several physical education classes in session taught by different teachers. Identify incidences, in percent of time or number of occasions, when the teacher utilized an individualized approach versus a collective, traditional approach. Write or discuss the conclusions you would draw relative to the learning outcomes.
   4. Visit an individualized approach school and interview the teachers, administrators, and students concerning the advantages and disadvantages of the system.
   5. Administer a questionnaire or opinionnaire designed to determine the opinions of various age groups (adults and students) on the teaching methods they experienced in physical education and the usefulness of what they were taught.
      Suggestions: The questions may be asked in the supermarket, street corner, or other gathering places of a cross section of people. The answers can be recorded on tape in an interview fashion or they may be pencil and paper responses. Respondents may be asked (1) to rank physical education in relationship to other school subjects, (2) to identify which sports they learned in school that they are now using, (3) to indicate how competent they feel they are in various skill levels, (4) to tell how the physical education teacher

*Highly recommended.

acted toward them, (5) to indicate how much individual attention they received in class.

Analyze the results in regard to the implications for instructional methods. A second population can be questioned, such as people participating in a YMCA or Park District program, to determine if they experienced a different physical education program in the schools.

6. Review teaching methods books written for physical education instruction from the 1940's to the 1970's. How do these authors accommodate individual differences?
7. Observe a film explaining individualized instruction.
8. Design an *input* experience of your own.

Practice:

1. Write out a philosophy of physical education which reflects an individualized humanistic approach to teaching. Write a philosophy of physical education which would reflect a traditional class (class-oriented, teacher-directed) approach to education. Contrast the two. Discuss these philosophies with another student or your teacher.
2. Write an anecdotal summary of those things you liked most and least about the teaching methods you experienced in a gymnasium class. Identify which events were humanistically oriented and which left you anonymous. Discuss your list with one or two others to see if they had similiar experiences and to discover how they felt about them.
3. Utilizing the goals of physical education instruction, describe how an individualized humanistic learning program could accommodate individual differences.
4. Discuss with a friend the factors and abilities one would need to learn how to learn physical education.
5. Review the implications of the evaluation part of this learning program. Knowing the desired end results, design a task for yourself which will help you accomplish the objectives and meet the evaluation criteria.
6. Design a practice task which will broaden the area of knowledge, understanding, and ability to explain the individualized humanistic approach.

Evaluation: You will be able to describe learning environments that facilitate and that inhibit self-actualization.

Rarely are we seated in a restaurant and not offered a menu. The menu includes a variety of foods to accommodate the tastes and appetites of all the patrons. Prices also vary to meet the pocketbook of the customer. When we purchase clothes we are presented with a variety of colors, sizes, and costs to suit our individual desires and needs. If we take a trip we have our choice of destinations by various means of transportation, departure times, and grades of luxuriousness. Similarly, automobiles, houses, appliances, and furniture are all designed for many different desires, needs, and economic means.

In our democratic society all the basic requirements of life—food, clothing, shelter, and mobility—have been produced to give the consumer a chance for individual expression. Private industry has recognized that survival in the competitive market is predicated on accommodating the individual needs and life styles of the consumer.

In so many facets of life the unique characteristics of the person are respected, yet for many decades only one dish has been offered on the educational menu. Everyone's learning environment was built in one style and all had to make do with the same tools and materials, without the freedom of choice one can enjoy in the real world.

Our forefathers saw education as a right of all and an essential need for societal improvement. They further acknowledged that education had to have an impact on the learner. Noted thinkers throughout the centuries—Locke, Rousseau, Descartes, Pestalozzi, Montessori, Whitehead, Dewey, Brunner—have all spoken of the need for education to be relevant to the age and time.

In our diverse and complex society, many avenues are open for citizens to seek economic security, leisure time, and their chosen life style. A single mold in the educational process will no longer do. Although authorities from many fields have spoken of this need for diversity in the educational process, you need only to look to yourself as an authority on YOU. You can probably recall some occasions during your education that were unendurable, as well as some bright moments when you were "turned on."

Have you reflected on what was occurring in the classroom or gymnasium when you were "turned off"? Maybe at times you wondered what the others saw that you didn't. Perhaps you are also aware that not all your classmates were equally interested when you were interested. Perhaps, when you were lost, you attributed that fact to your being dumb— or in the case of others to their being dumb or not interested.

Every subject in the curriculum has its critics. But quite often it is not the subject matter that students do not like, but the teaching method. The potency of the subject matter lies in how it is brought to bear on the individual learning it. That which we don't learn we often dislike.

Organizing the subject matter and learning environments and determining teaching methods to accommodate each student's learning pattern are necessary to effect learning. The best objectives and curricular offerings remain unfulfilled if they do not beneficially alter the behavior of the learner.

Students do not learn in a vacuum. All that occurs around them and to them affects their attitude. That which encourages a positive attitude toward the subject matter and learning process will enhance the learning. Conversely, that which leads to neutral or negative attitudes reduces the intended learning product.

Students can easily become locked onto an educational merry-go-round. Seated on a fixed horse, they go around rising and lowering to measured and repetitive cadence, passing the same scenery. The initial novelty is soon worn off. Imagination is stifled and enthusiasm is dulled once the student realizes he can not break out of the mechanically controlled circuit. It has become obvious that all educators must continually infuse the educational process with relevance to each student's needs and interests. The student must be permitted involvement in and responsible control of his or her learning environment to explore new ways to pursue knowledge and be allowed room for self-fulfillment.

If teachers believe in the educational value of physical education, great pains must be taken to ensure that each student will profit from the instruction. Nothing is taught until it is learned. The methods of inducing learning are as important and diverse as is the curriculum. There must be congruence not only between the curriculum offered and the student's interest and ability, but also between the teaching strategy, the learning settings, and/or with the student's learning characteristics. Decisions made about the learning environment are just as crucial as those made about what is to be learned. This aspect of the learning process is often left to chance. Students are often maneuvered around in the gymnasium with conformity or discipline control as the criterion, rather than with what will foster maximum learning. Discipline will be forthcoming when students are actively involved in a meaningful learning process.

Educational emphasis has shifted from rote repetition of subject matter to include learning the *process* of educating and the *how* of learning skills. The gymnasium organization must allow for flexible interaction of the students with the subject matter, other students, and the teacher. Helping students accept the responsibility of their own learning changes the role of the students and the teacher. The student is not only the recipient of fixed knowledge, but is also at times the initiator of learning projects and the evaluator of the learning outcomes. The teacher becomes not only the authority and "fountainhead" of fixed knowledge, but the encourager of creativity and independence in the students. The roles of both become *dynamic* rather than *static*.

The dimensions of learning are broad, yet specific; are diverse, yet integrated. The student in physical education must be educated in skill development, creativity, emotional and social maturation, and intellectual understanding of the principles operative in physical fitness and motor learning. As each of these areas is mastered in a meaningful and rewarding way, students' motivation for continued study will grow. Each of these objectives has implication as to how the learning program will be organized or formed according to each student's stage of development.

WHAT IS MEANT BY INDIVIDUALIZED INSTRUCTION?

Let us look at the words "individual," "individuality," "individualize," "individuation,". and "instruct." Webster[1] defines these words as follows:

Individual:	Not divisible; of one essence ... of the character of an individual, or indivisible entity
Individuality:	The quality which distinguishes one person or thing from another
Individualize:	To make individual ... to treat or notice individually
Individuation:	Process by which an individual develops his peculiar character
Instruct:	To impart knowledge to, especially methodically; teach

Thus, bringing the individual into focus we find we have to impart knowledge to an indivisible being who has a quality which distinguishes him or her from another. This being will be treated individually by a process which will develop his or her own peculiar character. Since we are talking about education, the knowledge imparted will be directed toward end products that are congruent with the morality of a democratic society and have appropriate utility of the learning product. We will treat or notice the students individually and utilize an individuation process for instruction.

Some attempts to individualize instruction have been made by removing the student from the group and allowing him to work independently on a task or program. This definition and learning mode are too narrow to be beneficial to all students' learning. Individualized instruction

---

[1]*Webster's New Collegiate Dictionary*, 2nd ed. (Springfield, Mass.: G. & C. Merriam Co., Publishers, 1959).

in the constructs of this book does not mean children will work constantly on their own or totally with program or machine learning aids. Rather, it is an attempt to structure a learning experience that will be congruent with a student's learning mode, achievement level, interests, and goals. The overall global objectives may be the same for all students; however, individualizing instruction relates to the various pathways individuals need to take to achieve the global goal or personalized goals.

HUMANISTIC INSTRUCTION

Programmed instruction directed to preconceived teacher-determined goals may have elements of individualization; however, it may not be humanistic. To be humanistic it must be personalized, and personalization can only be accomplished by a person. The teaching-learning act is actually a personal relationship extending to the teacher, the student, and the student's peers. Patterson suggests:

The good teacher is not an instructor, who simply provides information, facts, and knowledge, but a facilitator of learning for the student. Good teachers are not those who are simply experts in subject matter, or experts in teaching methods, or curriculum experts, or who utilize the most resources, such as audiovisual aids. The best teacher is one who, through establishing a personal relationship, frees the student to learn. Learning can only take place in the student, and the teacher can only create conditions for learning. The atmosphere created by a good interpersonal relationship is the major condition for learning.[2]

He also states that authenticity or genuineness, respect, and empathic understanding together make the humanistic teacher.[3]

When the teacher generates a humanistic atmosphere in the gymnasium, the elements of threat and disharmony dissipate. As students grow in their knowledge of facts and skills, they must also be directed toward growing as persons. The affective and cognitive aspects of learning are as crucial for self-actualization as is psychomotor development.

The teacher using the humanistic approach must be aware of the total student. It should not be forgotten that as a human being, the student is capable of thinking, creating, and feeling. To overlook any of these areas is to fall short of generating a humane learning environment.

INDIVIDUALIZED HUMANISTIC INSTRUCTION

Establishment of the learning program starts with the individual rather than with the class. At times it may be necessary administratively to assign students to specific teachers and at designated times, but decisions made for administrative feasibility may not facilitate learning. And even such grouping does not demand that the group be treated as a common whole.

Most teachers do individualize the instruction to some extent. They may give special instructions to certain students or allow some variety in the roles the students play in the class. Students may be working on different skills at different times. These and other adjustments to the individual needs within a class may be intentionally planned for or may occur incidentally as a need arises. Often this individual attention to one student may take place at the expense of the others because the overall plan of instruction does not allow for individual pacing and involvement.

A desirable learning environment will allow the individual to progress through the learning program with a large measure of self-direction

---

[2]C. H. Patterson, *Humanistic Education* (Englewood Cliffs, N.J.: Prentice-Hall, Inc., 1973), p. 98.
[3]Ibid., p. 110.

and involvement. The teacher facilitates the learning by identifying the knowledge and involvement tasks *with* the student and not at the expense of other students. These tasks take into consideration where the student is on the learning continuum, the student's mode of learning, the appropriate feedback information needed, the student's interest in the subject matter, and his or her own goals. There are many resources available to the student: the teacher, visual aids, other students, differentiated practice periods and learning tasks, and evaluation opportunities.

Individualizing instruction in the context of this book is a total process. The steps toward individualizing units are sequential and interdependent. It is essential to maintain the integrity of the components of the system—neither omitting steps nor pacing them unnaturally—however, the length of the unit or the time allotted for the task can be altered to suit the situation. If it is not feasible for an entire unit to be placed on an individualized basis, some phases of that unit may be individualized. These may be in the form of tasks or reciprocal styles of teaching as Mosston[4] describes.

The object of the individualized humanistic approach is to get the student involved in the learning process by doing, thinking, and feeling with all facets of his or her being. The student will not merely be manipulated to recite, mimic, or commit skills and knowledge to rote memory nor be allowed to wander aimlessly toward a whimsical goal that may never yield results. Rather, involvement in and responsible control of learning environments will be permitted. Even some universal goals of physical education which all pupils must attain should be pursued in a manner unique to the way the student learns. Within the context of the global goals, students would be encouraged to develop specific, intermediary or unique ones. The teacher would help the student to find the most productive pathway to the agreed-upon goals. Hopefully, the program will encompass learning the *process* of self-education—learning *how* to learn, as well as learning the foundations for mastery of the subject matter.

LEARNING HOW TO LEARN

Because the success of this program is greatly dependent upon the student's ability to be self-directing, certain cautions should be recognized. Students must be taught skills needed in self-directed behavior. Whether they learn these skills is largely dependent upon their motiva-

4Muska Mosston, *Teaching Physical Education* (Columbus, Ohio: Charles E. Merrill Publishing Company, 1966).

tion. Seeing fun, challenge, enjoyment, and success in each lesson will encourage the student to *accept the responsibility of his own learning* and take *pride* in his accomplishments.

Students experiencing the traditional class-centered teacher-directed approach which regiments them into an anonymous role with the teacher directing all the actions usually have not learned to be self-directed. When these reins are released, some students feel they may do as they please at the expense of other students and of learning. Carefully structured environments must be provided wherein the students understand what is expected of them and how they can proceed in the learning process. Otherwise they may feel lost and confused. The teacher must determine the length of time and complexity of the learning that each student can tolerate. It is important that success experiences be quick in coming. As short, productive tasks are accomplished, longer ones can be attempted. The need is to help the student set an appropriate pace to accomplish a task and provide a supportive environment to help direct the student toward his or her goal. The degree to which a student needs an interpersonal support system is an individual matter.

All subjects have undergone knowledge explosions. It has become apparent that schools cannot teach everything a student must know for a lifetime. Therefore, it is important that everyone learn the processes involved in learning.

In the past several years the physical education curriculum has vastly changed. Students educated in the 1940's to 1970's did not learn soccer, lacrosse, or fencing. Neither were they exposed to yoga, self-defense, or modern jazz. Probably golf, tennis, and badminton were not included in the high school curriculum. The President's Council on Physical Fitness and Sports in the fall of 1972 surveyed 1,939 men and 1,936 women, aged 22 or over, to determine their physical fitness patterns, knowledge, and opinions regarding physical education. Although the majority of the respondents had a positive attitude toward their physical education in school, only 3 percent presently participated in body-building or physical fitness programs through a health club or organization. While in school the dominant sports in which men competed were baseball, basketball, football, and track and field. The women participated in baseball, basketball, softball, and volleyball. (*Physical Fitness Research Digest*, Series 4, No. 2, President's Council on Physical Fitness and Sports, April 1974.) In the school education of these adults, little attention was paid to the skills of lifetime sports such as tennis, swimming, bowling, golf, for example. As we grow older our changing interests and economic situation make more sports accessible. Physically educated adults ought to be able to learn these new activities mainly by their own effort.

At this point we cannot project which skills and games will be taught in the twenty-first century. If students do not learn how to continue their education and do not have instilled in them a desire to learn on their own, the schools of today will be setting up their students for educational obsolescence.

PHILOSOPHY OF EDUCATION AND TEACHING METHODOLOGY

Educational goals have constantly changed throughout the decades, and consequently, so have teaching methods, subject matter, and student roles. The following is a brief and simplified summary of educational goals and the prevalent teaching styles used to attain them. If you are interested in delving further into the influence philosophy has on teaching method, you should read philosophy of physical education and methodology books.

In the 1920's physical education consisted mainly of calisthenics. Students were taught exercises and Indian club routines by mass drills. The teacher led the exercises which the students did in unison. Little emphasis was placed on individual enjoyment, differentiated programs, evaluation, or knowledge about the activity. Similarly, in other subjects the emphasis was on rote memorization of the foundational skills of reading, writing, and arithmetic. Students were judged by how well they could recite the exact information the teacher had taught them. Little time was spent on problem solving, creative activities, or enrichment.

The method of teaching was teacher-oriented. The teacher decided what the student should learn and taught by demonstration or by giving lectures. The students were to imitate the teacher as best they could.

During the 1930's and 1940's education was directed toward life adjustment—the vocational and political world—and cooperative social behavior—conformity to group standards. Perhaps the need for cohesive social behavior was the result of the Great Depression of the Thirties and World War II.

Physical education made its contribution to this educational goal by emphasizing team sports. Squad drills and team sport play were the modes of instruction. Some differentiation of student roles came about in the designation of team captains and team positions, and the captains were given some control over their teams' efforts and learning. Sportsmanship, leadership, and followership were added to the curriculum, because student interaction was necessary in team play. This interaction had to be governed by rules. It was assumed that this learning had carryover values into other phases of life.

Generally, however, the teaching methods placed the majority of the students in a passive role. Each pupil got an equal amount of time for skill drill practice in squads, game play, and exercises. Rarely was there a differentiation of activity according to the student's needs. For example, each student took one shot at the basket when his turn came in line. Whether he made the basket or not, he went to the end of the line to await his next turn.

Little attention was paid to the components of motor learning. Exercises and practice repetitions were the same for all. The number of repetitions chosen were often too many for some and not enough for others. As they were usually done in unison with the cadence called out by the teacher, the teacher found it difficult to be the organizational leader and a corrector of individual errors at the same time. Most of the thinking about the activity remained with the teacher, thus, opportunities for self-directedness were stifled. Yet, this method met some tenets of democracy: all students were treated as equals, and cooperative behavior resulted in total conformity for the good of the group effort. Mosston[5] refers to this teaching method in his spectrum of teaching styles as the command method.

With the student unrest later in the Sixties, individual human worth became the focus of the educational goals. Many writers were beginning to see the need to draw the individual out of a group context.

[5]Mosston, *Teaching Physical Education.*

This was not to be a freedom *from* responsibility, but rather, a freedom *for* responsibility. It was postulated that for students to be responsible citizens they must have an opportunity to learn and practice how to govern their own behavior and be self-directive in their formative school years.

Brunner, Holt, Rogers, and Silberman, among others, pointed out that all students were not alike and failure to learn was not solely the student's fault. Rather, it was the teacher who may have selected the wrong learning modes for the failing, disinterested child. Individualized and humanistic education reached the theory stage.

Early attempts to individualize instruction relied on programmed learning or independent study opportunities. Programmed learning organizes the subject matter in sequential fashion, allows the student to pace his learning, and fosters learning independent of the teacher's immediate surveillance. This form of instruction, however, is still teacher-controlled, with the teacher determining the mode of learning and its goals. For those students who have sufficient self-motivation, goals congruent with the learning program, and need for independence, this mode of learning can be beneficial. However, some students need a stronger personal support system and differentiated learning needs and find this form of independent study or programmed learning nonproductive.

During this time, physical education added to its curriculum individual sports, many of which are termed lifetime sports. Elective or selective physical education curriculum opportunities exist quite extensively. It now remains to expand this concept from the curriculum level to the teaching-learning process, individualizing not only *what* the student learns, but *how* he learns it. This adds the humanistic element to teaching.

The prevailing philosophies for physical education have thus ranged from education *of* the physical to education *through* the physical. Now we are emerging into a broader role, adding the dimensions of process and individual self-actualization.

Figure 1–1 indicates that the more directive and dominant the teacher is, the more passive the student is in his learning role.

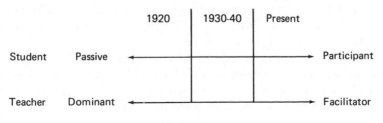

Figure 1–1

CHANGES IN THE ROLES
OF THE TEACHER AND STUDENT

Teaching is essentially a communication activity. The organization of this communication depends upon who is being communicated with —the class or the individual student. Every communication effort is a *one*-to-*one* relationship. The variable is: how *big* is the *one?* We can group things or people into units of varying sizes and components; when components are grouped they lose their individual identity and assume a common identity.

For instance, we can treat the school as one unit, although it has many different students, teachers, administrators, and goals. We speak of the school as having a specific reputation without regard for the deviation that exists among its component individuals.

We can focus on a class as the unit of one. All components of that class can be anonymous in the treatment of that class. The teacher is an indivisible unit of one. An individual student's response to the teacher's questions is only an expression of what that student has perceived or achieved; the *class* cannot return the communication conversation collectively as one. The teacher can make assumptions that if one student learned, then this knowledge or skill is common to all in the class. If it is not, then the student who didn't learn is at fault in some way.

Generally speaking, the principal views the school as a unit of one, as the teacher views the class. But the student views only himself or herself as the unit of one. The individual student can only assess learning as it exists within that individual, and cannot generalize about the unit as do the teachers and principals.

The principal can feel success in his job if he can say the school is "good." This may be based on the fact that 51 percent of the teachers or students are "good" by some predetermined standard. The teacher may feel success because the majority of her students appeared to have learned what she tried to teach. However, the student who has not learned cannot join in the feeling of success. That learning experience has been a failure to that student. There is little consolation in the fact that a classmate learned. Further, knowing that others have succeeded only heightens the feelings of frustration, and to be the "dummy" in a bright class is not conducive to building self-actualization. Also, if there is a dummy in the class, the "class" cannot be bright.

All schools require orderly behavior, a desire for learning to take place, and persons in decision-making roles. Also, in all schools students have to be assigned to teachers for instruction. The questions are: what constitutes orderly behavior and learning; who should be involved in the decision-making process; and how should students be assigned to teachers for instruction?

In the traditional school where the administrator views the school as a unit of one and the teacher views the class as one, orderly behavior demands a lack of social interaction among the students. Teachers must also conform to common specific patterns of instruction, because learning is measured by the collective standing of the school on normative standards and is generally factual in substance. Involvement in the decision-making process is restricted to the administration with some minor input from the faculty. The students are organized into classes of equal sizes for instruction of equal time duration.

However, in an individual-focus school, orderly behavior comes from within the student, who is allowed responsible natural interaction with other learners, the teachers, and the subject matter. Learning is measured in terms of each individual's success and includes knowledge of how to be self-directed. The decision-making process is broadened to include meaningful input from students, teachers, and community citizens. The students are organized for instruction according to their learning needs and the nature of the material to be learned. Time allotments are dependent upon the student's needs and the subject matter. Figures 1–2 and 1–3 indicate these differentiations.

The implications of these structures for the learning environment are apparent. In the individualized humanistic gymnasium, students would be given an opportunity to seek knowledge in a differentiated way—sometimes as a large group, other times in small-group settings, and often in a partner or individual effort. The teacher and students can act as tutors if the need exists.

Figure 1–4 indicates the differences in the roles of the principal, teachers, and students in the traditional collective-focus school and the individual-focus school.

Schools that try to accommodate individualized instruction have altered their organizational scheduling. Flexible student groupings, differentiated time allotments for subject mastery, and opportunities for independent or tutorial instruction are evident in the flexible-modular schedule schools, Multi-Unit elementary schools, Model Schools Project of the National Association of Secondary School Principals, open classrooms, and open-campus schools. In many cases subject matter has been organized on a continuous progress basis, whereby individual learning programs can be engaged in sequentially and the student is not confined to an artificial amount of material to be covered within a fixed time.

Rarely can a different method of instruction be successfully superimposed upon the old structure. A complete break from the traditional

TRADITIONAL COLLECTIVE FOCUS SCHOOL

DESIRE:

Orderly Behavior

Lack of social interaction in the learning process—other-directed, external control

Learning

Collective standing of the students or normative tests
Directed toward teacher-directed goals, knowledge, and skill

Decision Making

Administrators
Teacher representatives
Student government representatives

ORGANIZATION OF THE STUDENT POPULATION:

Classes

Compartmentalized classes of equal numbers of students

30	30	30	30	30
30	30	30	30	30

Time Allotments for Instruction

Equal time allotments for each subject

Figure 1–2

INDIVIDUAL-FOCUS SCHOOL

DESIRE:

Orderly Behavior

Responsible, natural interaction with subject matter and communication with teachers and peers—self-directed, internal control

Learning

Individual success—directed toward subject matter and self-directed goals

Decision Making

Administrators

Teachers

Student government representatives

Individual students

Community

ORGANIZATION OF THE STUDENT POPULATION:

Classes (learning groups)

Differentiated assignments depending upon the requirements of the students and the subject matter

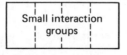

| Large group | Small interaction groups | Individual conference |

Time Allotments for Instruction

Differentiated on the basis of student need

Figure 1–3

RESPONSIBILITY AND INVOLVEMENT ROLES

	Traditional	Individual	
Principal	Disciplinarian Budgeter Scheduler Goal setter	Initiator Conductor Evaluator	Learning system
Teacher	Goal setter Authoritarian Evaluator Disciplinarian	Facilitator Resources Consultant Reinforcer	Learning environment
Student	Receiver Conformer Reciter	Initiator Interactor Accepter of learning responsibility Evaluator	Learning program

Figure 1–4

organization is preferred. However, the gymnasium organization can be adjusted. The gymnasium must become a motor-learning laboratory with the space utilized to accommodate the resources, practice areas, and game courts. Chapters 5 and 6 indicate how the gymnasium activity can be organized for individualizing instruction.

CURRENT GOALS OF PHYSICAL EDUCATION

The content and intent of physical education are not within the scope of this book; however, the authors would be remiss to overlook the desired outcomes of their individualized humanistic teaching-learning model.

Over the years the subject matter of physical education has matured. Foundational research has given direction to physical education content. Through the study of physiology of exercise it has been proven that regular exercise is necessary for the maintenance of organic vigor. The absence of exercise contributes to the degeneration of the vital systems of the body and speeds up the aging process. Psychological studies indicate that physical activity offers a release from mental tension. Specialists in motor learning have offered theories regarding how movement is learned, refined, and made permanent. Educational research has contributed to

the knowledge of how people are affected by learning environments. All these areas must be accommodated in the teaching-learning process.

The American Alliance for Health, Physical Education, and Recreation published in 1965 a pamphlet, *This Is Physical Education*, which states the current view of the contributions of physical education to the total education of the person.

> The old exercise period known as *physical training* has been transformed into a more comprehensive and complex subject called *physical education*. Its new content is a sequence of experiences in which children learn to move as they move to learn more about themselves and their world. The experiences are designed to serve five major educational purposes:
>
> To HELP children learn to move skillfully and effectively not only in exercises, games, sports, and dances but also in all active life situations.
>
> To DEVELOP understandings of voluntary movement and the ways in which individuals may organize their own movements to accomplish the significant purposes of their lives.
>
> To ENRICH understanding of space, time, mass-energy relationships, and related concepts.
>
> To EXTEND understanding of socially approached patterns of personal behavior, with particular reference to the interpersonal interactions of games and sport.

To CONDITION the heart, lungs, muscles, and other organic systems to respond to increased demands by imposing progressively greater demands upon them.

This, then, is physical education—the modern school subject in which children and young adults study the properties of their own idea-directed movements.[6]

More recent position papers have been formulated by the AAHPER, stating the qualities essential to elementary and secondary school physical education. In the *Guidelines for Secondary School Physical Education* is the following:

Physical education is that integral part of total education which contributes to the development of the individual through the natural medium of physical activity–human movement. It is a carefully planned sequence of learning experiences designed to fulfill the growth, development, and behavior needs of each student. It encourages and assists each student to:

DEVELOP the skills of movement, the knowledge of how and why one moves, and the ways in which movements can be organized.

LEARN to move skillfully and effectively through exercise, games, sports, dance, and aquatics.

ENRICH his understanding of the concepts of space, time, and force related to movement.

EXPRESS culturally approved patterns of personal behavior and interpersonal relationships in and through games, sports, and dance.

CONDITION the heart, lungs, muscles, and other organic systems of the body to meet daily and emergency demands.

ACQUIRE an appreciation of and a respect for good physical condition (fitness), a functional posture, and a sense of personal well-being.

DEVELOP an interest in and a desire to participate in lifetime recreational sports.[7]

Regarding the instructional program the following is stated:

The instructional program has as its foundation a common core of learning experiences for all students. This core of experiences must be supplemented in ways that serve the divergent needs of all students— the gifted, the average, the slow learner, and the physically handicapped. It must be geared to the developmental needs of each pupil.

The program should provide for a reasonable balance in those activities commonly grouped as team and individual sports, aquatics, gymnastics, self-testing activities, dance and rhythms.

[6]AAHPER, *This Is Physical Education* (Washington, D.C.: American Alliance for Health, Physical Education and Recreation, 1965), p. 3.
[7]AAHPER, *Guidelines for Secondary School Physical Education* (Washington, D.C.: American Alliance for Health, Physical Education and Recreation, 1970), p. 4.

Sequential progression in the specific skills and movement patterns involved in the activities included in the above grouping is essential.

There should be opportunity for elective learning experiences within the required program.

The acquisition of knowledge and understandings related to the development and function of the human body, and the mechanical principles of human movement is necessary.

Learning experiences (physical activities) should be designed to foster creativity and self-direction and to encourage vigorous activity which includes emphasis on safety procedures.

Physical fitness—agility, balance, endurance, flexibility, and strength —should be developed.

Experiences which reinforce the development of behaviors, attitudes, appreciations, and understandings required for effective human relationships are important.

Special opportunities should be offered for those students who find it difficult and uncomfortable to adjust to the regular program because of physical, social, or emotional problems.

The program should present basic skills which can be employed in a comprehensive intramural, interscholastic, and recreational program for all girls and boys.[8]

The beliefs of this Alliance relative to the elementary school instructional program are as follows:

We believe:

1. A well-conceived and well-executed program of physical education will contribute to the development of self-directed, self-reliant, and fully functioning individuals capable of living happy, productive lives in a democratic society.

2. A comprehensive physical education program for all children has as its foundation a common core of learning experiences. This common core of learning is concerned with efficient body management in a variety of movement situations. It serves the divergent needs of all pupils—the gifted, the slow learner, the handicapped, the culturally deprived, and the average—and is geared to the developmental needs of each child.

3. The program must be planned and conducted to provide each child with maximal opportunities for involvement in situations calling for mental, motor, and emotional responses which will result in optimal and desirable modifications in behavior: skills, knowledges, and attitudes.

4. A variety of learning experiences should be planned and carried

[8]AAHPER, *Guidelines.*

out to emphasize the development of basic concepts, values, and behaviors associated with the ultimate goal for the physically educated person.

5. Curricular content should be so organized that levels of learning in attitudes, understandings,* and skills are recognized and can take place in a sequential and developmental arrangement.

6. The instructional program should be designed to: (1) encourage vigorous physical activity and attainment of physical fitness; (2) develop motor skills; (3) foster creativity; (4) emphasize safety practices; (5) motivate expression and communication; (6) promote self-understanding and acceptance; and (7) stimulate social development. It should include such experiences as basic movement, dance, games, practice in sport skills, stunts, and tumbling work with large and small apparatus. When possible, the program should include aquatics. Each must be so structured that it is interrelated with the others, permitting children to generalize from one learning experience to the next.

7. To deal effectively with the whole child, many styles of teaching must be brought to bear on the learning situation. These include both teacher-directed and self-directed learning. If learning is to be personalized and concerned with the cognitive and affective domains, problem-solving as a teaching strategy becomes vital.

8. To foster the development of generalizations and key concepts, a range of instructional aids as well as teaching styles must be employed. Innovative use of audio-visual materials, large and small group instruction, individual help, and interdisciplinary approaches must all be considered.

9. Opportunity should be provided for participation in organized intramurals and such extramural programs as play days and sport days. These should be designed to serve the purpose of the class instruction phase of the program.[9]

The following list suggests the broad dimensions of knowledge to be imparted in order to physically educate the students adequately.

CURRICULAR DIMENSIONS

Understanding Self

Physiology of exercise
Status of oneself
Physical growth patterns

*Knowledge and Understanding in Physical Education, AAHPER (Washington, D.C., 1969).

[9]AAHPER, *Essentials of a Quality Elementary School Physical Education Program* (Washington, D.C.: American Alliance for Health, Physical Education and Recreation, 1970).

Physical potential

Improvement and maintenance techniques

Psychology of sport

Creative endeavor

Joy in movement

Socialization

Competition-cooperation

Appreciation of others' abilities

Movement in society

History of sports

Cultural aspects of sports

Commonality of human movement

Game rules

Leadership-followership

Personal involvement, sportsmanship, and enjoyment in subject matter

Skill Development

Balance

Joint action

Locomotor forms

Rhythm

Qualities of movement

Force production and reception

Relaxation

Skill integration

Concepts
Space, time, direction, weight, distance, dimension, force, flow (actual and illusory)

Spatial awareness, depth perception, motor perception

Strength and endurance

Flexibility

Recreational competency

Awareness of Variables

Physical environment
Water, ice, cold, heat, ground, air, suspension, body build

Psychological environment
Hostility, competitiveness, security, insecurity, temperament

Process Skills

Determining objectives

Mechanical analysis of movements

Commonalities and differences between and among movements and games

Evaluation of movement

Solving movement problems

Relating to other fields

Physics, biology, mathematics, history, art, drama, music, reading, literature

Identifying the content to be taught is a relatively easy task. The test of a good facilitator is whether he can establish a learning environment that is conducive to the student's learning mode. It is the affective curriculum which establishes whether or not the student learns what is desired.

The affective curriculum refers to all the feelings, experiences, and judgments the student makes, hence, learns, as he is engaged in the learning environment. You may believe you are teaching a boy to play and enjoy basketball, but he may find the experience unrewarding and decide that basketball is an undesirable game for him. As he fails to learn the skills and to play the game in competition with others, his self-image may be lowered. Thus, he is learning something other than what you planned. Figure 1–5 graphically indicates the dimensions of learning.

Learning is not always a positive event. We can learn not to like activities if the learning environment is counterproductive. Figure 1–6 indicates some of the factors that stimulate or adversely affect the learning.

The authors predicate the individualized humanistic approach on the following beliefs:

PREMISES FOR THE INDIVIDUALIZED HUMANISTIC TEACHING MODEL

- Physical Education has a body of knowledge essential to the physical, cognitive, and psychological growth of the child.
- Children differ in:
  1. How they learn
  2. Their rate of growth and pace of learning patterns
  3. Their physical and psychological constitution
  4. Their interests and life-style goals
- Children learn attitudes from the environment around them.
- Learning environments must encourage self-directedness for the learning to be complete and ongoing.
- The teacher-student relationship must be a trusting one.
- The student's self-concept must be enhanced.

Students should:

- Learn how to learn motor skills

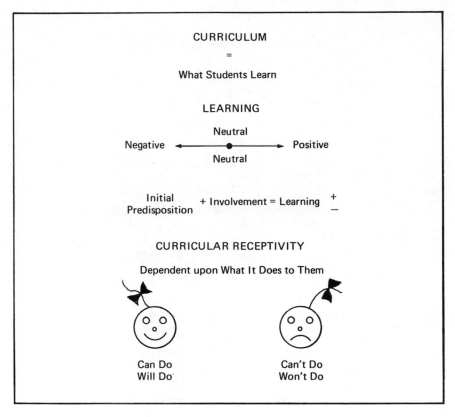

Figure 1–5

Dimensions of Learning

- Accept the responsibility for their own learning
- Have an interest in learning
- Acquire useful skills for maintaining organic vigor and for recreational use
- Improve their self-image
- Develop good social interaction skills
- Feel self-reliant
- Value physical education

SUMMARY

Individualized humanistic instruction refers to a teaching model that considers the pupil as a co-participant in the teaching-learning act.

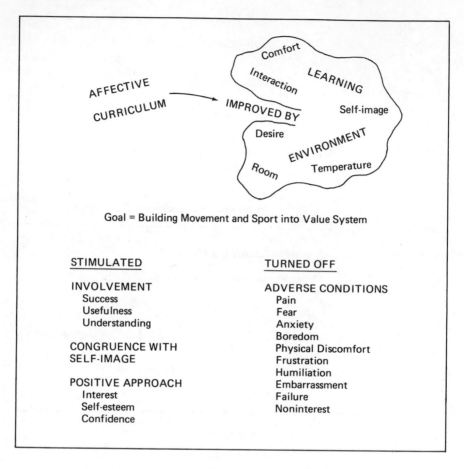

Goal = Building Movement and Sport into Value System

STIMULATED	TURNED OFF
INVOLVEMENT	ADVERSE CONDITIONS
Success	Pain
Usefulness	Fear
Understanding	Anxiety
	Boredom
CONGRUENCE WITH	Physical Discomfort
SELF-IMAGE	Frustration
	Humiliation
POSITIVE APPROACH	Embarrassment
Interest	Failure
Self-esteem	Noninterest
Confidence	

Figure 1–6

Factors Affecting Learning

The student's totality is respected as a thinking, caring, feeling person capable of teaching himself or herself, given a humanistic learning environment. It is necessary to become self-directed so that education can be continued long after formal schooling is completed. If the thinking and directions for actions come all from the teacher, little is learned that will be useful when the teacher is out of the picture.

Individuation is the process by which one is allowed to develop one's own uniqueness. Instruction can be individualized in a variety of ways and degrees. Some forms, such as programmed learning, allow the student control over the pacing of the learning; however, such programs often are limited to one mode of learning and one learning goal.

Humanistic teaching incorporates an individual prescription identified with the student. This prescription accommodates the student's learning mode, position on the continuum of ability and achievement, specific needs, and degree of involvement necessary to accomplish the goal. It utilizes a variety of teaching methods and resources. The one-to-one relationship of student and teacher helps the teacher to understand the student while the student comes to regard the teacher as an interested facilitator of the learning. Learning and teaching relationships with other classmates provide the learner with immediate feedback concerning process, while the student-tutor or observer develops insight to observe and evaluate performance. The humanistic atmosphere allows the student to have responsible control over process as well as product.

The prevailing philosophy of education influences the content and mode of teaching. When the desired outcome was to have the student memorize and imitate the skills or knowledges, a direct teaching style was employed. The teacher gave the information and controlled the student's learning program. The student responded with little thought of the *what* and *how* involved in the learning. The current philosophy of education places the student and his or her total development in focus, accommodating an individual's thinking, creating, and feeling capacities. To do this the student must be viewed apart from other classmates.

The roles of the teacher and student change as one views the student independently of the class. The teacher becomes a facilitator of learning and develops a unique learning environment for each pupil. The student becomes an initiator, interactor, and evaluator of his learning program. He accepts with the teacher the responsibility of his own learning because the student has had a part in the planning of his program.

Gymnasium activities can be reorganized for this new approach. The gymnasium becomes a motor learning laboratory, where a student can pursue skills and knowledge through both personal and technical resources. Time for mastery of skills and game play is not fixed. Instead, pacing is fluid and dictated by each student's needs, rather than being group-oriented.

The global objectives to which the learning is directed are those defined by the American Alliance for Health, Physical Education and Recreation. These goals emphasize foundational skills, knowledge and understanding of concepts and human movement, social growth, and organic fitness. They are to be attained through learning experiences that foster creativity and self-direction and that accommodate individual differences.

Important in attaining curricular receptivity is the affective curriculum—the students' feelings about what they are learning and the impact it is having upon their ego and self-image. Learning can be negative, neutral, or positive depending upon the learning environment. What one student may find satisfying and fun may be oppositely viewed by another. Hence, it is important that each student experience a learning environment that is conducive to his feelings of self-worth and dignity and is productive toward his positive success.

The individualized humanistic approach is based upon the premises that students differ in a variety of ways, students learn attitudes from the environment around them, self-directedness is an essential goal of education, teachers and students must be in a trusting relationship, and the student's self-concept must be enhanced.

REFERENCES

American Alliance for Health, Physical Education and Recreation. *Essentials of a Quality Elementary School Physical Education Program.* Washington, D.C.: AAHPER, 1970.

American Alliance for Health, Physical Education and Recreation. *Guidelines for Secondary School Physical Education.* Washington, D.C.: AAHPER, 1970.

American Alliance for Health, Physical Education and Recreation. *Knowledge and Understanding.* Washington, D.C.: AAHPER, 1969.

American Alliance for Health, Physical Education and Recreation. *Organizational Patterns for Instruction in Physical Education,* Washington, D.C.: AAHPER, 1971.

American Alliance for Health, Physical Education and Recreation. *Programmed Instruction in Health, Physical Education & Recreation,* Washington, D.C.: AAHPER, 1969.

American Alliance for Health, Physical Education and Recreation. *This is Physical Education,* Washington, D.C.: AAHPER, 1965.

BROWN, G. I. *Human Teaching for Human Learning.* New York: The Viking Press, Inc., 1971.

BRUNER, J. S. *The Process of Education.* Cambridge, Mass.: Harvard University Press, 1961.

CLARK, H. H. ed. "National Adult Physical Fitness Survey," *Physical Fitness Research Digest.* Washington, D.C.: President's Council on Physical Fitness and Sports, 4:2 (April 1974).

HEITMANN, H. M. "Rationale for Change," *Organizational Patterns for Instruction in Physical Education*. Washington, D.C.: AAHPER, 1971, pp. 1–36.

HEITMANN, H. M., ed. "The Whole Thing," *Journal of Health, Physical Education & Recreation*. Washington, D.C.: AAHPER, May '73, pp. 21–36.

HELLISON, D. *Humanistic Physical Education*. Englewood Cliffs, N.J.: Prentice-Hall, Inc., 1973.

KLAUSMEIER, HERBERT J., et al. *Individually Guided Education in the Multiunit Elementary School—Guidelines for Implementation*. Madison, Wisc.: Wisconsin Research and Development Center for Cognitive Learning, 1970.

LAVARONI, C. W. *Humanity*. Belmont, Calif.: Fearon Publishers, 1970.

MOSSTON, M. *Teaching Physical Education*. Columbus, Ohio: Charles E. Merrill Publishing Company, 1966.

"New Physical Education," *Journal of Health, Physical Education & Recreation*. Washington, D.C.: AAHPER, September 1971, pp. 23–37.

"The Now Physical Education," *Journal of Health, Physical Education & Recreation*. Washington, D.C.: AAHPER, September 1973, pp. 23–29.

PATTERSON, A., AND E. C. HALLBERG. *Background Readings for Physical Education*. New York: Holt, Rinehart and Winston, Inc., 1965.

PATTERSON, C. H. *Humanistic Education*. Englewood Cliffs, N.J.: Prentice-Hall, Inc., 1973.

ROGERS, C. *Freedom to Learn*. Columbus, Ohio: Charles E. Merrill Publishing Company, 1969.

SILBERMAN, C. E. *Crisis in the Classroom*. New York: Random House, Inc., 1970.

STROM, R. D., AND E. P. TORRANCE. eds. *Education for Affective Achievement*. Chicago: Rand McNally & Company, 1973.

2

Students: The Clients

INSTRUCTIONAL UNIT FOR CHAPTER 2

Learner's Diagnosis

Directions: Read the questions below. Write out, discuss, or mentally review your answers. If you believe that you know the information, check the "yes" column. If you are not sure of the answer, check the "no" column. After reading the questions and deciding your knowledge, check the accuracy of your answers by reading the summary at the end of this chapter. If you answered a question incorrectly, change your answer to the appropriate column.

Can you

Yes	No	Questions
		1. Explain the influence of body build and temperament upon activity selection?
		2. Explain why general age characteristics are not absolutely true descriptions of each child at any point in time?
		3. Explain how experience and achievement can differ in children?
		4. State circumstances in which ability can be affected?
		5. Indicate how physical capacity could affect success in certain sports?
		6. Identify the various learning modes or characteristics that individuals may possess?
		7. Explain how attitudes are formed and the effect attitudes have on learning?
		8. Indicate how a student's goals and interests can affect his or her learning?
		9. Relate the extent to which individual students may desire social interaction?

Yes	No	Questions
		10. Give circumstances relative to how cognitive curiosity can affect learning in physical education?
		11. State Maslow's hierarchy of needs?
		12. Identify the many variables that can exist in one child versus another?

Suggested Prescription

Directions: Count the number of checks you have placed in the "yes" column. When the percentages are determined, you may increase your knowledge and skill by using the suggested Learning Program activities recommended in the Input and Practice columns. Input and practices not listed offer additional learning options.

Results	Input	Practice
More than 80%	#1, 5, 6	#1, 2 or 3, 4
60% to 80%	#1, 2, 3 or 4, 5	#1, 2, 3, 4
40% to 60%	#1, 2, 3, 4, 5	#1, 2, 3, 4
Less than 40%	#1, 2, 3, 4, 5, 6	#1, 2, 3, 4

Learning Program

Directions: Select any or all of the activities listed below. These are designed to increase the reader's awareness of individual differences in students.

Proposed Learning Objective: The learner will be cognizant of and be able to identify unique characteristics of students which may be operative in their learning. An awareness of the implication of these differences for instructional modes and learning programs will be gained.

Input:

*1. Read Chapter 2 of this book.

2. Read selected articles in the references at the end of the chapter.

3. Develop a list of sport and dance activities. Give this list to your classmates or other students and have them rank the activities according to how well they either liked or disliked the activities. They can also indicate which they haven't had and, of those, which they would like to learn. Analyze in the light of congruence or diversity of the respondents' likes and dislikes.

   Suggestion: Ask why they liked or disliked the activity. Is there agreement? Do some students like activities others do not?

*4. Identify specific teaching modes you have experienced (drills, lectures, discussion, research methods, independent study, interaction tasks with others). Rank the method you enjoyed or learned from most. Is there a clear ranking or do some have an equal rank depending upon the circumstances? Have several other people rank them. Do they agree with you?

*5. Identify the sensory modes through which you learn.
   Can you follow oral directions without seeing a picture? View a demonstration and perform without an accompanying explanation?
   Can you see a demonstration once and perform the skill?
   Can you do a new skill without someone helping you?
   Do you mind having a more skilled peer watch you as you learn a new skill?
   Do you feel cognitively challenged in a problem-solving task, or are you frustrated if the teacher does not tell you how and why?

   Suggestion: Find a skill you do not know in sports or dance. Try to learn it by the suggested ways listed above. Have several others try it. What method was best for you? Was that method the same for the other students? Analyze what this means about differences in learning styles and modes.

6. Observe a class of students who are about the same age. How many differences can you find in body build, temperament,

*Highly recommended.

achievement, physical capacity, learning style, attitudes, interests, and social and cognitive needs?

Suggestion: Discuss with the teacher of the class how she perceives these differences among her students. Analyze the differences that may be inherent in the child who is succeeding and the child who is not.

7. Observe a group of various varsity sport athletes. Can you tell by looking at their body builds the sport they are associated with? Are there deviations in body builds? What seems to account for their success?

8. List some dual or team sports. Ask several people to what extent they would like to learn the sports. This could be ranked in a continuum from "not at all" to hobby level to amateur or professional standards. Do people have preferences?

9. Ask a student having difficulty learning a skill why he believes he isn't successful at it. Is it lack of coordination, strength, motivation, interest, etc.?

10. Ask an individual sport contestant why he didn't choose to become a team sport player and vice versa.

11. Design an input experience of your own.

Practice:

1. Identify circumstances that would make one "need" stronger than another when learning a sport.

2. Take several people of different body builds who have never "put the shot." Teach them shot putting. Assess the attributes of the ones who learned more quickly and who put the shot farthest. Try to assess the learning product in the light of why some did better than others. Was it interest, probability of success as perceived by the learner, and/or physical characteristics that were operative?

3. Take four or five 9-year-old children who have never played jacks and teach them the game. Assess their quickness to learn in the light of physical readiness, motivation, interest, and the learning mode. How intense was each in watching you and the others in order to improve his or her skill? How many questions did each ask or how many times did they ask you to do it again? What conclusions can you draw about age group readiness and learning styles?

4. Design a practice of your own. Any of the above can serve as a model; just use other criteria for observation, other skills, or other people.

Evaluation: You will be observant of differences in students and will be able to identify probable learning needs or problems which may result from unique characteristics of the learner.

Since the child is the focus in the individualized humanistic approach to instruction he must be studied in a variety of aspects. Each component of an airplane is constructed to serve a particular function independently; but it is only the way these components are put together that gives them the capacity to fly. Hence, the truism: the sum of the whole is greater than the sum of its parts.

So it is with each student. Each has a physical structure, temperament, and intelligence. For each of these components, some generalities can be observed. However, the student's humanness is a special blend of all the components interacting with each other in a unique and special way. The degree to which these attributes reflect the norm is dependent upon the modifiers called experience and personal interaction. Using the basic components to perform tasks of doing and thinking will yield a continuum of failure to success. The actions, judged by the doer in reference to a conceived internal model or by an outside person, influence the doer's self-concept in a variety of settings, and affect the doer's feelings about the actions.

In studying the component categories below, you should keep in mind that a continuum exists within and among the existing elements. Where the attribute is on the continuum and the strength or degree to which it is present make for uniqueness in each pupil.

PHYSICAL AND TEMPERAMENT DIFFERENCES

It has always been obvious that we all have unique physical characteristics. Hippocrates suggested that differences in actions occur among people because of physiques and temperament. Further, he hypothesized that there was a relationship between the two. His typology was twofold. He classified physiques as short and thick or long and thin. Temperament classifications paralleled the four basic elements of air, water, fire and earth. Hippocrates further suggested that the predominance of one of the four humors (liquids which may refer to what is now called the endocrine system) which he believed to be within the body would determine the temperament of the individual.

In 1824 a Frenchman, Rostan, classified physiques into four types: digestive, muscular, cerebral, and respiratory. In 1909, Viola, an Italian anthropologist, added the classification of body measurement. More recently, in 1921, Ernst Kretschmer, a German psychiatrist, gave rise to constitutional psychology while studying mental disorders. He classified body types as asthenic (frail and linear), athletic (muscular and vigorous), and pyknic (plump). To these three categories he added a fourth called dysplastic—physiques that have deviant aspects. His work postulated a connection between temperament and physique type in the mentally ill as well as normal individuals.

Modern constitutional psychology has been forwarded by Sheldon whose technique of somatotyping classified body build into three basic types: endomorphic, mesomorphic, and ectomorphic. A measurement system was established to assess the degree of each of the three attributes an individual possessed. Studies and measurements of thousands of men and women showed that some characteristics which could be termed maleness and femaleness could occur in either sex. Sheldon further named categories of temperament as viscerotonia, somatotonia, and cerebrotonia. These terms recognized a link between the physique type and the temperament.

What is pertinent here for physical educators is that the categories of physique and temperament may relate to the way the person moves, to the person's desire for movement, and to his or her facility to move. In addition, it implies a relationship between how the individual reacts to the world and that individual's reaction to outside forces. The extent to which any of the typing systems are absolute, and the connection between temperament and physique, can be questioned. But the work is definitive enough to suggest that something may be operative in the students' receptivity to movement education which is related to their body build and temperament.

BODY BUILD AND TEMPERAMENT RELATED TO SPORT SELECTION

Experimenters have been able to establish that certain traits of personality and temperament occur more frequently in athletes than in nonathletes. Also, they have found certain common personality traits in participants of similar sports, which differ from those in participants of other sports.

Using the Thurstone Temperament Inventory, Heitmann (1966) found that in a group of freshmen and sophomore high school girls, those scoring high on the AAHPER Youth Fitness test were significantly higher on the *Active trait* than were those in the low group. The high motor fitness group characterized themselves as preferring to work and move actively and rapidly. They liked to "be on the go" and were restless whenever asked to be quiet. The opposite was true for the low group. Significant differences were found also for the *Vigorous trait* between the high and low groups. The high motor fitness group preferred physical activity using large muscle groups and great expenditures of energy. Furthermore, they enjoyed physical sports. The girls in the lower group preferred less physical activity.[1]

How much the personality influences the selection of a sport or how much the nature of the sport influences the participant is not completely known. Steinhaus at the Colloquium on Exercise and Fitness stated:

> Whether the fitness induces change in the psyche or the psyche change in the fitness, or whether both are due to a common force behind both will no doubt [also] become clear with time. Presently it appears that athletic ability is found in association with greater ego strength, dominance, relative freedom from anxiety, outgoingness, below average guilt proneness, extroversion, self-sufficiency, and little of that which is ascribable to an over-protective home environment.[2]

It does stand to reason that our body build suits us more for one sport than another. The quality of buoyancy is helpful for swimming, and long legs and litheness contribute to the runner's success. Tallness and agility make basketball easier, while stockiness may be more suitable for football. Even within a team sport various positions may call for different builds. In football a tackle would need stockiness and force; an end, agility and running ability; the quarterback, less bulk but more agility and precision.

In the area of temperament, a soccer goalie must remain unafraid as the offense prepares to attack the goal; a forward need not be as fearless, but must be agile and have aggressive attack qualities.

Along with the gross body build attributes are the variables of neurological organization and sensory discrimination. Cratty summarizes studies regarding perception as follows:

[1]H. M. Heitmann, "Teacher Effectiveness in Relationship to Motor Fitness and Temperament Groupings" (unpublished Doctoral dissertation, Springfield College, 1966).
[2]A. H. Steinhaus, "Summary and Comments," *Exercise and Fitness* (Chicago: Athletic Institute, 1960), p. 234.

Perceptual differences are found between athletes and non-athletes. Slight to moderate differences in peripheral vision, ability to track moving objects, depth perception, and figure-ground acuity have been found, generally favoring the athlete over the non-athlete.[3]

It is unrealistic to think that every child will have the attributes to excel at all sports or all positions. Teaching programs that assume students can perform equally well in all areas set certain students up for failure. Some educational value may accrue from a student trying various sports and team positions, such as an appreciation for the many factors involved. But not to be allowed to pursue what one is most suited for makes learning nonrelevant to the participant. It is as illogical as trying to make a bass sing soprano in a music class.

PHYSICAL GROWTH PATTERNS

Growth patterns depend to a large extent on heredity and environment. Illness, nutrition, sleep patterns, exercise, and endocrine functions all can affect the rate of growth and maturation. Children within an age group can be at varying stages in their physiological or psychological development.

[3]B. J. Cratty, *Motor Behavior and Motor Learning* (Philadelphia: Lea & Febiger, 1967), p. 103.

Readiness for learning is sequential and progressive. Instruction in tasks for which the proper growth and neurological foundations are not present becomes frustrating to the learner. Withholding instructional assistance when the readiness is present may delay the acquisition of the appropriate learning, hence, arrest the development of the child. Variations in the physical growth are particularly noted at the beginning of new stages of development, upon entering school and at the onset of puberty.

Each person seems to have his or her own biological and psychological time clock which brings readiness at different times. Teachers must be alert to the unique patterns demonstrated by the pupil and must differentiate the learning tasks and facilitate an environment that will be conducive to the pupil's passing through each level so that sequential development can be assured.

EXPERIENCE AND ACHIEVEMENT BACKGROUNDS

Any given group of students today may represent a great variety of backgrounds. Mobility is now a way of life. Toffler states in *Future Shock*, "Between March 1967 and March 1968—in a single year—36,600,000 Americans (not counting children less than one year old) changed their place of residence."[4] With this amount of mobility it is difficult to characterize any student as being typical of the place where he is currently. Furthermore, some children have been allowed a great deal of freedom and have experienced successful activity, whereas others have been curtailed by overprotective parents, or confining environmental or health factors. Thus, experiences can be so varied that generalities about preceding instruction, home or community environmental factors, or future needs cannot be made.

Piaget has identified four stages of development: sensory-motor, pre-operational, concrete, and formal. The child's early activities are intuitive in nature and rely on trial and error. During this pre-operational stage, which concludes sometime between the ages of 6 and 7, the child builds an experience background for the next stage. The concrete third stage is operative at the time the child enters school. Real objects or symbols can be manipulated when they represent things the child has experienced in the stage of trial-and-error exploration. Within the dimensions of the experimental background, problems of a cognitive or motor nature can be solved. If the pre-operational period of trial and error was limited the child will be handicapped in his ability to draw relationships

---

[4]A. Toffler, *Future Shock* (New York: Random House, Inc., 1970; Bantam Books, 1971), p. 78.

and conclusions in the concrete stage. The fourth or formal stage should be operative when the child is between 10 and 14 years of age. In this stage the child can deal in hypothetical symbolic relationships unrelated to his concrete experiences.

Physical education learning programs must incorporate learning tasks that will help the child to move into new stages when readiness exists—that is, when the previous stages have prepared the child for the next stage.

Hence, students can be different, not only in their gross motor achievement but also in their ability to utilize the attained skills in a mature and integrative fashion. Ability to conceptualize game strategy is dependent upon easier concrete experiences. Some students, regardless of age or isolated skill development, must be given an additional period of time to correct their backgrounds.

There is also diversity within each individual. A student may have accomplished a high degree of achievement in one aspect or activity in physical education and lower levels in others. Diagnostic testing on a variety of fundamental criteria could give a performance profile for each student. The student's longitudinal progress in one activity could be plotted on a performance graph. Progress could also be recorded horizontally in a variety of activities. Cross checking the basic areas of success and failure could reveal which areas may be deterring achievement.

ABILITY DIFFERENCES

Innate motor ability factors have been researched and identified. These factors are generally considered to be agility, dynamic balance, static balance, flexibility, dynamic or slow control of range of joint motion, and speed of movement. Strength ability can be dynamic, static, or explosive. Neurological development can affect ability. Psychological factors of persistence, aspirations, and social needs can also influence the development of ability.

These basic traits exist at various levels within each individual and are somewhat dependent upon the physical structure and attributes of each person. For instance, static strength is related to the potential girth of the muscle and the range of joint motion to the individual's structure of the joint. Specific sports and movements require these factors in various degrees and combinations. Motor ability tests can give a broad, generalized diagnosis of a student's ability to perform. If a score is low, more definitive testing should be undertaken to identify specifically whether the problem is lack of strength, poor coordination, obesity, poor vision, or a lack of motivation.

PHYSICAL CAPACITY

Students, because of varying physiological capacities, experience, or psychological constitution, may exhibit different capacities or tolerance for exercise. Those with a great capacity for exercise profit from tasks that challenge their potential. Others need tasks commensurate with a lower capacity, with gradual increases as the capability improves.

Differences can be predetermined by one's cardio-respiratory capacity or muscular density or girth. Some students may have a potential for quick bursts of speed or energy production, but cannot sustain the effort very long. Others can more naturally undergo physical activity for a long period of time. This can be the difference between the sprinter and marathon runner.

Students with handicaps may have limited capacities. Each handicap will present special needs. These students have, however, the same basic physical, psychological, and social needs as do normal children. The handicapped child should be offered meaningful programs with tasks that are not contraindicated for that condition.

LEARNING CHARACTERISTICS

Learning is affected by the way the student organizes the learning input and how he relates it to his past experiences. In cognitive learning, some students are aurally oriented and others are visually oriented; still others may need conceptual interaction with mental imagery. This is also true in motor learning, which is further complicated with the addition of sensory or kinesiological orientations. Each of these methods may be needed by all students in differing amounts at different times in the learning process.

In addition to the way students receive instruction they are affected by how and from whom they receive it. Some students need a supportive environment; others desire a minimum of teacher control or interaction. Many students with low achievement or potential seem to desire teachers who exhibit sympathy or empathy in their interaction with the student; the highly skilled students seem to desire a greater interaction with the subject matter.[5] Coffman states, "the more difficulty students have with classwork, the more likely they are to value teachers who are helpful and understanding."[6] He further concluded from his study that:

[5]M. J. Morris, "Selected Teacher Qualities Desired by High School Girls" (unpublished Master's Thesis, Springfield College, 1969).

[6]W. E. Coffman, "Determining Students' Concept of Effective Teaching from Their Ratings of Instructors," *Journal of Educational Psychology*, 45 (May 1954), p. 277.

> [Empathy] ... seems to include more than a tribute to simple friendliness or to the instructor's tendency to be easy. Here is student recognition that good teaching often requires an awareness of problems learners encounter, a willingness to be patient with student limitations, and appreciation of the world of the student as well as the world of the scholar.[7]

You must, therefore, vary your approach to the student depending upon where he is on the continuum of need for dependence or independence. His place on this continuum may change at various stages in the learning process. Rarely can one teaching style affect positive and maximum learning in all students.

Goldberg's research supported the assumption

> ... that a pupil's learning is, in large measure, a function of the kind of teaching to which he is exposed. Thus, the extent to which a pupil masters a given set of academic tasks reflects not only his attitudes and aptitudes, but also the appropriateness of the particular approach by which he is taught.[8]

Some students can see a model performance and quickly grasp the gross motor framework, remember it, and approximate it with relative

[7]Ibid., pp. 280–81.

[8]M. L. Goldberg, *Adapting Teacher Style to Pupil Differences* (New York: Horace Mann-Lincoln Institute, March 11, 1963, Mimeograph), p. 1.

speed. Others may need constant reminders of the model. Perhaps they can see only parts at a time. Readily accessible models must be available to them in the form of pictures, loop films, or video-taped models. Other students may need printed instructions accompanying the visual picture. Still others may profit from audio-taped instructions which they can re-play when desired.

Temperament may also affect the way a learning program is paced. We seem to have a unique time clock which innately governs the speed at which we feel comfortable when moving or thinking. An imposed pacing may be too slow for some or too fast for others, frustrating those who have difficulty keeping up, while boring others.

ATTITUDES

Attitudes can be diverse among people and may also be complex within an individual. Generally, attitudes can be *cognitive*, relating to one's belief or knowledge of a subject; these are evaluative beliefs, and may be favorable or unfavorable, or desirable or undesirable. Other attitudes may come from *feelings* or emotions, such as pleasing or displeasing, liked or disliked. *Action* tendencies of an attitude refer to the behavioral readiness one associates with the attitude; these attitudes determine whether one acts positively or negatively.

Attitudes exist in varying degrees and may be altered according to circumstances. A continuum may exist relative to the three components of attitude sets. At a given time, one's belief about an object (cognitive) may be strong, while feelings about it may be less strong, and the action tendencies may be neutral, depending upon the circumstance and prudence of exhibiting the attitudes.

Seldom do attitudes exist in isolation of circumstance. Asking a person's attitude toward physical education may yield a variety of answers depending upon knowledge the person has of the subject, feelings regarding past experience and desire to act toward it. A parent, when asked if physical education is important for school children, may give a favorable response; but when asked to rate school subjects on a continuum of ten points, physical education may rate at the lower end, behind reading, writing, and arithmetic. When a student is asked how he enjoyed physical education his response will be in terms of how it affected him; he may not reveal his real attitude if it is negative and his desire to "say the right thing" for various reasons is stronger.

In an attempt to discover if success in achievement (skill and knowledge) produced favorable attitudes toward physical education, Heitmann[9] discovered that some students who were successful in improving their achievement scores revealed a dislike for the experience. The rewards were not commensurate with the effort demanded by the teacher in order to attain them. Their reaction was to the method used and the predetermined goals set by the teacher.

Attitudes can be influenced by others and by outside forces. Ray,[10] studying attitudes of high school girls toward physical education, concluded that attitudes of girls with low physical fitness scores were significantly lower than those of girls with high physical fitness scores. Also, the parents of these girls held attitudes that correlated with those of their daughters.

Students' attitudes toward the relevance of the subject matter or learning tasks affect their receptivity toward the learning. Learning environments that are unproductive or threatening to their self-image are likely to generate negative attitudes. Positive attitude development must be ongoing and be part of each daily lesson objective.

INTERESTS AND GOALS

Interest can heighten motivation, thus speed learning. Allowing students to select activities according to their goals and providing for a variety of experiences which will allow any degree of involvement the students desire can heighten motivation.

An individual's actions are a reflection of his wants and goals.

> The degree to which wants are regularly satisfied or chronically frustrated helps determine the strength and primacy of these wants and the readiness with which other wants may emerge in an orderly developmental sequence.
>
> For any given want there may be many different appropriate goals. Which particular goal develops for a given individual depends upon cultural values, biological capacity, personal experience, and availability in the environment. If fully appropriate goals are lacking, the individual may develop substitute goals, which may, in time, become primary goals in their own right. Prolonged action toward remote goals is sustained by the achievement of intermediate goals.[11]

The desire to satisfy one's wants and goals becomes one's interest.

[9]H. M. Heitmann, "Teacher Effectiveness in Relationship to Motor Fitness and Temperament Groupings."

[10]B. J. Ray, "Attitudes of High School Girls and Their Parents Toward Physical Education" (unpublished Doctoral dissertation, Springfield College, 1968).

[11]D. Krech, S. Crutchfield, and E. Ballachey, *Individual in Society* (New York: McGraw-Hill Book Company, Inc., 1962), pp. 78–79.

Students: The Clients   **49**

Interests can vary from day to day or year to year. We find interest in those activities in which we will probably be successful. Our interests may or may not be directed toward our primary goal at all times. Interest in one goal may be diverted momentarily as something else may catch our fancy; it may even be a springboard to another goal. An interest can be dulled if the pursuit of it strictly closes out all other options and interests; or we may find that it is no longer to our liking. Learning programs that do not allow for divergent goal-seeking deny the humanness of the learner.

The activity goal itself may be less important than the activity's usefulness in attaining another goal. For instance, a boy may show an interest in dancing only because it will help him to get a date. A girl may pursue a slimnastics program with great energy, not for the healthful, organic vigor gained but to have a socially acceptable figure. Others may select activities because friends participate in them and they don't want to be left behind.

Neumann[12] surveyed 600 high school girls regarding their likes and dislikes in physical education. Their ranking of fifteen items placed their likes at (1) "the activity itself," (2) "good personal relationships with classmates," and (3) the "amount of activity in class." The "level of personal skill achieved" rated eighth and "amount of basic knowledge and understanding you attained" rated ninth. When rating their dislikes the "teacher's manner of teaching" ranked number one.

Kneer administered to 1,200 high school girls in physical education, a goal-revealing device entitled *Your Goals in this Class*. She concludes that: "Students indicated a preference for the social goals of being with friends, having freedom to learn, and new experiences. The physical well-being goals of fitness and skill achievement were ranked last."[13] A study conducted by Dotson and Stanley[14] to determine the values of physical activity perceived by male university students revealed that the male students placed pursuit of vertigo (sensation of movement) and catharsis above health and fitness. It should be remembered that although generalities can be made from a group population, individual differences do occur among people. If you wish to facilitate learning in all students you must be sensitive to the masked and expressed goals of each student.

Within physical education the global goals can be fulfilled by en-

12A. Neumann, "Comparison of Two Motivational Factors in Girls Physical Education" (unpublished Master's thesis, George Williams College, 1973).

13M. E. Kneer, "Influence of Selected Factors and Techniques on Student Satisfaction with a Physical Education Experience" (unpublished Doctoral dissertation, University of Michigan, 1972), p. 83.

14C. O. Dotson and J. Stanley, "Values of Physical Activity Perceived by Male University Students," *Research Quarterly*, 43:2, May 1972, p. 153.

gaging in activities which are more congruent with the students' interests, wants, or goals, keeping in mind that interests and goals can change.

SOCIAL DIVERSITY

All people are usually in need of some human affiliation. However, some students have a strong need for social interaction, while others prefer to be more selective in their social activities. Interaction with others is explored from one's own frame of reference. As social experiences increase through trial and error, the child becomes selective, seeking a comfortable fit between himself and others. At times a young boy likes to play and learn alone; other times he may desire one person for the special attributes that person possesses; another time he may prefer someone else.

Rarely are our social needs static. At times a child may be in total harmony with certain children, and then they may spin apart as needs and interests change.

Our desire for social interaction also varies from day to day. Flexibility to accommodate a student's need for any day can be built into the learning program. When communication between participants is desired, reciprocal or cooperative student learning can be facilitated. Students who already have a bond may enter into mutual assistance more readily than if the participants are strangers. At other times students may prefer to learn with others on an achievement criterion.

Some students are naturally "loners" and prefer to preserve their own privacy. There need not be anything abnormal about this trait. They usually select sports or activities where they can compete individually against another person or their own past performance. Being forced into cooperative effort is distasteful to their nature and when they do conform to such participation it is often at the expense of enjoyment.

Social development is not always linked with physical development. Some students may progress faster in their social development than others. Readiness for various roles of leadership, followership, and cooperative endeavor varies from student to student.

COGNITIVE INTERACTION

Some students have a high cognitive interest and may be motivated by learning tasks that will stimulate their intellectual curiosity. Others may be thwarted if too much emphasis is placed on the cognitive aspects of a sport skill. Respecting a student's cognitive desires can be accommodated in individualized learning.

Structuring learning tasks which bring cognitive interaction with the subject matter can contribute to the understanding of the process involved in education. Somewhat dependent upon knowledge gained in other subjects, students can make a transfer of the principles. Those whose interest and inquiry-desire are low need tasks of short duration and easy solving processes. Others may seek a learning program heavily weighted on learning through induction, deduction, and conclusion inference.

Summarizing research relating to fitness, academic performance, and intelligence, Cratty stated:

> To challenge more intelligent youngsters and to elicit their best effort in physical activities, one must present them with games which contain an intellectual challenge. The rules must be reasonably complex or the teacher must provide opportunities for the children to experiment with different rules, new apparatus, or even the invention of new games.[15]

HIERARCHY OF NEEDS

Despite the complexity of the human being, we all possess common needs, although to varying degrees. Maslow (1943) has speculated that a hierarchy of needs exists for all. These needs are identified as:

1. Physiological needs of hunger, thirst, and so on.
2. Safety needs for security.
3. Belongingness and love needs for affection or identification.
4. Esteem needs for prestige, success, self-respect.
5. Self-actualization need for self-fulfillment.

It is his belief that the "lower" needs must be fulfilled before the next "higher" need can be developed. When the physiological needs are adequately attended to, more creative and enriching goals can be attained. A person may move up and down the hierarchy as the circumstances demand.

In the teaching of gymnastics to all students the hierarchy of needs may deter some from attaining the highest goal. The end products of moves on a piece of gymnastic apparatus may be self-fulfillment, creativity, and joy of success and effort. But some students may be stopped from this desired product because of the safety needs. Insufficient strength, neuromuscular patterns, or obesity may make some gymnastic skills a threat to the person's safety. Inept moves on the balance beam or modern dance floor may be an affront to the student's need for self-esteem.

[15]B. J. Cratty, *Teaching Motor Skills* (Englewood Cliffs, N.J.: Prentice-Hall, Inc. 1973), p. 99.

The same principles of safety and self-esteem may be violated in the learning of other sports as well. Certainly there are some aspects of all sports that the beginner or those with minimal attributes could learn, but the learning environment must be sensitive to the student's need for self-esteem and security.

It is generally accepted that all people want the following:

Physical good health—but circumstances and attitudes may cause the person to be at various levels either intentionally or subconsciously. Some may be fanatic on the subject of nutrition; others may satisfy their health needs as a necessary evil.

Secure environment—but security for one may be boredom for another. Some have a very high tolerance for risk taking while others prefer less personal—physical or mental—risk. Some skilled tennis players would not enjoy high diving. The enjoyment of walking or hiking may vary from a walk around the block to mountain climbing.

Belongingness—but the extent varies. Some seek peer, teacher, parent, or team approval. Others choose different persons or groups to identify with. And some are satisfied with more private fulfillment.

Esteem needs for prestige, success, self-respect—but the levels to which people aspire differ. Some students feel successful with "C" grades; others are more achievement-oriented and must earn "A's," be elected captain, or be singled out for praise. Some may seek esteem in one area of endeavor and care little about it in another.

Self-fulfillment—but this also means different things to different people.

Each student's unique characteristics must be assessed by you, the facilitator, in order to allow the pupil to feel comfortable and have the greatest possibility for success in the learning program.

Motivation can be influenced by all the factors discussed in this chapter. In addition, there may be other conditions that affect a student's success. These may be tolerance of stress, reaction to temperature, aesthetic appearance of the environment, and cultural values, to name only a few. The facilitator of learning must be continually sensitive to all that may be operative within each student.

SUMMARY

People seek to express themselves in ways unique to their own special combination of personal traits. Our inherited characteristics are modified by environment experiences. Each child possesses a myriad of component elements—some universal, some divergent from others. No child reflects the hypothetical norm.

Body build and temperament make a person more suitable for one sport activity than another. Each body build has certain characteristics that facilitate participation in particular sports. Temperament can suit a person more for certain positions on a team as well as for one sport over another. Traits of passiveness, aggressiveness, vigorousness, reflectiveness, and sociability color the student's receptivity to the role he is to play in the activity and learning program.

Physical growth patterns differ from one individual to another. General age characteristics do exist, but variations are observable within an age group. Each person seems to possess his own biological and psychological time clock which brings readiness at different times.

Experience and *achievement* backgrounds differ in many regards. The mobility of people today makes it difficult to assume that any group of students has similar geographic, social, or economic backgrounds. Ready access to lakes, oceans, or pools encourages aquatic skill, whereas deserts or mountains encourage different skills. Achievement reflects experience in successful activity. Some children because of nonsuccessful activity or overprotective parents may have ceased their exploration before an adequate experiential background has been formed. Piaget has theorized that young people progress through learning stages of trial and error, awareness of cause and effect, concrete operations dealing with real things or symbols, and finally in abstract thinking unrelated to actual experience. An absence of a rich background in the preceding stages inhibit the motor and cognitive growth of the child.

Basic motor ability components are related to individual structure and neurological integration. The development of these ability components can be affected by psychological factors. Specific sports and movements use these factors in varying degrees and combinations. Diagnostic testing for the degree to which the ability is present can be undertaken. However, if a student scores low on one of the components, further testing should be done to determine if remediable problems exist which are influencing performance.

Students differ in *physical capacity* for movement. Cardiovascular or muscular endurance may be governed by respiratory capacity or muscle girth. Maximum potentials would differ.

Individual *learning styles* reflect the way the student gains an idea of what he or she is to do and reflect how the student processes the information. Students may be visually oriented, aurally oriented, or sensory oriented. Some students require more interpersonal interaction, greater feedback, or a more supportive environment than other more independent students.

The receptivity the student has for any given activity or learning environment is dependent upon that student's *attitude*. This attitude is his reflection of the way the subject matter is brought to bear on the student: its relevancy to the individual, the degree of success that can be attained, how congruent it is with one's value system, and how it contributes to self-esteem. Negative attitudes may be privately held if expression of them is threatening to the student. No circumstance is experienced without some attitude being internalized.

People seek goals that have an interest to them. *Goals* and *interests* can vary and may change at any time. Some students may wish only a cursory exposure to certain sports while desiring a greater involvement in others. Furthermore, attainment of the goal may be for primary reasons—such as the internal pleasure of participating—or for secondary reasons—such as participation with friends or attainment of notoriety.

Our need for *social interaction* can vary from one day to the next or can be a somewhat constant pattern. Some pupils may prefer activity unrelated to cooperation with others, while some do not like to participate alone. Some students may desire social and cooperative interaction only with selected persons.

The degree to which one needs or desires *cognitive* interaction can vary. For some, movement patterns happen almost spontaneously; others enjoy cognitive interaction with the motor skill. Students with intellectual curiosity need to know why and how, and their minds must be put to work if the movement skills are to be challenging and fulfilling.

Maslow has identified a *hierarchy of needs* which exist in all people: (1) physiological needs, (2) safety needs, (3) belongingness and love needs, (4) esteem needs, and (5) self-actualization needs. In each need there is a continuum related to satisfying the need. Some are content to achieve what others may term average or minimal, but within each person is the desire to meet what he believes to be adequate for himself.

Recognizing the great diversity that exists among and within students, you must be sensitive to helping your students select learning programs that are consistent with their individual qualities.

REFERENCES

BRUNER, J. S. *The Process of Education*. Cambridge, Mass.: Harvard University Press, 1961.

CARTER, J. E. LINDSAY. "Somatotype of College Football Players," *Research Quarterly*, 39 (1968), 476–81.

————. "The Somatotype of Athletes—A Review," *Human Biology*, 42 (1970), 535–69.

COFER, C., AND W. JOHNSON. "Personality Dynamics in Relation to Exercise and Sports," W. Johnson, ed., *Science and Medicine of Exercise and Sports*. New York: Harper & Row, Publishers, 1960.

COFFMAN, W. E. "Determining Students' Concepts of Effective Teaching from Their Ratings of Instructors," *Journal of Educational Psychology*. 45 (May 1954), 277.

CRATTY, B. J. *Movement Behavior and Motor Learning*. Philadelphia: Lea & Febiger, 1967.

DANIELS, J. "Physiological Characteristics of Champion Male Athletes," *Research Quarterly*, 45: 4 (December 1974), 342.

DOTSON, C. O., AND W. J. STANLEY. "Values of Physical Activity Perceived by Male University Students," *Research Quarterly*, 43:2 (May 1972), 148–56.

GOLDBERG, M. L. *Adapting Teacher Style to Pupil Differences*. New York: Horace Mann—Lincoln Institute, March 11, 1963 (Mimeographed).

HARRIS, D. V. *Involvement in Sport: A Somatopsychic Rationale for Physical Activity*. Philadelphia: Lea and Febiger, 1973.

HARRIS, D. V., ed. *Women and Sport*. Proceedings from the National Research Conference on Women and Sport. The Pennsylvania State University: Penn State HPER Series, no. 2, 1973.

HEITMANN, H. M. "Teacher Effectiveness in Relationship to Motor Fitness and Temperament Groupings." Unpublished Doctoral dissertation, Springfield College, 1966.

————. "Organizational Patterns to Facilitate Physical Education Instruction," *Illinois Journal of Education*, 62: 2 (March 1971), 40–43.

HOLT, J. *How Children Fail*. New York, N.Y.: Dell Publishing Co., Inc., 1964.

————. *How Children Learn*. New York, N.Y.: Dell Publishing Co., Inc., 1966.

KANE, J. E. "Personality Arousal and Performance," *International Journal of Sports Psychology*, Vol. 2, no. 1 (1971).

————. "Psychological Correlates of Physique and Physical Abilities," E. Jokl and E. Simon, eds., *International Research in Sports and Physical Education*. Springfield, Ill.: Charles C Thomas, Publisher, 1965.

————. Personality and Physical Abilities," *Contemporary Psychology of Sport*. Proceedings of the Second International Congress of Sport Psychology. G. S. Kenyon, ed. Chicago: The Athletic Institute, 1970.

KENYON, G. S. "A Conceptual Model for Characterizing Physical Activity," *Research Quarterly*, Vol. 39 (1968).

KEOGH, J. "The Relationship of Motor Ability and Athletic Participation in Certain Standardized Personality Measures," *Research Quarterly*, 30 (December 1959), 444.

KNEER, M. E. "Influence of Selected Factors and Techniques on Student Satisfaction with a Physical Education Experience." Unpublished Doctoral dissertation, University of Michigan, 1972.

KRECH, D., S. CRUTCHFIELD, AND E. L. BALLACHEY. *Individual in Society*. New York: McGraw-Hill Book Company, Inc., 1962.

KRETCHMER, E. *Physique and Character*. New York: Harcourt, Brace & Co., Inc., 1926.

MASLOW, A. H. "A Theory of Human Motivation," *Psychological Review*, 50 (1943), 370–96.

MORGAN, W. P. "Selected Psychological Considerations in Sports," *Research Quarterly*, 45: 4 (December 1974), 374.

MORRIS, M. J. "Selected Teacher Qualities Desired by High School Girls." Unpublished Master's thesis, Springfield College, 1969.

NEUMANN, A. "Comparison of Two Motivational Factors in Girls' Physical Education." Unpublished Master's thesis, George Williams College, 1973.

NOAR, G. *Individualized Instruction: Every Child a Winner*. New York, N.Y.: John Wiley & Sons, Inc., 1972.

O'NEILL, W. F. *Selected Educational Heresies*. Glenview, Ill.: Scott, Foresman and Company, 1969.

PLOWMAN, S. "Physiological Characteristic of Female Athletes," *Research Quarterly*, 45: 4 (December 1964), 349.

POLLOCK, M. "Physiological Characteristics of Older Champion Track Athletes," *Research Quarterly*, 45: 4 (December 1974), 363.

PURDY, J. G. "Computer Analysis of Champion Athletic Performance," *Research Quarterly*, 45: 4 (December 1974), 391.

RATHS, LOUIS E., MERRILL HARMIN, AND SIDNEY B. SIMON. *Values and Teaching*. Columbus, Ohio: Charles E. Merrill Publishing Company, 1966.

RAY, B. J. "Attitudes of High School Girls and Their Parents Toward Physical Education." Unpublished Doctoral dissertation, Springfield College, 1968.

RIESMAN, D., N. GLAZER, AND R. DENNEY. "Tradition-Direction, Inner-Direction, and Other-Direction," *Selected Educational Heresies*, William F. O'Neill, ed. Glenview, Ill.: Scott, Foresman and Company, 1969.

SHELDON, W. *Varieties of Temperament: The Psychology of Constitutional Differences*. New York: Harper and Brothers, 1942.

SILBERMAN, C. E. *Crisis in the Classroom*. New York, N.Y.: Random House, Inc., 1970.

SIMON, J. A., AND F. SMALL. "An Instrument for Assessing Children's Attitudes Toward Physical Education," *Research Quarterly*, 45: 4 (December 1974), 407.

SINGER, R. N. "Athletic Participation: Cause or Result of Certain Personality Factors," *Physical Educator* (1967).

SLUSHER, H. S. "Personality and Interest Characteristics of Selected High School Athletes and Non-Athletes," *Research Quarterly*, 35 (December 1964), 539–45.

SMITH, D. "The Relationship Between Ratio Indices of Physique and Selected Scales of the Minnesota Multiphasic Personality Inventory," *Journal of Psychology*, 43 (April 1957), 325–31.

SMITH, L. E. "Personality and Performance Research: New Theories and Directions Required," *Quest*, Winter Issue (January 1970).

STEINHAUS, A. H. "Summary and Comments," *Exercise and Fitness*. Chicago: Athletic Institute, 1960.

TOFFLER, A. *Future Shock*. New York, N.Y.: Random House, Inc., 1970 (Bantam Books, 1971).

3

Teachers:
The Facilitators

INSTRUCTIONAL UNIT FOR CHAPTER 3
Learner's Diagnosis

Directions: Read the questions below. Write out, discuss, or mentally review the answers. If you believe that you know the information, check the "yes" column. If you are not sure of the answer, check the "no" column. After reading the questions and deciding your knowledge, check the accuracy of your answers by reading the summary at the end of this chapter. If you answered a question incorrectly, change your answer to the appropriate column.

Can you

Yes	No	Questions
		1. Define teaching?
		2. Describe four characteristics of a desirable learning climate?
		3. Explain the roles of facilitators?
		4. Describe differences between traditional teachers and facilitators?
		5. List three major competencies of facilitators?
		6. Describe teaching ability?
		7. Explain differences between teaching strategies and teaching behaviors?
		8. Explain goals of good interpersonal relations?
		9. List interpersonal skills needed by a facilitator?
		10. List at least three sources of professional growth opportunities?

Suggested Prescription

Directions: Count the number of checks you have placed in the "yes" column. When the percentages are determined, you may increase your knowledge and skill by using the suggested Learning Program activities recommended in the Input and Practice columns. Input and practices not listed offer additional learning options.

Results	Input	Practice
More than 80%	#1, 4, 11	#5
60% to 80%	#1, 4, 6 or 7, 11	#3 or 4, 5
40% to 60%	#1, 2 or 3, 5 or 6, 7	#2, 3 or 4
Less than 40%	#1, 2 or 3, 5 or 6, 10	#1, 3, 4

Learning Program

Directions: It is suggested that the reader attempt to follow any and all suggestions in this learning program. They are designed to improve the reader's knowledge and understanding of practice procedures and skill in developing meaningful learning experiences to facilitate physical education instruction.

Proposed Learning Objective: The learner will understand the characteristics, roles, and competencies of facilitators as evidenced by demonstrated efforts to seek learning experiences designed to help him or her acquire ability as a facilitator of learning.

Input:

   *1. Read Chapter 3 of this book.

   2. Read Chapter 9, "Becoming a Teacher," in Bucher, Koenig, and Barnhart, *Methods and Materials for Secondary School Physical Education.*

  *Highly recommended.

3. Read Chapter 2, "Characteristics of Successful Physical Education Teachers," in Miller and Massey, *Methods in Physical Education for Secondary School.*
4. Read selected references given at the end of this chapter.
5. Interview a teacher and/or facilitator. Prepare a list of questions which will give you some insights as to the roles, characteristics, competencies, and professional growth of teachers.
6. Observe a teacher and/or facilitator in action. Look for the roles played, the characteristics exhibited, the learning climate generated, and the competencies shown.
7. Read selected portions of books listed in this chapter's references which relate to humanistic teaching.
8. Attend a professional workshop and/or convention.
9. Browse through several professional journals.
10. Complete the exercises suggested in the article by Marian Kneer, "How Human are You?" in June 1974, *Journal of Health, Physical Education & Recreation*, pp. 32–34.
11. Plan an input of your own.

Practice:

1. Arrange to visit a campus counselor for the purpose of assessing and/or improving your interpersonal relations ability.
2. Join a professional organization for physical education.
3. Teach a micro-lesson, have a colleague or friend observe your teaching behavior, using the Interaction Analysis Observation device described in Chapter 12.
4. Give directions to a small group. Encourage the group to ask questions if they do not understand the directions. Have someone note the kind and number of questions.
5. Execute strategies #7 and #70 in Simon, Howe, and Kirschenbaum, *Values Clarification.*
6. Plan a practice of your own.

Evaluation: You will be able to teach a small group a skill task which they will learn at the 80 percent or better mastery level. Eighty percent or more of the students will respond positively as to their satisfaction with the experience.

To the student, the most important worker in a school is the teacher. It is the teacher who has the most intimate and direct contact with the student, who serves as the mediator between the "present" student behavior and the "changed" student behavior, and who is the most dynamic force in a relatively static physical learning environment. And it is the teacher who, in a flexible, responsive, and understanding way, helps the learner to become rational, responsible, and autonomous.

Teachers, like students, come to the teaching-learning setting with their own unique interests and needs. However, it is to be expected that teachers will exhibit those characteristics that are required in the teaching procedure. Since a school exists for the benefit of the learner, the teacher's options and preferences must be restricted.

Heitmann, studying teaching effectiveness, determined that (under traditional teaching):

> Teachers interact with and teach to a segment of their class. They do not affect all girls in a physical education class equally. Teachers should become aware of their limitations and seek to improve their range of effectiveness.[1]

Individualized humanistic instruction frees the student from teacher characteristics that may be counterproductive to learning and from environments that cater to the instructor's personal preferences in curriculum and methodology. It is the teacher who must adjust the total learning environment to provide the individual students with congruence between where they are and where they are going. The teacher must exercise professional knowledge, but the learner may have many personal options to fulfill the specified objectives.

DEFINITION

Teaching is deliberately managing the learning environment and learning activities in such a way as to bring about desired changes in behavior. In this book, this process is called individualized humanistic facilitation of physical education. This system sees you, the teacher, as a change agent, who relies on helping and enabling behavior, rather than on controlling behavior, to reach the goals of education. Since learning requires activity by the student, the term "facilitator," rather than "teacher," more precisely describes the function of teaching.

Charles Galloway and Edward Mulhern state:

[1]Helen Heitmann, "Teacher Effectiveness in Relationship to Motor Fitness and Temperament Grouping" (Doctoral dissertation, Springfield College, 1966), pp. 178–79.

If the goal of rational autonomy is to be achieved it seems likely that it will succeed in situations where teachers and support personnel have first achieved this goal for themselves.[2]

Facilitating the learning of students is a difficult and complex task. It is more than acquiring a storehouse of knowledge and skill to be spewed forth in a singular delivery system relying on demonstration and explanation; and it is more than providing mass drills in a locked-time pattern type transaction. The facilitator must be a student in his/her field, differing from learners mostly in experience and in the ability to structure and execute learning programs. Your success as a facilitator will rely mainly on you as a person. Successful educational experiences are always directly traceable to good teachers, who free the student to learn through establishing a meaningful personal relationship.

CHARACTERISTICS OF FACILITATORS

In the past good instruction was assumed if the teacher displayed certain characteristics. These characteristics were wrapped in terms such as:

Good personality
Good health
Leadership ability
Professional attitude
Neat appearance
Skill in activities
Intelligence

Certainly such characteristics are still important but they only describe a *good personable teacher*. Good instruction is characterized by a climate that the student perceives to be fair, firm, friendly, and fun. This climate is made possible when the teacher's behavior or actions are based on his or her belief in the value of each student.

Actions that are *fair* do not require that you like all students equally well, but rather that you treat or interact with each empathetically and that your treatment be consistent for all. It is important that your behavior exhibit your respect for the student as a unique human being. Respect must be reciprocated; students respect the teacher-facilitator who provides a consistent atmosphere and who dependably applies specified learning conditions. *Firmness* contributes to the learner's feelings of security concerning the dimensions and direction of progress toward his goals. *Friendly* behavior does not negate your personal preference for

---

[2] Jack Frymier, *A School for Tomorrow* (Berkeley, Calif.: McCutchan Publishing Corporation, 1973), p. 255.

some students or your feelings of displeasure. However, each student is dependent on your help. Help cannot be given in a hostile environment. Students respond to warmth and concern. When hostile feelings are felt, they should be acknowledged and discussed as a problem to be mutually solved. The pursuit of learning goals requires personal commitment which may result in temporary feelings of physical, emotional, and social deprivation. *Fun* is perceived by students as your ability to place their deprivations in proportion and to structure conditions that will foster a feeling of joy, genuineness, and mutual sharing.

The degree to which the characteristics of good personality, health, leadership, professional attitude, appearance, skill and intelligence influence good instruction has not been validated. It is conceded that these characteristics contribute toward achieving behavior that is conducive to successful teaching and will make you fair, friendly, firm, and fun in the mind of the student.

ROLE OF THE FACILITATOR

Your role as the facilitator requires you to be the instructional planner, leader, and evaluator. These roles are methodological operations which will be discussed later. However, the traditional teacher role is carried out in a narrow and tightly controlled manner, whereas the facilitator role is marked by openness and fewer constraints to guide learning. Operational roles for the traditional teacher emphasize leadership. The emphasis for the facilitator role is on the planning operation. The relative importance of these roles under both systems is illustrated in Figure 3–1.

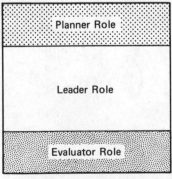

Proportion of Emphasis Placed on the Roles of the Traditional Teacher.

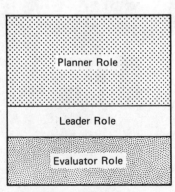

Proportion of Emphasis Placed on the Roles of the Facilitator.

Figure 3–1

The traditional teacher's role is authoritarian in nature for the purpose of controlling the learning environment. The teachers apply whatever disciplinary measures are deemed necessary to insure that knowledge and skill are transmitted. The traditional teacher is the decision maker, presenter of information, director of activity, enforcer of rules, and manager of the learning climate. Physical education teachers often carry out these roles with immense physical and psychological distance between themselves and the students. Students pursue the learning program without asking and knowing why, and consequently learn to assign physical education instruction as something apart from actions and thought. A measure of teacher competence is predicated upon an orderly, neat, quiet, and restrictive climate.

The traditional teacher's role as an evaluator is to assign a grade which indicates the level of student learning, either in relation to the entire class (norm referenced) or in proportion to the teacher's goals (criterion referenced). It is the belief of the authors that the traditional teacher role has "turned off" many students and has failed to physically and mentally educate the student-client. The need for activity persists in the students, but the educational value of physical education seems to elude them. It is no wonder that research[3] has indicated that the activity itself is considered to be the most valued by students, and that skill acquisition, fitness, and good health were ranked less valuable.

[3]Charles Dotson and W. J. Stanley, "Values of Physical Activity Perceived by Male University Student," *Research Quarterly*, 43:2 (1972) 148–56.

The role of a facilitator, on the other hand, is to enable the students to reach goals which are important to each of them. Control is shared by the facilitator and the learner. You provide the student with learning programs that give feedback for guidance and control. Consequently, you are free to offer more personal attention and to support the learning process. The activity area may look disorganized, but close inspection will reveal widespread involvement of students pursuing the achievement of a plethora of learning outcomes. Instead of being the major source of information, the facilitator is also a diagnostician, who can ascertain, develop, and prescribe learning experiences that will be most helpful and productive for the learner.

The role of the facilitator as an evaluator is to determine when the student has reached his terminal objectives. Grades are considered unimportant. However, the reality of the present educational system requires

that grades be given. Therefore, grades are assigned upon the portion of the goals reached in whatever amount of time is available.

COMPETENCIES

A baker must know what ingredients contribute to a good loaf of bread. In addition, the baker must be skillful in selecting the proper pans, amount of dough for the pan, proper ovens and oven temperatures, and baking time. And finally, he must know how these ingredients are to be put together so they will interact properly. Baking methods are an important link in transforming the interacting ingredients into a changed substance called bread.

As physical educators, you must possess these same three competencies to transform behavior: (1) knowledge and skill in physical education subject matter, (2) teaching ability or methods, and (3) meaningful interpersonal relations or interaction. Regardless of the process used to help people to learn, all three competencies must be present. The differences in the various approaches to physical education are often more of emphasis in one or more of these areas. The process of facilitating learning in physical education requires that all three of these competencies be equally present.

Subject Matter Knowledge and Skill

As a physical educator, you must be a master of the substance of the discipline's body of knowledge as well as the associated activity skills. You must possess an understanding of the human body and how it functions, knowledge and skill in a variety of physical education type activities, and an understanding of how motor skills are learned.

Professional preparation programs have tended to provide adequate learning opportunities in the first two areas mentioned; however, the understanding of how motor skills are learned often occurs with insufficient experiences. The facilitator must have this knowledge in order to develop effective delivery systems and transactions requiring task analysis competency. Task analysis involves classifying skills and identifying the critical components of a skill task. According to Robb,[4] specified activity skills may be distinguished on the basis of space and time environments, pacing, prior movement state, type of movement, feedback source, and objective. Ability to analyze critical skill components will guide the sequencing and selecting of tasks for each individual student.

[4]Margaret Robb, *Dynamics of Motor Skill Acquisition* (Englewood Cliffs, N. J.: Prentice-Hall, Inc., 1972), pp. 144–46.

Even if you lack skill in a particular activity or sport, you can still completely understand the various skill components and their relationship to skilled performance. Your knowledge of subject matter should include familiarity with a multitude of media for any activities for which you are a facilitator.

Teaching Ability

Facilitating physical education utilizing an individualized humanistic approach requires that you acquire understanding and skill in all possible teaching strategies and behaviors. *Teaching strategies* refer to your ability to plan a variety of delivery systems and practice transactions to help the learners reach their physical education goals. Teaching strategies include the ability to utilize a variety of methods—reading, observing, listening, and investigating through the use of a multitude of media such as books, films, sound tapes, video tapes, and computers. The facilitator must also possess a thorough knowledge and understanding of the available media and the ability to use it properly. In addition you should be able to plan practice experiences which are self-contained, interactive, discovery-based, and independent in nature.

Your *teaching behavior* should display ability effectively to clarify and respond to questions, solicit questions and information, give corrections and affirmative feedback, express acceptance, give positive or negative opinions, and express nonverbal actions and feelings. The application of strategies and behaviors to the learning act will involve personal, task, and institutional decisions. Further discussion and explanation of teaching ability for the facilitator will be found in subsequent chapters.

The acquisition of skills necessary for helping students learn and benefit from the subject matter of physical education will be at best a never-ending task. You are urged to practice facilitating learning early in your professional experience and in settings with which you will normally be associated. Facilitating instruction is a relatively new art which is dynamic and constantly in search of procedures that will result in efficient learning and achievement of student goals.

Interpersonal Relations

The wellspring of motivation lies in the human relations competencies. Most professional preparation institutions provide learning experiences to master the art and science of teaching physical education through subject matter and field teaching experiences. Unfortunately, human relations is often left to chance acquisition. Research has increasingly pointed to the impact of the affective—feeling domain—on learning. Dr. Herbert Greenberg, author of *Teaching with Feeling*, says:

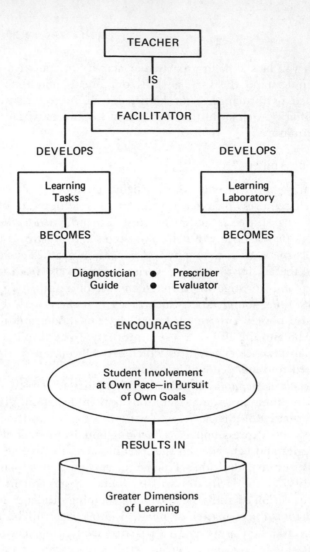

Facilitating instruction is a relatively new art which is dynamic and constantly in search of procedures which will result in efficient learning and achievement of sudden goals. No matter how much emphasis is placed on such other qualities in teaching as educational techniques, equipment, technology, or buildings, the humanity of the teacher is the vital ingredient if children are to learn.[5]

What makes us human as teachers is the way we interact with students; the "fit" between teacher values and student values is processed through interpersonal skills such as:

[5]Herbert Greenberg, *Teaching with Feeling* (Toronto, Canada: Macmillan Co., 1969), p. 20.

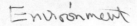
Environment

1. Knowing and trusting each other.
2. Accurately and unambiguously understanding values.
3. Influencing and helping through instructive confrontation and cooperative behavior.
4. Constructive resolving of problems and conflicts.

These skills, which can be developed, are dependent upon your ability to *trust, communicate, understand,* and *cooperate* with students. Kneer[6] found that when interpersonal relations training was provided for teachers, their students were significantly more satisfied with the teaching-learning experience than were students of teachers without special training. Furthermore, student achievement in skill and knowledge was slightly improved. Your role as a planner, instructor, or evaluator cannot proceed effectively without knowledge and skill in interpersonal relations.

Trust. Trust means willingness to risk hurting feelings which relate to your self-concept and the role of others as worthwhile human beings. Trust is absolutely essential between student and facilitator. It is promoted by creating a climate relatively free of betrayal, rejection, and fear of failure. Consequently, a trustful facilitator will develop learning conditions that build acceptance, support, and hope. Learning sequences should be perceived by the student as achievable, and difficulties should be met with mutual concern for success and understanding. The single most important act to build trust is based on the highest compliment possible to another human: an expressed expectation that the person is trustworthy—that the student is responsible and self-directive, able to select meaningful goals, and willing to work with you to reach these goals. There will no doubt be some violations of trust, but with experience and careful analysis, violations will become rare.

Communication. Effective verbal and nonverbal communication is vital to understanding between student and facilitator. Helpful communication depends upon listening skill and upon ability to respond succinctly and accurately. Often students fail to respond in a responsible and directed manner because of faulty perception of the implication of words or actions. Precision in expressing verbally and nonverbally is an art that must be developed through conscious effort and practice.

Inaccurate communication is the result of a gap between what is sent and what is received. There are several possible reasons for this gap: (1) emotional and social implications such as attitudes or prejudices; (2) differing frames of reference; (3) inappropriate use of the language; (4) nonverbal expressions; and (5) environmental interference. Four tech-

[6]Marian E. Kneer, "Influence of Selected Factors and Techniques on Student Satisfaction with a Physical Education Experience" (Doctoral dissertation, University of Michigan, 1972), pp. 84–85.

niques may be employed to clarify your own messages. First, state the message, and then repeat it using more channels, such as writing in addition to verbalizing. Second, include all background information, yet be specific. Next, personalize the message by using "I" and "my"; take the risk of being responsible for your statements. And, finally, attempt to make your verbal statement congruent with your nonverbal cues and actions.

Non-verbal messages often communicate feelings which reinforce or contradict what is said verbally. You no doubt have experienced a teacher stating "I'll be happy to help you!" as she/he nervously looks at her/his watch. People tend to believe behavior—which is harder to hide.

Although honesty in communication is vital to good interpersonal relations, honest messages that are risky or hurtful should be carefully constructed; the speaker should take responsibility for the message and should explain the feelings involved. There is no easy pathway to effective communication.

Understanding. Understanding requires that you put yourself in the students' place and become sensitive to their perceptions and feelings, that you try to see their attitudes, beliefs, and values. Ambroze Brazelton, speaking at the Secondary School Physical Education Conference of the Illinois Association for Health, Physical Education & Recreation, stressed the need for "educaring" educators: that is, educators who are aware of student needs, dedicated to helping the student, free of negative feelings toward students, and able to help the students to develop their best talents. Physical educators would not attempt to teach a psychomotor skill without knowing how the body moves and the influence of growth and development upon learning. Similarly, they should not attempt to relate to a student without understanding the student's affective being.

An effective facilitator must provide nonthreatening learning conditions. Tensions, fear, and anxiety inhibit learning. Reduced threat and increased understanding come from your respecting students and sincerely wanting the best for them. It is impossible to facilitate learning if you are preoccupied with our own problems and frustrations. Your self-concept must be healthy if you are to have the perspective and confidence necessary to relate to the multitude of human differences.

Cooperation. Cooperation involves listening, responding, communicating, enabling, supporting, and giving, in a nonthreatening atmosphere. Cooperative behavior requires willingness to know, accept, create, and provide multiple pathways, experiences and problem solutions to help achieve stated goals of the learner. To be cooperative, one must be open to new ideas, processes, and practices. The student must be viewed as a partner in the teaching-learning process and not as an enemy who is in competition with your personal peace, time, and desires. As a matter of fact, the latter goals are more often outcomes of cooperative behavior.

BEING A PROFESSIONAL

Professional development should be lifelong. Facilitators, like all persons, differ in experience, education, and personal preference and have differing personal values and goals. Therefore, no one channel is acceptable for all. Many options for improvement of instruction are available: in-service training may be provided by the employing school, graduate courses, professional meetings, personal professional reading, and participation in workshops and research. The amount and frequency of involvement is a personal matter. However, many schools will require certain professional growth experiences as contingencies for employment, tenure, and salary increases. The option of renewing and growing is not open to choice. You, as a professional facilitator of physical education, are responsible for providing the best possible service to your clients—the students. The commitment to professional improvement is expected of you.

SUMMARY

Facilitators of learning are the most important workers in a school. They represent the flexibility and response needed to shape the educational environment to help the learners achieve their goals. The facilitator must be willing to adjust the curriculum, environment, and instruction to the needs of the student rather than to the facilitator's own preferences.

Teaching is defined as deliberately managing the learning environment and activities to bring about desired changes in behavior. Facilitation refers to helping and enabling the learner rather than imposing teaching. The key to good teaching or facilitating is positive interpersonal relations: the teacher's characteristics should create a climate perceived by the learner to be fun, fair, friendly, and firm.

The roles of the facilitator are planner, instructor, and evaluator. Both the traditional teacher and the facilitator carry out these roles, but the emphasis for the facilitator is placed in planning as opposed to leading in the teacher role. Facilitators plan extensively to permit the learner to give leadership to his own learning. The facilitator spends less time controlling group behavior and, therefore, has more time for personal interaction with each learner. Evaluation is criterion-referenced rather than norm-referenced as in traditional teaching. Achievement of mutually agreed upon goals at the mastery level is paramount.

Three major competencies are required for facilitators: (1) knowledge and skill in subject matter, (2) facilitating ability, and (3) meaningful interpersonal relations interaction. All three are equally important. *Knowledge and skill* in physical education subject matter includes understanding the human body, being able to perform a variety of physical education type activities, and understanding how motor skills are learned. *Facilitating ability* includes ability to plan a variety of delivery systems and practice transactions. Teaching strategies refer to ability to utilize a variety of methods to transmit information to the learner through a variety of media and to structure practice experiences which are self-centered, interactive, discovery-based, and independent in nature. Teaching behaviors are defined as interaction skills to guide learning within the teaching-learning setting. *Interpersonal relations* are crucial to process the interaction of subject matter and teaching ability. The flexible role of the facilitator is manifested in (1) knowing and trusting students, (2) accurately and unambiguously understanding values, (3) influencing and helping through instructive confrontation and cooperative behavior, and (4) constructive resolving of problems and conflicts. Achieving these skills requires ability to trust students, to communicate accurately and responsibly, to understand the learner's feelings, and to cooperate in a helpful manner.

Professional development is a never-ending process. A facilitator must avail himself of appropriate ongoing professional learning experiences to provide the best possible service to students. These learning experiences are available through in-service education, professional organizations, graduate work, reading, observing, and researching.

REFERENCES

Brown, G. *Human Teaching for Human Learning*. New York: The Viking Press, Inc., 1972.

Bucher, C., C. Koenig, and M. Barnhard. *Methods and Materials for Secondary Physical Education*. St. Louis: The C. V. Mosby Company, 1970.

Dotson, C., and W. Stanley. "Values of Physical Activities Perceived by Male University Students," *Research Quarterly*, 43: 2 (May 1972), 148.

DUNN, R., AND K. DUNN. *Practical Approaches to Individualize Instruction*. W. Nyack, N.Y.: Parker Publishing Company, 1972.

FRYMIER, J. D. *A School for Tomorrow*. Berkeley, Calif.: McCutchan Publishing Corporation, 1973.

GREENBERG, H. *Teaching with Feeling*. Toronto, Canada: Macmillan Co., 1969.

GREER, M., AND B. RUBINSTEIN. *Will the Real Teacher Please Stand Up?* Pacific Palisades, Calif.: Goodyear Publishing Company, Inc., 1972.

HARRIS, T. *I'm O.K., You're O.K.* New York: Harper & Row, Publishers, 1967.

HEITMANN, H. M. "Teacher Effectiveness in Relationship to Motor Fitness and Temperament Grouping." Unpublished Doctoral dissertation, Springfield College, Springfield, Mass., 1966.

HELLESTON, R. *Humanistic Physical Education*. Englewood Cliffs, N.J.: Prentice-Hall, Inc., 1973.

JOHNSON, D. *Reaching Out*. Englewood Cliffs, N.J.: Prentice-Hall, Inc., 1972.

JOHNSON, R., AND S. JOHNSON. *Assuring Learning with Self-Instructional Packages*. Philippines: Self-Instructional Packages, Inc., 1973.

KNEER, M. E. "How Human Are You?" *Journal of Health, Physical Education & Recreation*, 45:6 (June 1974), 32.

———. "Influence of Selected Factors and Techniques on Student Satisfaction with a Physical Education Experience." Unpublished Doctoral dissertation, University of Michigan, Ann Arbor, Mich., 1972.

LAVORNI, C. *Humanity*. Belmont, Calif.: Fearon Publishers, 1970.

MILLER, A., AND M. MASSEY. *Methods and Materials for Secondary School Physical Education*. Englewood Cliffs, N.J.: Prentice-Hall, Inc., 1963.

PATTERSON, C. H. *Humanistic Education*. Englewood Cliffs, N.J.: Prentice-Hall, Inc., 1972.

ROBB, M. *Dynamics of Motor-Skill Acquisition*. Englewood Cliffs, N.J.: Prentice-Hall, Inc., 1972.

ROGERS, C. *Freedom to Learn*. Columbus, Ohio: Charles E. Merrill Publishing Company, 1969.

SIMON, S., L. HOWE, H. KIRSCHENBAUM. *Values Clarification*. New York: Hart Publishing Co., 1972.

STROM, R., AND E. TORRANCE. *Education for Affective Achievement*. Chicago: Rand, McNally & Company, 1973.

4

Learning:
The Product

INSTRUCTIONAL UNIT FOR CHAPTER 4

Learner's Diagnosis

Directions: Read the questions below. Write out, discuss, or mentally review the answers. If you believe that you know the information, check the "yes" column. If you are not sure of the answer, check the "no" column. After reading the questions and deciding your knowledge, check the accuracy of your answers by reading the summary at the end of this chapter. If you answered a question incorrectly, change your answer to the appropriate column.

Can you

Yes	No	Questions
		1. Define learning?
		2. Name four learning theories?
		3. Explain behaviorism?
		4. Explain experientialism?
		5. Explain cybernetics?
		6. Explain functionalism?
		7. Describe what makes individualism humanized?
		8. Describe two major aspects of humanistic approach?
		9. Describe predetermined learning plans?
		10. Describe dynamic interaction learning conditions?
		11. List four learning domains?
		12. List stages of learning?
		13. List five influences on the nature of learning?

Yes	No	Questions
		14. Give two major reasons for forgetting?
		15. List four procedures to promote remembering?

Suggested Prescription

Directions: Count the number of checks you have placed in the "yes" column. When the percentages are determined, you may increase your knowledge and skill by using the suggested Learning Program activities recommended in the Input and Practice columns.

Results	Input	Practice
More than 80%	#1, 6	#5
60% to 80%	#1, 4, 5	#3, 4
40% to 60%	#1, 2, 5	#2, 3, 4
Less than 40%	#1, 2, 3, 4	#1, 2, 3, 4

Learning Program

Directions: It is suggested that the reader attempt to follow any or all of this learning program. It is designed to improve knowledge and skill in understanding and applying learning theory and procedures to facilitate physical education.

Proposed Learning Objective: The learner will be able to structure teaching-learning conditions which will permit students to attain a mutually agreed upon skill objective.

Input:

*1. Read Chapter 4 of this book.
2. Attempt to teach yourself a novel skill. Analyze the stages you experienced in your learning and list the procedures that helped you to learn.

*Highly recommended.

3. Observe someone learning a skill and follow steps in #2 above.

4. Read selected references listed at the end of this chapter.

5. Propose an input of your own.

6. Read the following for in-depth understanding of learning theories as proposed and practiced by physical educators:

Behavioristic .... D. Siedentop and B. Rushall, *Development and Control of Learning in Sports and Physical Education.*

Cognitive .... D. Gallahue, P. Werner, and G. Luedke, *Moving and Learning.*

Cybernetic ...... R. Singer and W. Dick, *Teaching Physical Education: A Systems Approach.*

Motor Learning .. B. Oxendine, *Psychology and Motor Learning.*

Practice:

1. Write out or discuss with friends several learning theories.

2. Write out or discuss with friends the structure for teaching physical education humanistically.

*3. Develop a learning objective from which you will plan alternative delivery systems and transactions which reflect at least three learning principles. Describe the desired terminal behavior.

4. Discuss #3 with instructor and/or friends.

5. Develop a practice of your own.

Evaluation: You will be able to develop a lesson agenda which will illustrate the functional learning theory utilizing the humanistic approach. The plan will feature alternatives based on motor learning principles and will provide for learner interaction. It will be verified by the instructor, a friend, or a student.

Learning is considered to be a product of education—the result of directed or undirected experiences. From the teacher's point of view,

*Highly recommended.

learning results from the mix of procedures and content interacting in appropriate doses with the student. The verification of the attainment of the product is measured by written and/or skill tests. But is it learning?

DEFINITION

Learning is defined as a more or less permanent change in behavior. Behavior is said to be changed if a new word is spoken with appropriate usage, a poem is memorized, a typewriter is operated, throwing speed is increased, or accuracy is gained. However, learning also includes gestures, the acquisition of preferences, prejudices, attitudes, ideals, and social skills.

Students of learning theory find it difficult to write a satisfactory definition of learning. Some define learning as improvement with practice, or profiting by experience; however some learning is not an improvement and may have undesirable consequences. A change of behavior may be the result of growth, fatigue, or other physiological developments and thus may not be learning at all. Hilgard and Bower propose the following definition:

> Learning is the process by which an activity originates or is changed through reacting to an encountered situation, provided that the characteristics of the change in activity cannot be explained on the basis of native response tendencies, maturation, or temporary states of the organism.[1]

Such a definition provides for innate behavior including unlearned activities such as reflexes, instinct, or imprinting. Behavior modified by growth or maturation, such as a bird flying, is not considered to be learning. However, many activities of man and nature are a result of a complex interplay of growth and learning. For example, children perceive basic movement patterns, then try to imitate them, but may not succeed until bone and muscle growth can sustain the selected activity.

Another cause of behavior change may be fatigue. Repeated actions over time result in work decrements, or changes in performance due to voluntary or involuntary response to bodily distress. Often a behavior change results from a process called habituation, which is reduced responsiveness to a repeated stimulus. An example is the ability to read and listen to a radio at the same time. Too much practice (repeated stimulus) may cause an athlete's performance to become less precise. This is due to less response to detail. Coaches refer to this performance decrement as staleness.

[1]Ernest R. Hilgard and Gordon Bower, *Theories of Learning* (New York: Appleton-Century-Crofts, 1968), p. 2.

Authorities agree that it is difficult to formulate a satisfactory definition of learning which covers or excludes certain activities and processes. For the most part learning is more or less a permanent change in behavior inferred from performance.

LEARNING AS A PROCESS—
DYNAMIC AND ONGOING

Some learned activities lead to other activities. If you can walk, you can solve many new problems without learning anything new. You merely apply the learned behavior. For example, once able to walk, you may learn to adjust the speed of the walk to accommodate environmental conditions, or create a walking action which solves some problem or preference.

The direction, intensity, and endurance in learning is dependent upon many variables: heredity, environment, and learning opportunities. Although controversy is rampant concerning the role and mix of these variables, their presence influences the behavior change as evidenced by performance. The influence of heredity and environment was discussed in the preceding chapters. We will now look at the third factor, learning opportunities.

LEARNING THEORIES

There are many theories concerning how one learns. However, by grouping according to basic similarities, three distinct theories emerge: association, cognitive, and cybernetic. A fourth theory is proposed which is a conglomeration of all learning theories. Hilgard[2] called such a theory functionalism. Since methods of instruction are imbedded in facets of learning theories, you should have a basic understanding of how learning occurs.

Association.   The association theory of learning holds that three main events must occur for learning to take place: a stimulus, a response, and a consequence. The stimulus can be internal, such as hunger, or external, such as a loud noise. The reaction, or response, may result in a consequence which will determine whether or not the action will be repeated. If the consequence is desirable, the likelihood of repeating the response is increased or reinforced. However, if the consequence is not rewarding, then the response may not be repeated. For example, suppose you foul an opponent in the act of shooting, and the referee notes the

[2]Hilgard and Bower, *Theories of Learning.*

ASSOCIATION OR STIMULUS RESPONSE THEORY

foul and enforces the penalty. The need to foul to prevent an advantage to the opponent is the stimulus, the fouling is the response, and the penalty is the consequence. Those who accept the major tenets of the association theory are often called behaviorists. The process of learning is referred to as conditioning and that of unlearning, as extinguishing. Thorndike, Gutherie, Watson, and Skinner are all behaviorists.

Utilization of the association theory often relies on certain laws. Thorndike is considered the founder of association theory. He proposed three laws. The *Law of Readiness* states the conditions necessary to be receptive to change. Repeating experiences to strengthen the response— for example, drills and lengthy practices—is a manifestation of the *Law of Exercise.* The *Law of Effect* refers to the consequences of the response; the use of praise, success, and personal satisfaction will strengthen the association between the stimulus and the response. The Law of Effect is often neglected or left to chance by teachers.

Association theorists believe that you learn as a result of forces exerted upon you. Critics of this theory express concern about whether one can solve problems or be creative under this system, because it uses command or direct teaching to foster learning and because it focuses on the end product rather than on the means.

Cognitive.   The cognitive theory of learning is based on perception. Advocates of this theory—often referred to as experientialists—believe that new learning takes place when sensory stimuli are interpreted in the light of past experiences. Behavior is explained in terms of how things

Learn- Problem solving
- Similarities from previously learned skills and concepts, rather
  then stressing facts and generalizations
Process oriented - emphasizes means as well as end product

CYBERNETIC
Emphasizes performance capibilities , limitations and adaptions
concerned with way experience is processed . Process must be controlled and
understood
FEEDBACK LOOP -effect and reinforcer
What Happened?
Process is important to achieve product

Functional- Any aspect of all three can be used

ASSOCIATION -

Process   Stimulus Response Consequence
           Stimulus Internal or external
           Response Consequence Positive or negative reinforcement

           Behaviorist
           Conditioning   Law of Readiness
                          Law of Exercise
                          Law of Effect

Learn - as a x result of forces exerted upon you

Critics - no problem solving
          command teaching to foster learning
          focuses on end product rather than on means

COGNITIVE
          Based on perception
          Experimentalists
Process - new learning takes place when sensory stimuli are interpreted
          in the light of past experience
          - control over what is learned is internal
          - insight, trial and error and experience are the processes of
          learning

COGNITIVE THEORY = PAST EXPERIENCE + SELF-CONCEPT

seem to a person. Thus the role of right and wrong is often left to a person's values. Control of what is learned lies within the person. Insight, trial and error, and experience are the processes of learning, rather than stimulus, response, and consequence.

Tolman, Combs, Lewin and Rogers are supporters of cognitive learning theory. They see self-concept as crucial to learning. Personal interest, needs, values, and goals are extremely important influences on what and how much is learned. A cognitive learning theory physical educator would utilize Mosston's problem-solving and creative styles.[3] This theory would emphasize similarities from previously learned skills and concepts, rather than stressing facts and generalization of responses. Indirect and more personal approaches are the chief instructional processes. Cognitive theory is process-oriented, emphasizing the means as well as the end product.

Cybernetic. The cybernetic theory or systems approach to learning is a more recent theory. It emphasizes performance capabilities, limitations, and adaptations. Although experiences are important to proponents of this theory, they are more concerned about the way these experiences are processed. If the processes can be controlled and understood, then learning can take place. The main thrust of learning is the feedback

[3]Muska Mosston, *Teaching Physical Education* (Columbus, Ohio: Charles E. Merrill Publishing Company, 1966), pp. 183–229.

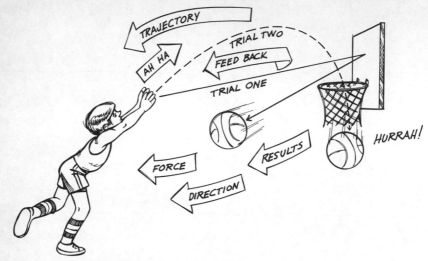

CYBERNETIC THEORY = FEEDBACK LOOP

loop, which is considered the effect and thus the reinforcer. Physical educators utilizing this learning theory would manipulate feedback to attain learning.

Cyberneticists deplore the aimlessness of the "shotgun" approach of cognitivists and doubt the learner's tendency to repeat a stimulus-response bond simply because of satisfaction, since satiation often dulls the effect. Wiener, Wilford, Fitts, Goody, and Smith are among the noted researchers in cybernetic learning theory. Descriptions of the theory are often presented through models, many of them based on information processing. The organization of bits and chunks of information is crucial. The physical educator who utilizes the guided discovery approach by asking, "What happened?" and then arranges practices to find out, is a proponent of cybernetic theory. This theory is oriented toward the fact that the process is important to achieve the product.

Functional. The functional theory of learning applies facets of association, cognitive, and cybernetic theories within the kaleidoscope of changing environments, experiences, and human needs. Proponents of this theory believe that any aspects of the three basic theories can be utilized as needed and decided by the learner with the guidance and advice of the instructor. The physical educator who utilizes this theory makes available a variety of learning alternatives to students. *Direct* teaching through lectures, commands, and imposed learning experiences may be used, as well as *indirect* teaching through tasks, problem-solving, and creative experiences. Tasks could be used to offer insights through trial and error; command-lecture-demonstrations could direct stimulus-response associations; and guided personal and social interaction methods could control feedback. These techniques could be used singly or in combination. The criterion for selecting the method or methods is the learner's needs. Functional learning theory is oriented to the learner's choice of the process that would be the most productive means to achieve the learner's goals.

Learning theories are the basis for teaching methods. Teachers have had difficulties in implementing any one theory since no one theory seems to explain how students actually learn. The cybernetic theory or "systems approach" has gained favor since it seems to be an objective basis for selecting from association or cognitive theories the processes best suited to the attainment of global goals. However, this approach places the instructor in the key decision-making position for assigning learning conditions stressing behavioristic theory. Singer[4] stresses that "the systems approach is not meant to confine the teacher to one teaching method or strategy; the learning conditions and instructional events to be presented will reveal a trend toward a prescriptive approach along behavioristic lines."

The humanistic approach utilizes the functional theory of learning. It does not confine you to any one teaching technique or strategy based on any single learning theory. It does require that you determine global goals for behavior change and that you develop tentative learning programs and diagnostic procedures which will bring about the change.

The functional theory is pragmatic and has demonstrated to successful instructors that "it works." The process is couched in the dynamics of positive human relations. The humanistic approach has been difficult to implement in a systematic way. Succeeding chapters will attempt to help you understand and learn structure and procedures (individualized instruction), utilizing the functional learning theory toward humanistic goals.

The basic assumption of individualized learning is predicated on the ideas postulated by Bloom and Carroll that aptitude is predictive of rate, but not necessarily the level at which a student could learn.[5] For example, if the amount of time allowed to learn a psychomotor skill is held constant—such as planning thirty minutes to learn the lay-up shot in basketball—then the varied student aptitudes for learning the skill will inevitably lead to differences in the amount of skill acquired. On the other hand, if each students received differentiated instruction and time based on his or her aptitude, then most could reach a mastery level.

[4]Robert Singer, *Teaching Physical Education: A Systems Approach* (New York: Houghton Mifflin Company, 1974), p. 20.
[5]As stated by J. Block in "Teachers, Teaching and Mastery Learning," *Today's Education*, LXIV (July 1973), p 34.

THE PROCESS

The process of learning in the humanistic system involves: (1) the content or the information and skills to be learned, (2) the structure and procedures to facilitate learning, and (3) the human relations interaction between teacher and student to mediate the first two. Figure 4–1 illustrates the components. The crucial aspect of the triangle is the human relations base. The interaction between teacher and students is the determination of differentiated treatment. The differentiated treatment can be learning through trial and error, through reinforcing conditions, or through a variety of interacting experiences.

Figure 4–1

The *structure of the process* is straightforward and essentially static. However, the *execution of the process* is dynamic and requires patience and trust. Trust is essential because the learner must be a partner in the decision-making process. Educators lament the difficulty in motivating a student to learn through prescribed methods and content. Motivation is imbedded in the personal needs, abilities, and incentives of the learner. We have already seen in Chapter 2 the myriad differences existing in any teaching setting. The structure features alternatives in *delivery systems* (plans or processes offering the information and experiences that will lead to planned objectives), *transactions* (practice events designed to fix the learning), and *objectives*.

Figure 4–2 schematically illustrates the structure of the learning process to be presented in this book. The predetermined conditions which are developed by the facilitator begins with your establishing the global goals for the course, module, or unit of instruction. These goals are translated into learning objectives for the various skills, knowledges, and feelings. Terminal objectives are identified for the various behaviors which will indicate to the student when his acceptable level of competency is reached.

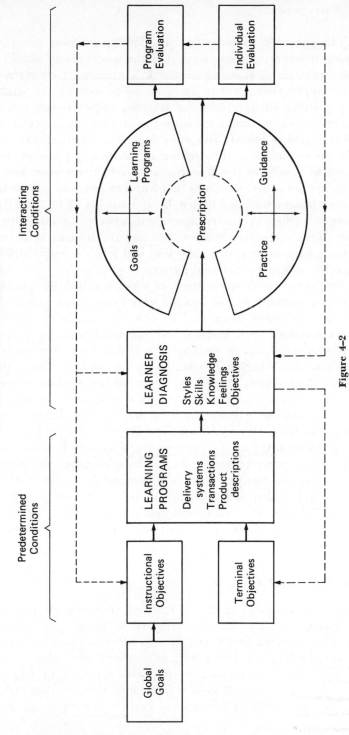

MODEL FOR
PHYSICAL EDUCATION INSTRUCTIONAL TECHNIQUES:
An Individualized Humanistic Approach

Interacting Conditions

Learning Programs

Goals

Prescription

Guidance

Practice

Program Evaluation

Individual Evaluation

Predetermined Conditions

LEARNER DIAGNOSIS

Styles
Skills
Knowledge
Feelings
Objectives

LEARNING PROGRAMS

Delivery systems
Transactions
Product descriptions

Instructional Objectives

Terminal Objectives

Global Goals

Figure 4–2

The next step requires that you develop learning programs which will suggest several possible ways that the student may obtain information and practice what is to be learned. The learning program will indicate the appropriate level of competency desired by the student. The final predetermined condition for learning requires that you select appropriate means to diagnose, with the student, his special aptitudes, interests, learning modes, and objectives. The application of the diagnosis is the beginning of the dynamic or interacting phase of the humanistic system. Results of the diagnosis are used in two ways: one, to select the appropriate course of action in a learning program and, two, to indicate any changes not anticipated by the teacher. The prescription for learning is reached by mutual agreement between the facilitator and the student. This agreement between you and the student is often a blend of behavioristic and cognitive learning and it is the *major difference* between cybernetic and functional theory.

The prescription is executed in what is called the guidance step. This step is carried on mainly in the school setting but may occur in any setting that facilitates learning. The behavior change or learning objectives are practiced with instructional assistance given by you, peers, or anyone who can assist the student in reaching his or her goals. You are free to give much personal attention to the student during this phase. When the desired level of learning is reached, the evaluation step begins. This step analyzes how well the terminal objectives are achieved. The degree of satisfaction with the learning may have implications for further learning and this step may become the diagnosis for the pursuit of additional learning listed in the prescription. The overall results of the student-facilitator interactions in the teaching-learning environment comprise the program analysis which will give insight to you concerning the adequacy and quality of the predetermined conditions. It will guide the revisions. Subsequent chapters will help you to acquire the learning you may desire concerning the humanistic system of teaching physical education.

WHAT IS LEARNED?

As long as stimuli are being received, responses are possible. When these responses change, then learning has occurred. Learning can be directed or undirected and it can be related or unrelated to stated goals. In a formal education system, such as a school, education is directed toward stated goals. The educational system attempts to achieve certain behavior changes that will sustain and improve the quality of life for all. It is generally agreed by educational experts that education is aimed at transmitting the culture and at developing the total potentiality of humans, including skills, knowledges, and feelings, so that each person will be open to change and be able to live existentially as a self-actualizing individual.

Physical education should give the student an understanding of the need to be physically fit and the ability to maintain a healthy and vigorous life. Since learning is both process and product, it is important that personal satisfaction result from the stimulation of play and exercise. The joy of activity is a product in its own right but is also an outcome which stimulates continued pursuit of activity. Continued involvement of society in gross movement experiences must be considered a major goal of physical educators since the outcomes of exercise and play are ephemeral.

Learning Classification. Educators are attempting to categorize behavior changes according to some classification system, or *taxonomy*. The changes are generally considered to be in three domains: cognitive or knowledge, affective or feelings, and psychomotor or skills. Many educators believe that there is a fourth domain called the social domain. Classifying learning assists the educator to understand the components of learning within each domain so that objectives, methods, and evaluation procedures may be planned and so that a more universal understanding of learning may be formed. The cognitive and affective taxonomies are well accepted and structured. Controversy over content and structure exists for the psychomotor and social domains. They will be discussed further in Chapter 5. It will suffice for now to say that these taxonomies are the basis for writing goals and objectives for learning.

Behavioral Objectives.   Within each behavior domain, three kinds of objectives are commonly used to guide the direction of the learning experience: global goals, learning objectives, and terminal objectives. *Global goals* indicate what is to be learned—for example, "tennis." *Learning objectives* guide how the learning will proceed within the global goal; "learning to serve" is a part of learning to play tennis. These objectives are normally planned by the teacher but are also planned by students when choice is provided to them. *Terminal objectives* specify the standards of performance of a learning objective: "Being able to serve seven of ten serves over the net and landing in right service court." Terminal objectives should be jointly agreed upon by the teacher and the student. Instruction is given in Chapter 5 to assist you in writing behavioral objectives.

As you can see, learning begins with the recognition of a relevant problem. Relevancy is related to the meaning or value that the acquisition of the knowledge, skill, or feeling may have for a person. Once the goal is accepted and the decision is made to pursue it, then the learning process is initiated. Suppose a student wishes to learn a psychomotor skill, such as the hook shot in basketball. The desire to pursue this goal may be rooted in the cognitive domain—hook shooting is an effective evasive skill for scoring; or the desire may be rooted in the affective domain because the learner enjoys the feeling experienced in observing someone attempt a hook shot. Skill is described as the ability to complete a task with ease and precision. The acquisition of the skill is achieved through conscientious effort and purposeful practice.

STAGES OF LEARNING

All learning is operationally described as following an input, processing, and output stage which is constantly evaluated in terms of error or success information called feedback. In the case of learning a motor skill, input is gathered from the receptor organs such as the auditory, visual, proprioceptive, tactile, or olfactory senses. Next, the input is processed in the central nervous system to gain meaning through coding, storing, and translating so that the output stage can be attempted by the muscular system. The output is evaluated in terms of the feedback received through the receptors and then reprocessed in the nervous system to adjust the performance of the skill so that it will more closely match the goal. This procedure is repeated through practice until the desired skill level or goal is consistently attained and automatically performed without the involvement of the central nervous system.

These stages may be described as *formulating a plan, fixing the learning* through practice, and continuing the process until the final stage, *automatic performance,* is achieved. Figure 4–3 illustrates the roles of the facilitator, student, and motor learning system during these stages.

In the plan-formulating stage, the student must come to understand the task and the sequence of components. Stage one of learning a basketball hook shot may be viewing films, pictures, or demonstrations, or reading a description, listening to an explanation, or receiving information from other sources or combinations thereof. Obviously, accurate sensory perception of the information is crucial; thus, the role of the facilitator is to enhance the crucial stimuli through cues and other attention-producing procedures. Care must be taken not to give too much information, because the immediate capacity of the translating system is limited. When planning delivery systems, the facilitator must make every attempt to control within the prescription the essence of what the student should attend to, since task understanding is paramount in the initial stage of learning.

Once the skill is understood, then practice can proceed to fix the performance sequence. The fixation stage is a kaleidoscope of changing

Learning Stages	Roles		
	Facilitator	Student	Motor Learning System
Formulating input plans	Delivery systems	Prescription	Receptors
Fixing learning	Transactions	Practice	Translation from feedback loops
Automatic performance	Terminal objectives	Terminal objectives	Ease, precision, few errors

Figure 4–3

Comparison of Learning Stages with Roles of the Facilitator, Student, and
Motor Learning System

patterns of action, thought, or feelings until the terminal objective is
attained. Instruction will be individualized and time required will vary
according to each student's specific aptitudes, physical needs, and personal aspirations. Cues, practice schedules, whole and part learning, serial
order sequencing, transfer, and feedback are important to fixing the learning. The basketball player attempting to learn a hook shot will now
be concerned with the timing or temporal pattern of the skill and will
be aided by attending to certain visual, auditory, and proprioceptive cues.
A student with high motivation and natural skill may be able to sustain
practice for a considerable amount of time. Since the hook shot is complex, certain parts of the skill may be practiced, as well as the entire
action. Many of these variations will be guided by previous learning. If
the student has learned similar skills such as pivoting, then perhaps the
similarity of that skill to the initiation of the hook may be transferable
and, thus, little practice may be needed. During practice the performer
will be attempting to analyze errors in terms of his or her understanding
of the task and terminal objective. Information concerning these errors
is received through the senses and compared with the learner's perception of the hook shot. This process is called feedback. Feedback may be
augmented by the facilitator, students, and other peers, movies, and
simulators. It is the single most important factor during this stage. Chapter 7 will discuss further how these aspects of motor learning can be applied to the acquisition of skills.

The final stage is automatic execution. The hook shot now is performed with ease, few errors, and maximum pleasure. It may be executed

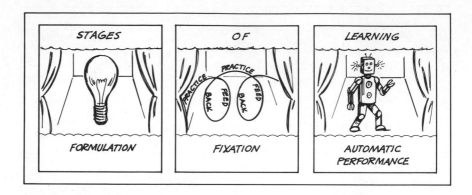

with little thought and as a result the learner may now turn attention to refinements such as the height of the jump. Continued practice is dependent upon the goals and objectives of the learner. Additional help and information concerning teaching procedures to assist learning this stage are presented in Chapter 8.

FACTORS AFFECTING SKILL ACQUISITION

The task of teaching is a difficult art because in spite of what is known about learning, the learner and the learning environment are never static. Constantly impinging on the teaching-learning act are variables regarding the content, personal conditions, perseverance, environment, and motivation.

Content. The learning task must be meaningful to students in that they must consider the task important to their immediate goals, and they must believe they will be able to succeed in learning it. One of the confounding problems is that the above factors may be present but not necessarily at the precise time that is selected for learning. Flexibility in the scope and sequence of pursuing learning programs is a useful strategy to overcome negative influences of personal preferences about content.

Personal Conditions. Many of these conditions have been discussed in Chapter 2. The immediate status of the learner's health, age, fatigue level, previous experiences, and anxiety state affect the success of the learning experience. These conditions may influence the pace and depth of the learning experience.

Perseverance. This factor controls the ability of the learner to sustain concentration and to eliminate interference of competing stimuli on the learning act. The value attached to the goals sought and the extent and nature of the success experience influence the ability of the learner to pay attention to the planned delivery system and practice events. You may augment this process by employing tactics that will force attention, such as introducing novel practice, unique rewards, and intense cueing procedures. Disciplinary measures such as reprimanding, withholding praise, withdrawing privileges, or removing a pupil from the learning environment are traditional procedures to force perseverance in attention and pursuit of the goal. However, learning theorists have found that positive consequences are far more effective. It is better to build trust in the value of your help than to rely on disciplinary measures.

Environment. There are many stimuli in gymnasiums or learning laboratories that relate to the planned learning event. The temperature and humidity tend to affect the amount of activity of the learner. Hot and humid conditions decrease activity, whereas cool, dry conditions increase participation. The appearance of the environment has similar influences on performance. Sufficient space and equipment, of course, are important, but the order, readiness, color, and lighting can arouse or diminish participation in the learning act.

Motivation. Regardless of the mix of aptitude, environment, and instruction, the fuse to ignite learning is motivation. Chapter 9 is entirely devoted to this most powerful tool. It is difficult, if not impossible, for people to commit themselves to the demands of learning if they can see no implications toward some basic need or motive. Even if the activity or skill to be learned is of value to the students, it is equally deterring if they view it as physically or intellectually beyond their ability. Incentives are valuable to tempt the learners to put forth the effort, and the learners must perceive the task as not too easy or too difficult to attain. The facilitator must design learning procedures that provide challenging success experiences and rewards that are congruent with the students' interests and needs.

SUSTAINING LEARNING

Since learning is described as a relatively permanent change of behavior, you may be wondering about forgetting. Theorists and researchers have not discovered any one factor that accounts for forgetting. Basically it may be attributed to two major factors: *disuse* and *repression*. When a behavior change is achieved but not practiced sufficiently, it is believed that the information, skill, or feeling fades from memory. This fading may also be the result of confusion caused by frequent practice of more recent, competing learning. This happens most often when the information or skills are very similar. For example, if you learned to play badminton, which stresses a flexible wrist, and then learned tennis, which emphasizes a firm wrist, you may tend to keep your wrist too firm when you return to playing badminton. The competing stimuli interfere with previously learned patterns. This interference is called negative transfer. Scientists recognize two types of interference: *retroactive inhibition* and *proactive inhibition*. Retroactive inhibition occurs when badminton is learned and then, after one learns tennis, badminton skills are forgotten. Proactive inhibition is operating when the previous learning of badminton interferes with the learning of tennis.

Another theory relating to disuse is the biochemical theory that learning produces RNA (ribonucleic acid), which encodes what is learned. However, study shows that RNA tends to disappear over time. Finally, the most accepted theory is based on what is called *channel capacity*. This theory holds that learning is held momentarily in a short-term memory, and if rehearsed long enough the behavior change will be transferred to a long-term memory store and will not be forgotten.

The repression theory, which was postulated by Freud, holds that learning that is unpleasant is avoided or unconsciously repressed. This idea coincides with positive reinforcement theory—the likelihood of one's repeating behavior that is satisfying.

You may sustain the students' learning by implementing certain conditions. First, provide frequent and sufficient practice. Extensive practice tends to encourage retention by strengthening stimulus-response bonds (association theory). Also, carefully organizing the experiences will help to stimulate recall by utilizing positive transfer sequences (cognitive theory). Studies have indicated that the beginning and ending learning experiences are remembered better than the middle portions. The middle part of the serial order is subject to two possible influences: one, proactive and retroactive inhibition, and two, the amount of time rehearsed behavior is in the short-term memory storage.

Finally, to avoid repressing, what is learned should be meaningful, relevant to the student's goals, satisfying, and pleasurable. The nature of the satisfaction tends to be more permanent when primary reinforcement or pleasure conditions are consequences of activity. These primary consequences may be joyful human relations, a feeling of control over one's destiny, and positive feeling of self-worth. Money, symbols of winning, praise, and avoidance of pain are secondary consequences and tend to be more satiating.

Additional applications of these strategies are explained in Chapter 11.

SUMMARY

Learning is defined as a more or less permanent change in behavior inferred from performance. Four learning theories are generally accepted: (1) *association* theory, which is used by behaviorists, utilizes the stimulus-response bond resulting from desirable consequences; (2) *cognitive* theory, which is used by experientialists, is based on perception of an experience which is analyzed by repeated trials and errors resulting in new information; (3) *cybernetic* theory, which is an information-processing theory, utilizes a systems approach to control feedback from trial and error and stimulus-response bond to change behavior; and (4) *functional* theory, in which all three of the above theories operate in any given situation, stresses human interaction between teacher and learner to bring about the learning desired.

The humanistic approach to teaching physical education utilizes the *functional theory* for predetermining learning conditions and guiding dynamic applications of instructional strategies. The humanistic approach does not confine you to any one teaching method or strategy based on any single learning theory. The goals of humanism are aimed at developing self-actualizing persons who are open to change and to continued learning. Content and methods are integrated to promote learning in physical education.

The structure of learning under the humanistic approach has two major aspects: predetermined learning and interacting conditions. Predetermined learning plans include: (1) behavioral objectives, (2) delivery systems, (3) transactions, and (4) evaluation plans. The dynamic or interacting conditions include: (1) learning diagnosis, (2) prescriptive learning programs, (3) practicing the transactions, and (4) analysis of learning in terms of agreed-upon criteria.

Learning is classified into four domains: cognitive, psychomotor, affective, and social. Taxonomies or classification systems aid in planning for learning sequences and determining objectives. Learning proceeds through three stages: (1) formulation of plans, (2) fixation of skill or learning through practice, and (3) the automatic stage, which approximates the objective. The acquisition of skill is influenced by the nature of the content to be learned, personal conditions, perseverance, environmental conditions, and motivation. Disuse and repression are major reasons learning is forgotten or extinguished. Remembering can be fostered by overlearning, selecting meaningful activities, eliminating interfering experiences, and carefully organizing the sequence of skill components.

REFERENCES

AAHPER. "The New Physical Education," *Journal of Health, Physical Education and Recreation,* 42:24 (1971), 39.

BLOCK, J. H. "Teachers, Teaching and Master Learning," *Today's Education.* NEA, 63:7 (1973), 30.

BLOOM, B. S. "An Introduction to Mastery Learning," in James H. Block, ed. *Schools, Society and Mastery Learning.* New York: Holt, Rinehart and Winston, Inc., 1974.

BLOOM, B. S., M. ENGLEHART, E. FURST, W. HILL, AND D. KRATHWOHL. *Taxonomy of Educational Objectives Handbook I: Cognitive Domain.* New York: David McKay Co., Inc., 1956.

BLOOM, B., H. HASTINGS, AND G. MADAUS. *Handbook on Formative and Summative Evaluation of Student Learning.* New York: McGraw-Hill Book Company, 1971.

CARROLL, J. "A Model of School Learning," *Teachers College Record,* 64 (1963), 723–33.

COMBS, A. W., AND D. SNYGG. *Individual Behavior.* New York: Harper & Row, Publishers, 1959.

CRATTY, B. *Movement Behavior and Motor Learning.* Philadelphia: Lea & Febiger, 1964.

FITTS, P., AND M. POSNER. *Human Performance.* Belmont, Calif.: Brooks/Cole Publishing Company, 1967.

GAGNE, R. *Conditions for Learning* (2nd ed.) New York: Holt, Rinehart and Winston, Inc., 1970.

HELLISTON, DONALD. *Humanistic Physical Education.* Columbus, Ohio: Charles E. Merrill Publishing Company, 1973.

HILGARD, E., AND G. BOWER. *Theories of Learning.* New York: Appleton-Century-Crofts, 1966.

JEWETT, A., S. JONES, S. LUNEKE, AND S. ROBINSON. "Educational Change Through a Taxonomy for Writing Physical Education Objectives," *Quest,* 15 (January 1971).

KRATHWOHL, D., B. BLOOM, AND B. BASIA. *Taxonomy of Educational Objectives: Handbook II: Affective Domain*. New York: David McKay Company, Inc., 1964.

MOSSTON, M. *Teaching Physical Education*. Columbus, Ohio: Charles E. Merrill Publishing Company, 1966.

PATTERSON, C. H. *Humanistic Education*. Englewood Cliffs, N.J.: Prentice-Hall, Inc., 1973.

ROBB, M. *Dynamics of Motor Skill Acquisition*. Englewood Cliffs, N.J.: Prentice-Hall, Inc., 1972.

ROGERS, C. *Freedom to Learn*. Columbus, Ohio: Charles E. Merrill Publishing Company, 1969.

SIEDENTOP, D., AND B. RUSHALL. *The Development and Control of Behavior in Sport and Physical Education*. Philadelphia: Lea & Febiger, 1972.

SINGER, R. *Motor Learning and Human Performance*. New York: The Macmillan Company, 1968.

SINGER, R., AND W. DICK. *Teaching Physical Education—A Systems Approach*. Boston: Houghton Mifflin Company, 1974.

PART II

HOW TO DO IT
DEVELOPING
LEARNING PROGRAMS

5

The Plan:
Static
Conditions

INSTRUCTIONAL UNIT FOR CHAPTER 5
Learner's Diagnosis

Directions: Read the questions below. Write out, discuss, or mentally review the answers. If you believe that you know the information, check the "yes" column. If you are not sure of the answer, check the "no" column. After reading the questions and deciding your knowledge, check the accuracy of your answers by reading the summary at the end of this chapter. If you answered a question incorrectly, change your answer to the appropriate column.

Can you

Yes	No	Questions
		1. Explain the major value of the unit plan?
		2. List at least five components of a unit plan?
		3. Define a behavioral objective?
		4. Define a global goal?
		5. Construct a learning objective?
		6. Construct a terminal objective?
		7. Explain a module or contract?
		8. Explain the value of a learning objective?
		9. List the major parts of a learning program?
		10. Explain the purpose of diagnosis?
		11. Construct a diagnostic plan?
		12. Develop a plan for disseminating material and record keeping.
		13. Construct a tentative 25-lesson I.I. (individualized instruction) block plan?
		14. Develop a lesson agenda for one day of #13?
		15. Develop a grading plan for an I.I. unit of study?

Suggested Prescription

Directions: Count the number of checks you have placed in the "yes" column. When the percentages are determined, you may increase your knowledge and skill by using the suggested Learning Program activities recommended in the Input and Practice Columns.

Results	Input	Practice
More than 80%	#1, 8	#7
60% to 80%	#1, 6, 8	#2, 3 or 4
40% to 60%	#1, 3, 4 or 5, 7	#1, 2, 3 or 4, 5
Less than 40%	#1, 2 or 3, 4 or 5, 6, 7	#1, 2, 3, 4, 5, 6

Learning Program

Directions: It is suggested that the reader attempt to follow any and all suggestions in this learning program. These are designed to improve knowledge and understanding of planning for individualized instruction and to promote skill in developing plans.

Proposed Learning Objective: The learner will be able to develop a complete individualized instruction unit of study.

Input:

 *1. Read Chapter 5 of this book.
  2. Read Mager, *Preparing Instructional Objectives.*
  3. Read Chapter 14 of this book, which gives samples of unit plans.
  4. Observe an individualized instruction class. Note activities of one or two of the students during an entire hour.
  5. Observe and discuss a Unit of Study plan with a colleague or faculty member.
  6. Read selected references at the end of this chapter.
  7. Observe at least two teachers' space and records management.
     Discuss with them any questions that you may have.
  8. Plan an input of your own.

*Highly recommended.

Practice:

1. Write a global goal, learning objective, terminal objective. Compare with samples given in this chapter.
2. Write a learning objective. Develop an outline of a possible module. Discuss its adequacy with a colleague.
3. Develop a diagnostic examination for a physical education activity of your choice. Discuss your plan with a colleague or faculty member.
4. Construct a prescription form for a physical education activity of your choice.
5. Sketch a tentative plan for facilitating a physical education activity of your choice using the humanistic approach.
6. Develop a 25-lesson block calendar for individualizing an activity of your choice.
7. Plan a practice of your own.

Evaluation: You will be able to develop a Unit Plan for facilitating an individualized humanistic instructional course for an activity of your choice. The plan will include the following:

1. Behavioral objectives:
   a. The global goal
   b. Examples of at least one learning objective, and a list of other possible subject matter topics
   c. Examples of at least one terminal objective
2. Learning program: Outline one module or contract, or prepare an agenda for a more flexible, open program
3. Diagnosis (describe or outline plan)
4. Prescription (describe or outline plan)
5. Guiding plans (list of topics)
6. Evaluation plan (describe or outline plan)
7. Operation procedures (explain only)

Individualized instruction begins with the student, not the group. Each student's learning program is planned and conducted on a one-to-one basis. Group instruction is utilized whenever several students are ready to practice a skill or task in a like way. Thus group structure would vary and is a tool to be used whenever students' needs appear to be similar. Student self-direction is the key to effective individual learning without the need for continual assistance from the facilitator.

Instructional techniques for physical education with an individualized humanistic approach are founded on the production of predetermined conditions or static plans which identify what it is possible to learn, how well it can be learned, and what procedures will help the student to learn it. What is to be learned, and how well, are delineated in stating purposes, objectives, and standards of performance. Assisting the learner requires the development of multi-variant processes to allow the learner to acquire knowledge and understanding, as well as to practice for reinforcement. These plans are predicated upon an assessment of the total teaching-learning environment and operational feasibility in terms of time, space, facilities, and instructional assistance.

Predetermined conditions developed by the facilitator provide a sound operational base from which a student may plan his approach to learning physical education subject matter. These conditions make available an initial source of experiential alternatives which may satisfy the student's own unique needs within the specific module selected for study. It should be noted that the opportunity to choose is not restricted or limited to the available alternatives. Major responsibility is given to the student to analyze his entry point and to determine how he will reach the desired goal. As a matter of fact, well-developed plans should stimulate students to conceive additional learning conditions and possibilities.

Static learning conditions are called unit plans. Lesson agendas are generated from the unit plan. The succeeding sections of this chapter will help you to acquire the ability to construct unit plans and lesson agendas.

UNIT PLAN

An instructional unit has six major provisions: (1) behavioral objectives, (2) learning programs, (3) diagnostic plans, (4) prescription development, (5) grading and evaluation program, and (6) operational procedures. The determination of these provisions is based on a comprehensive analysis of the subject matter, the learner, and the environmental influences. Additional help for decision making will be found in Chapter 10.

Behavioral Objectives. A behavioral objective is a collection of words, statements, or symbols which describe the desired visible activity by a student after learning. Obviously, objectives give direction to the entire teaching-learning endeavor. Directions for planning require identification of what, how, and to which degree the learning is to proceed. Theorists use various terms to refer to types of behavior objectives.

The *global goal* is the general purpose of the course. Examples of global goals are as follows:

> Students will learn to play tennis.
>
> Students will be able to play golf.
>
> Students will be able to ski.

Notice that the statement is structured to identify *who* (the student) will be doing *what* (the activity).

How a student will reach the global goal is specified in what are called *learning objectives*. Some educators refer to learning objectives as instructional objectives. Learning objective refers to the learner's outcome, whereas the instructional objective specifies how the facilitator will reach the outcome. Examples of learning objectives are as follows:

> Students will be able to:
>
> execute three types of tennis serve
>
> hit a slice tennis serve
>
> serve accurately

It can be seen that learning objectives delineate the global goal into various integral components. Since behavior objectives describe the type of behavior to be observed, verbs must be used which will accurately identify the final product of the endeavor. Chapter 4 indicated four types of learning domains: cognitive, affective, psychomotor, and social. The writing of learning objectives becomes easier and more precise when verbs are used that reflect the categories appropriate to the portion of the global goal to be learned. Figure 5–1 presents the sequential hierarchy in the three behavior domains in which categories have been identified.

When writing a learning objective, you would identify the category of learning and select a verb that represents that category. For example, within the cognitive domain:

> Know tennis rules   (recalling)
>
> Umpire a game   (applying)

DOMAINS		
Cognitive*[1]	Affective*[2]	Psychomotor*[3]
Recalling Comprehending Applying Analyzing Synthesizing Evaluating	Receiving Responding Valuing Organizing Characterizing	Perceiving Imitating Patterning Adapting Refining Varying Improving Composing

Figure 5–1

Perhaps the knowledge is related to strategy, in which case an example might be:

Analyze the opponent's defense	(analyzing)
Select the best offense	(evaluating)

A similar procedure would be used to write an affective learning objective. A learning objective for a football module might be:

Attend football games regularly	(valuing)
Organize football practice	(organizing)
Accept defeat graciously	(characterizing)

An example of a psychomotor learning objective for a golf module might be:

Putt with accuracy	(patterning)
Putt on an undulating surface	(adapting)
Chip with a quarter swing	(varying)

[1]Benjamin S. Bloom., ed, *Taxonomy of Educational Objects, Handbook I: Cognitive Domain* (New York: David McKay Co., Inc., 1956).

[2]David Krathwohl, *Taxonomy of Educational Objectives: Handbook II: Affective Domain* (New York: David McKay Co., Inc., 1964).

[3]Ann Jewett, et al. "Educational Change Through a Taxonomy for Writing Physical Education Objectives," *Quest*, XV (January 1971).

Figures 5–2, 5–3, and 5–4 present a list of verbs appropriate for the various learning domains and levels of classifications.

COGNITIVE DOMAIN					
Recalling	Comprehending	Applying	Analyzing	Synthesizing	Evaluating
Write List Recall	Transfer Interpret Construct Change Explain	Explain Solve Solicit Employ Use	Identify Select Compare Differentiate	Create Make Compose Devise	Describe Discern Investigate Judge

Figure 5–2

AFFECTIVE DOMAIN				
Receiving	Responding	Valuing	Organizing	Characterizing
Know Understand Perceive Follow Accept	Answer Echo Choose Gather Visit Argue Mimic	Desire Depend Threaten Believe Rely upon Support Subscribe Want	Arrange Coordinate Establish Classify	Typify Represent Identify

Figure 5–3

PSYCHOMOTOR DOMAIN			
Perceiving	Imitating	Patterning	Adapting
Try Know Note	Copy Mimic Imitate	Follow Repeat Hit Catch Stroke	Adjust Allow Adapt
Refining	Varying	Improving	Composing
Smooth Combine Integrate	Change Alter	Develop Improve	Make Create Invent Design

Figure 5–4

The process of writing learning objectives begins with identifying the subject matter in the learning program and then analyzing the tasks in terms of their basic domain categories. Actions are indicated by stating the verb that best implies the behavior. It should be noted that performance involves more than one domain and category. No learning is really void of implications of other types of learning. Figure 5–5 illustrates this procedure for a badminton module. The degree of breakdown is a matter of facilitation preference based on the degree of sophistication desired.

Both the learner and the facilitator need to know when the desired goal is reached. *Terminal objectives* specify the degree of proficiency at-

Subject Matter	Possible Verbs
Grips (Forehand and Backhand)	Hold, grasp
Strokes Clears (Overhead, Forehand, Backhand) Drops (Overhead, Forehand, Backhand) Smashes (Overhead, Forehand, Backhand) Nets (Overhead, Forehand, Backhand) Drives (Overhead, Forehand, Backhand)	Hit Strike Smash Direct Swing Guide Stroke Initiate Adapt
Serve High long Low short	Guide Direct
Defense Singles Doubles	Position Analyze Apply
Offense Singles Doubles	Follow Position Analyze
Rules	Know, apply, analyze, comprehend
Strategy	Analyze, develop, create
Appreciation of game	Value, enjoy, cooperate

Figure 5–5

Badminton Task Analysis

tained by identifying the appearance and evidence of successful acquisition of the learning objective. Specifications to describe the desired performance level are called standards or criteria. In addition, conditions under which the goal is to be performed must be spelled out. Here is an example of a terminal objective:

> The student will be able to hit a pitched ball for a base hit 25% of the time during a tournament.

The first part of the statement identifies the terminal behavior and is, therefore, a learning objective; however, "for a base hit 25 percent of the time" describes the observable evidence. The last portion, "during a tournament," is a condition which sets the acceptable circumstances. Standards of performance may deal with quantitative variables such as distance, time, accuracy, speed, and consistency; or with qualitative variables such as form and appearance. Conditions specify environment, constraints, and exclusions.

You may wish to open-end a terminal objective so that the exact standards of performance and conditions can be personalized on the basis of each student's entry level and goals. For example:

> Hit a golf ball with a midiron _____ yards _____% of the time while playing in a _____ (place).

Or you may specify conditions *only*:

> Hit a golf ball with a midiron _____ yards _____% of the time during the prescribed practice in class.

The values of behavioral objectives are as follows: (1) They convey to the learner the possible learning necessary to reach the desired global goal and at the same time define for the facilitator the inherent subject matter that must be processed to provide the learner with the needed information and practice. (2) They describe the dimensions of the learning goals. (3) They provide a verification that learning has occurred and thereby serve as an objective evaluative means for both the facilitator and the learner.

Thus, the initial stages of developing a unit plan are as follows:

1. Identify the global goal or purpose of the unit.
2. Analyze the knowledge, skills, and feeling components.
3. Write learning objectives using appropriate verbs which define the action of the learner for each component of the goal.
4. Write terminal objectives by adding to the learning objectives, the standards of performance and conditions which will describe the acceptable level of performance.

Learning Programs. Learning programs form the bridge between learning objectives and terminal objectives. These "bridges" may be group-centered or individualized. Group teaching provides a singular approach to learning via teacher-directed explanations, demonstrations, and drills in which all students are expected to participate. Within an individualized teaching-learning setting several courses of action may be pursued singly or in combinations. Different students may be (1) working on different tasks toward different goals, (2) using a variety of learning materials or equipment to reach similar goals, (3) practicing the same task in individual or group settings, (4) pursuing assistance from different resource personnel: facilitators, aides, peers, leaders, or paraprofessionals, (5) studying via different methods, discovery, and independent practice, and (6) using varying amounts of time to achieve mastery. The degree of structure or control for individualized humanistic physical education is dependent upon student readiness for responsibility, the situation, the facilitator's ability, and perhaps, the type of activity.

A student may work as an individual or as a member of a group. The teacher may use some class-prescribed activities as well as provide a degree of individual choice. For example, a class may be taught as a group one day, be completely individualized another, or be a combination of the two on still another. However, individual learning, where a variety of opportunities for obtaining the reference pattern and practice are available, will need some form of a self-contained package. This self-contained package is referred to as a module or contract that includes all possible options and directions. The module may take from a few minutes to several hours to complete. It may be used singly or in combination with other modules. When the learning program is used singly, it is often referred to as a mini-course. Several mini-courses based upon

independent components of a sport or movement art are made available
to the learner, through verbal directions or through written cards. Basketball may be comprised of mini-courses in ball handling, shooting, defensive play, offensive play, rules, officiating, and strategy. The prescribed
activities provide the learners with small, readily mastered segments of
the unit of study, as well as active involvement options, feedback, and
opportunity to learn at the pace most suitable to each of them. These
functions are executed through the following components:

1. Statement of learning objectives   (Purpose)
2. Delivery system   (Information input)
3. Transactions   (Practice)
4. Terminal objective   (Evaluation)

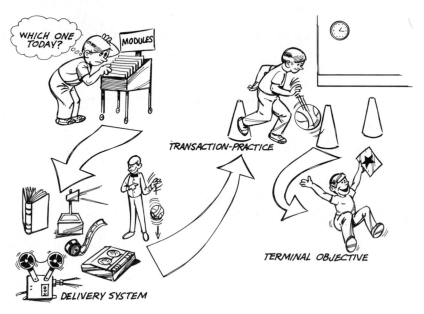

The process of writing a learning program begins with a selected
learning objective and its concomitant terminal objective. A variety of
media options are written which will generate and maintain interest,
introduce relevancy, provide consideration of human variables, enable
the student to choose what will be learned and how, and permit the student to assume responsibility for most of the learning. The activities
whereby students may obtain information and help is called a *delivery
system*. The next chapter will give detailed directions and examples of
how to construct such learning options. However, it is recommended that

delivery systems provide opportunities for the acquisition of information through actions, reading, listening, observing, and discussing. The specific options will be dependent upon the resources available, such as:

Space: Gymnasiums, corridors, other rooms, fields
Resources: Library, media, books, filmstrips, loopfilms
Professionals: Student leaders, paraprofessionals, parents

Once the delivery system is constructed, your next step will be to develop practice tasks, called *transactions*. Transactions serve to give the learner a chance to apply the information. In addition, they supply the learner with feedback to reinforce the learning. Chapter 7 gives extensive directions to guide the construction of transactions. The learning module should provide a variety of transactions so that the learner may select practice experiences which are best suited to his or her most productive pathway to learning. Possible practice choices should include self-contained, interaction, discovery, and independent-type tasks.

The final component of the learning program or module is the terminal objective or evaluation criteria, discussed earlier in this chapter. The verification that the standards of performance and conditions have been met may be specified or left open depending upon the facilitator's wishes. Proof may be accepted from the learner, another student, a paraprofessional, or the facilitator. If the facilitator assumed major responsibility for monitoring the achievement, less time will be available to give guidance to the total teaching-learning environment. Chapter 8 offers additional help for evaluating student performance. Figure 5–6 is an outline for a learning module.

The module should be presented to the student in an attractive and readily understandable format. Directions and size of print should be appropriate for the reading and interest level of the overall group. Generally, a class characterized by low reading ability and perseverance will need simple directions and well-illustrated modules. The programs may be printed on reusable poster boards or cards, or printed for personal use. Plans must be made to keep a record of the achievement of the terminal objectives. The operational procedures section of this chapter deals with record systems.

Developing learning modules takes time, and the learning options may not always be as productive as planned. These concerns should not deter you from doing the best you can, even if the desirable variety of options are not produced. Adjustment in the learning activities of the module may be made while the unit or course is in progress or before

Topic		
Name _____ Date _____		
Learning Objective:		
Safety Cautions:		

Delivery System: (Input)	Attempted	Completed
1. Read		
2. Listen		
3. Observe		
4. Discuss		
Transaction: (Practice)		
1. Self-contained		
2. Interaction		
3. Discovery		
4. Independent		
Terminal Objective:		
Comments:		

Figure 5-6

Learning Module

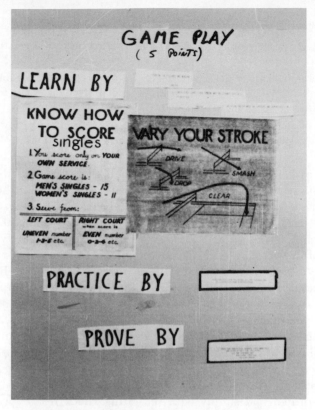

the next presentation of the unit of instruction.

Although learning programs are intended for use with individualized instructional programs, they can also provide uniform instruction for a large number of students. They can be arranged or sequenced in a variety of formats and students may be free to select the order in which they wish to pursue them. A number of modules may be specified to meet the course requirements. The emphasis is placed on *student learning* rather than on the *teacher teaching*. Learning modules direct the student learning more so than does the facilitator. Nevertheless, the facilitator is essential to give surveillance over all the learners' activities. The quality of the entire learning program and the personal professional assistance must create an environment that will inspire total student participation. An important feature of a learning program is active participation experiences designed to be enjoyable and challenging. Even though learning modules are segments of complete learning programs, the facilitator is still necessary to guide, encourage, diagnose, and manage the learning experiences of each student.

In summary, the development of a learning module follows these steps:

1. Select learning objectives for the unit based upon the needs and abilities of the class.
2. Develop as many delivery systems and transactions as possible with the available facilities, space, resources, and professional help to assist the learner to reach his desired goals.
3. Reproduce the modules in a format that is conducive to fostering maximum student interest, understanding, and participation.

It is assumed in humanistic individualized instruction that the facilitator and student have come to an agreement concerning the modules to be learned. When the system used is more or less formalized so that a payoff in terms of points or credit toward a grade is promised, the module is often referred to as a contract. Most contracts specify only the terminal objective. Figure 5-7 is an example of contracts.

Diagnostic Plans. You will notice in the individualized humanistic learning model presented in Chapter 4 that the change from static conditions to dynamic conditions was at the learner diagnosis phase. The goal of diagnosis is to help the learner and facilitator select learning objectives and experiences that will achieve the end product. An examination is required to gain the insight to arrive at the correct decisions. This examination may be in the form of written or skill tests designed to determine entry aptitudes, learning styles, interests, and needs; or it may be less sophisticated and simply be a self-rating check list as presented at the beginning of each chapter in this book. Figure 5–8 is an example of a simple diagnostic test given to a group of high school students.

The extent of the diagnosis depends upon the amount of previous knowledge about the learner which is available, time constraints, need, and expediency. Regardless of the nature of the diagnosis, information must be obtained which will help the learner and facilitator determine a personal prescription for learning. Figure 5–9 is an example of a more sophisticated basketball diagnosis examination which will supply only aptitude information. If this type of diagnosis examination is used, extensive choice should be given to the learner to select differentiated learning experiences, environments, and time. Your diagnostic evaluation plans should be structured to give you insight into the following: experience, learning mode, understanding, interest, and skill.

Prescription. When the facilitator has obtained sufficient information, a program of study is suggested to the student. This program is called a prescription. The form of the prescription may be designed to suit the specific situation. However, it must clearly indicate the learner's entry point, learning program, and terminal objectives. It is not feasible to print the entire learning program on the prescription form, but the exact skill or knowledge to be learned should be made known to the

ARCHERY CONTRACTS

Grades in this course shall be based upon the following:
1. Successful completion of Contracts 1, 2 and 3
2. Complete written test with at least 70% accuracy
3. The number of points that you accumulate

      A = 50 points
      B = 40 points
      C = 30 points
      D = 20 points

Contract 1. Be able to brace and unbrace a bow. (5 points)

Contract 2. Demonstrate ability to nock an arrow and draw the bow in good form. (5 points)

Contract 3. Be able to hit the target with five arrows out of six at 20 yards. (5 points)

Contract 4. Be able to score 25 points with six arrows from a distance of 20 yards. (5 points)

Contract 5. Be able to hit the target with four arrows out of six at 30 yards. (5 points)

Contract 6. Be able to score 30 points with six arrows from a distance of 20 yards. (5 points)

Contract 7. Be able to hit the target with three arrows out of six at 40 yards. (5 points)

Contract 8. Be able to score 20 points with six arrows from a distance of 30 yards. (5 points)

Contract 9. Be able to score at least 30 points with six arrows from a distance of 30 yards. (5 points)

Contract 10. Be able to score 10 points with six arrows from a distance of 40 yards. (5 points)

Contract 11. Be able to score at least 20 points with six arrows from a distance of 40 yards. (10 points)

Contract 12. Be able to score 300 points or more on a Junior Columbia Round. (15 points)

Contract 13. Be able to score at least 250 points on a Junior Columbia Round. (10 points)

Figure 5–7

student either verbally or in writing. Figure 5–10 is an example of a prescription which provides a record of the student's entry point, a list of all possible modules or skills to be mastered, a procedure for indicating which are to be learned, and a system of recording completed modules.

The facilitator tentatively completes the prescription based upon the diagnostic examination. The dynamic conditions of the learning process begin exactly at this juncture. A conference is held with the student

BADMINTON DIAGNOSIS

Name _____

Class _____ Hour _____ Date _____

Directions: Please answer the questions below as accurately as possible. Your answers will be helpful to plan with you ways which will help you to learn badminton.

Yes	Some	No	Questions
			1. Have you ever played badminton?
			2. Have you ever hit a badminton shuttlecock?
			3. Have you ever been given badminton instruction?
			4. Are you looking forward to learning badminton?
			5. Do you consider yourself skilled in sports?

If you answered yes or some to questions 1, 2, or 3, please rate your ability and knowledge of the badminton skills below:

Skill/Knowledge	Beginner	Amateur	Pro	Comments
1. Serving				
2. High clearing shots				
3. Net shots				
4. Drop shots				
5. Drives				
6. Smashes				
7. Rules				
8. Strategy				

What kind of assistance would be most helpful to you in this class? (Check)

_____ Drills _____ Teacher demonstration and instruction _____ Work on own

_____ Help from classmates _____ Lots of pictures _____ Other

(You may check more than one. If you checked Other, please explain below.

Figure 5–8

Diagnostic Test Sample

BASKETBALL ASSESSMENT

Name _____ Date _____

Purpose: This assessment is designed to help you and your instructor plan a learning program in basketball that will help you the most.

Directions: There are 3 parts to this assessment. Part 1 is a series of basketball skill tests, part 2 is game play ability, and part 3 is a rules and strategy quiz.

For Part 1, find four classmates and follow the directions for skill test as written in the test booklet. Record your results in the Part 1 space below.

For Part 2, find a classmate to tally the items to be assessed while you are playing basketball in class.

The instructor will give the entire class the quiz.

Part 1 Skill Tests

Test	Time	Points	Percentiles
Bounce and shoot			
1/2 Minute shooting			
Push pass			
Dribbling			

Part 2 Game Play

Offense	Tallies	Defense	Tallies
Points scored		Steals	
Passes		Interceptions	
Screens		Rebounds	

Comments: (Feel free to write anything here that would be helpful to satisfy your interests and desires for this class.)

Figure 5–9

Diagnostic Test Sample

117

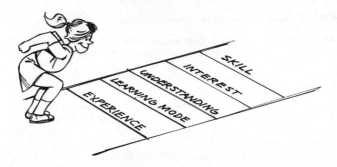

DIAGNOSIS

EXPERIENCE · LEARNING MODE · UNDERSTANDING · INTEREST · SKILL

for the purpose of seeking agreement between the teacher and student. The student's feelings concerning the prescription, questions about the course, additional suggestions, and the student's role in being responsible for learning are discussed. The prescription should be open to discussion and modification at any time.

Evaluation.   Your unit plan should include the procedures you will use to evaluate performance and assign credit or grades. Chapter 8 offers considerable help and insight for developing this aspect of the instructional unit. Whatever the plan, it is recommended that the grades be criterion-based rather than norm-based and that the system be clearly communicated to the learners at the onset of the course. Grades may be determined on the percentage of learning modules completed, task or contract points, final knowledge and skill tests, or combinations of these plans. Since modules and learning programs specify terminal objectives and a means to verify achievement, they may well serve as self-evaluative assessments for the students. Utilization of transactions will provide a continuous evaluation program for the learner to guide his progress throughout the unit.

Operational Procedures.   The final component of a unit plan will deal with procedures for managing and scheduling the course. Students move about with direction and with structure even though the class may not appear to be so ordered. Management plans must include provisions for dissemination of modules or learning program, record keeping, managing equipment, space, media, and safety. A system is needed whereby learning programs are readily available to the students. File folders, file boxes, pigeon holes, or booklets are all possible provisions to solve this problem. Records of student progress also may be kept in folders or file boxes, or recorded on a master record chart. Any system that can readily store the information and be easily made available should be workable. How to arrange a media management plan will be explained in the next chapter.

BASKETBALL
STUDENT ASSESSMENT FORM

Name _____ Year _____

Advisor _____

Summary of Accomplishments

Skills	Teaching	Extra

Planned Points _____ Large Group* _____ Written Tests* _____

Completed Tasks _____ Small Group   1   2   _____

Grade   _____   Individual 1, 2, 3, 4   _____

Diagnosis:	No further work	Some additional work	Beginning level
Passing			
Dribbling			
Shooting			
Offense			
Defense			
Rules			
Strategy			

Comments:

Prescription: Using the test results, students are to cross off skills which they can Perform. (Use a series of vertical lines.) Draw a diagonal line through tasks listed below which are to be learned in class. Draw a diagonal line from the opposite direction when the task has been completed. (This should form an X.) Each task or contract listed below has a corresponding task sheet to assist you to acquire the skill. Place the task sheet in your folder when completed.

PASSING 1	DRIVING 2	FAKES AND MOVES 3
Baseball pass Chest pass Overhead	Crossover	Jumpshot fake Rocker step Drop step fake
3 points	2 points	4 points
PASSING 4	SHOOTING 5	REBOUNDING 6
Bounce pass from dribble Flip pass from dribble	Conventional layup shot Stationary From dribble From pass	Jumping Protecting Blocking Clearing
2 points	3 points	3 points

*Required

Figure 5–10

Sample Prescription

DRIBBLE 7	SHOOTING 8	OFFENSE 9
Control Speed 2 points	Layup crossover Layup crossunder 5 points	Against man to man defense 4 points
DRIBBLE 10	SHOOTING 11	OFFENSE 12
Crossover change Reverse pivot change 2 points	1 hand push 2 hand set 3 points	Against zone 4 points
DRIBBLE 13	SHOOTING 14	DEFENSE 15
Cross behind change 2 points	Jump shot Hook 3 points	Man-to-man 4 points
DRIVING 16	SHOOTING 17	DEFENSE 18
Free throwing 2 points	Jump shot Turnaround Inside power 3 points	Zone 4 points
COACHING 19	COACHING 20	OFFICIATING 21
In class 2 points	Outside of class 4 points	In class 2 points
OFFICIATING 22	WRITTEN TEST 23	WRITTEN TEST 24
4 points	Officiating 8 points	Rules Strategy 88+ = 25 70+ = 20 points
STUDENT PROPOSAL	STUDENT PROPOSAL	STUDENT PROPOSAL
TEACHER PROPOSAL	TEACHER PROPOSAL	TEACHER PROPOSAL

Figure 5–10 (*cont.*)

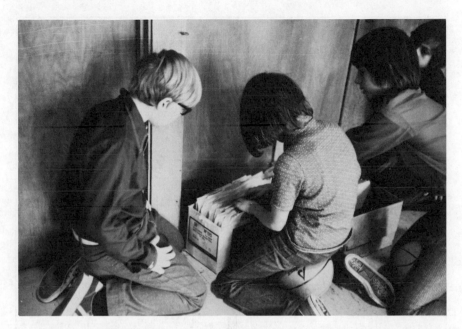

Space should be arranged to maximize its use to the students. Areas should be specified for practice, play, study, and evaluation. Figure 5–11 is an example of a space management plan. This plan might also include provisions for student or professional assistance in setting up the equipment, media, and records. Safety provisions should follow those recommended for the specific activity. Plans for communicating them to the students and enforcing them during the conduct of each learning experience should be developed.

It is possible to individualize instruction in a variety of teaching-learning environments: indoors, outdoors, and in small or large spaces. Exact provisions for overcoming unique problems are difficult to propose. However, if the activity is held outdoors, learning modules or tasks may be attached to a clipboard located near area markers, in boxes, or in a control area on benches. Media may need to be centered inside the building in the library or in a room adjacent to the field and provision for its use made on a rotating basis. A group may be assigned time to gain information while some practice and others play. A similar pattern may be used inside where little space is available.

Whether indoors or outdoors, recording results may be a problem in certain situations. It may be helpful to define a single recording area or to minimize paper work by recording results on a posted master record chart.

If the unit must be restricted to a certain number of lessons, a

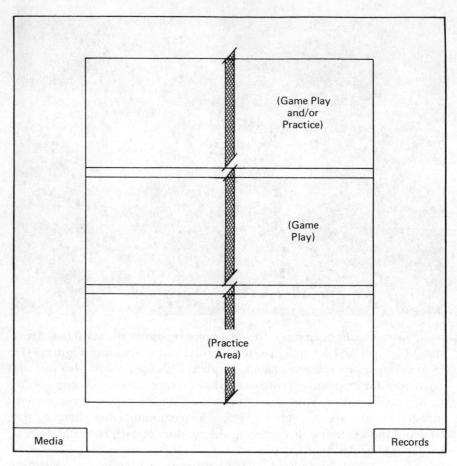

Figure 5–11

Sample Space Management Plan

calendar or block plan should be drawn up to properly plan the time that is available. An individualized instructional calendar may be less structured than a traditional teaching plan, but provisions for special help, instruction, practice, evaluation, and tournaments should be tentatively scheduled. The block may be written in list or calendar form. A twenty-lesson course might be blocked as in Figure 5–12.

Figure 5–13 is an outline to guide the development of a unit of study for facilitating physical education.

LESSON PLANS—AGENDAS

Individualized instruction simplifies the writing of lesson plans. If modules or contracts are used, all students will be working independently

Week	Monday	Tuesday	Wednesday	Thursday	Friday
1	Orientation Diagnosis	Diagnosis Play game	Conferences Play game Practice	Conferences Play game Practice	Practice Play game Movie
2	Play ──▶ Practice (learning programs) ───────────────────────────────▶ Special group instruction sessions as needed ─────────────▶				
3	Class tournament ───▶ Practice (learning programs) ───────────────────────────────▶ Special/Expert		Conferences	Conferences	
4	──▶ ──▶				
			Skill and knowledge tests	Summative conferences	

Figure 5–12

UNIT PLAN OUTLINE

1. Description of the situation (facilities, students, time, media, equipment)

2. Behavioral objectives (global goal, learning and terminal objectives)

3. Learning programs (topics and format)

4. Diagnostic plans (form and procedures)

5. Prescription plans (form and conference plans)

6. Evaluation plans (form, basis)

7. Operational procedures

    a. Supply plan
    b. Records
    c. Block calendar
    d. Laboratory management (arrangement and help)
    e. Safety

8. References

Figure 5–13

on varying phases of their own prescription. They will be selecting and pursuing delivery systems and transactions, reporting achievements, seeking assistance as needed, and working at their own pace. Consequently, a single lesson plan is not possible. What is needed is an agenda which designates the sequence of assigned practice and play time, special help, special events, and evaluation for each student or group of students. Such a plan appears in Figure 5–14.

The format of a lesson agenda may be any arrangement that is convenient and useful. Lesson agendas may be written on index cards that fit into a pocket or written more formally and placed on clipboards for ready reference. Preparing an agenda is helpful in determining the most

---

LEARNING AGENDA

Activity _____ # _____ Date _____

Equipment Needed: Usual media and supplies

Special Objectives: Improve game play by encouraging utilization of learned skills

Activity	Space Assignment	Special Instruction	Time
Organization	Post directions on bulletin board	Play schedules	0
Game play	Group A. 10:00-10:15 B. 10:15-10:30 C. 10:30-10:45	Encourage use of defense modules	15 each (45)
Practice	Groups B,C. 10:00-10:15 C,A. 10:15-10:30 A,B. 10:30-10:45	Individual work on module	30 minutes each group (45)
Special instruction	Open to anyone interested Invite Mary, Sue, Bill (10:20-10:25)	Crossover layup shot Stress pivot	5 minutes

Comments/Evaluation:

Figure 5–14

efficient use of time, space and instruction. Furthermore, it serves as a reminder of the plan, and provides a record of the experience and its assessment as a foundation for immediate and future planning.

CASE STUDY

SETTING:	Urban high school
CLASS SIZE:	38 freshmen boys (average of 32 were present)
ACTIVITY:	Basketball—twenty lessons
SKILL LEVEL:	25% beginners, 50% average, 25% skilled
FACILITIES:	1 regulation court (baskets on sides to permit two cross court courts)
EQUIPMENT:	1 ball to 3 students

The instructor has arranged class time to permit practice and play each day. For the first ten lessons, one-third of the time will be spent on new skills, one-third practicing previously introduced skills and one-third on game play. The instructor introduces general basketball skills by demonstration and explanation: inside shooting, outside shooting, driving, passing, individual and team offensive and defensive skills, and rules. Within each general skill, beginning to advanced skills are presented. Students are encouraged to practice via self-contained and interaction tasks covering three skill levels within a general skill. Students may select the level that they believe they need or that is of interest to them. Task sheets are posted on the wall. Students check off a skill on a master sheet when they have completed it.

Beginning with the eleventh lesson, a tournament is held. Practice continues on one cross court on any skills not mastered. Each student plays in the tournament two out of every three lessons. While students are practicing or playing the game, the instructor is giving individual guidance to any student who seeks or seems to need help. Advanced students may elect to pursue coaching-type skills which require helping the less skilled students. An observer will note that all students are involved and little or no waiting for a turn to practice is evident. Some students are working on shooting, some on dribbling, some on feinting maneuvers, and some on passing. Occasionally a little horseplay develops which is immediately investigated and solved by the facilitator.

Grades are based on points earned by completing tasks, plus the successful completion of a written test.

SUMMARY

The individualized humanistic approach to facilitate physical education requires the production of a course unit or plan of instruction which contains well-constructed pre-determined or static learning conditions. These conditions are based upon the facilitator's assessment of the total instrumental and affective environment and provide a secure operational base from which students may plan their approach to learning physical education activities.

The unit plan has six major provisions: (1) behavioral objectives, (2) learning programs, (3) diagnostic examination, (4) prescriptive procedures, (5) evaluation plan, and (6) operational procedures.

A *behavioral objective* is a collection of words, statements, or symbols which describe visible activity by the student after learning. These objectives give direction to the entire course of study by requiring a priori decisions concerning the what, how, and the level of learning that is to proceed. A global goal identifies the purpose of the course. A learning objective describes how a student will reach the global goal. Learning objectives are developed from the analysis of the subject matter and constructed to describe the learning by using verbs selected from the appropriate category of the three learning domains of knowledge, skill, and feelings. Terminal objectives specify the degree of proficiency attained by identifying the appearance and evidence of the learning. Proficiency is specified in stated standards and performance conditions. Standards of performance variables may be distance, time, accuracy, speed, consistency, and form. Behavioral objectives are valuable directives to the learner to guide, to evaluate, and to verify performance achievement.

Learning programs are comprised of delivery systems and transactions and form the bridge between the learning objective and the terminal objective. They may be operationalized by the development of self-contained packages or be presented in an open, loose-type structure. Modules or contracts contain complete directions for the student to learn at his pace and by self-direction. These directions include: (1) learning objective, (2) delivery system, (3) transactions, and (4) terminal objective. The delivery system and transactions provide a variety of options so that learners may select experiences that will best suit their own needs. Even though learning programs serve as the instructional mode, the facilitator's assitance is needed to guide, encourage, diagnose, motivate, and manage the learner and his experiences in the teaching-learning setting.

The *diagnostic plan* provides the means to shape the predetermined or static learning conditions to the learner so that instruction may be dynamic and flexible. The plan should be an evaluative examination to supply whatever information is needed about the learner's goals, aptitude, and background.

The *prescriptive program* is the product resulting from the selection of learning programs based upon the diagnosis. It is normally a mediated statement, by the student and facilitator, of the specific learning program and objectives.

The *evaluation plan* is criterion-referenced and utilizes the self-assessing transactions and terminal objectives as the crux of the assigned grade.

The *operational procedures* include the plans for managing and scheduling the course. These plans include provisions for disseminating and collecting information, for the care of equipment, for space and media, and for maintaining a safe learning environment.

Specific lesson agendas are generated from the unit plan. However, since individualized instruction learning programs are adequate guides and resources for student pursuit of their goals, lesson plans become agendas of activities.

REFERENCES

AAHPER. "The New Physical Education," *Journal of Health, Physical Education and Recreation*, 42 (1971), 24–39.

AAHPER. "The Now Physical Education," *Journal of Health, Physical Education and Recreation*, 1972.

AAHPER. "The Whole Thing!" *Journal of Health, Physical Education and Recreation*, 44 (1973), 21–36.

BLOOM, B., M. ENGLEHART, E. FURST, W. HILL, AND D. KRATHWOHL. *Taxonomy of Educational Objectives Handbook I: Cognitive Domain*. New York: David McKay Co., Inc., 1956.

BUCHER, C., C. KOENIG, AND M. BARNHARD. *Methods and Materials for Secondary Physical Education*. St. Louis: The C. V. Mosby Company, 1970.

CASSADY, R. AND S. CALDWELL. *Humanizing Physical Education, Methods for Secondary School Movement Programs*. Dubuque, Iowa: Brown Publishing Co., 1974.

DUNN, R., AND K. DUNN. *Practical Approaches to Individualize Instruction*. W. Nyack, N.Y.: Parker Publishing Co., 1972.

FRYMEIR, J., AND C. GALLOWAY. "Individualized Learning in a School for Tomorrow," *Theory into Practice*. Columbus, Ohio: Ohio State University, Vol. XIII, 2, 65–70.

GRONLUND, NORMAN. *Stating Behavioral Objectives for Classroom Instructors*. New York: The Macmillan Company, 1970.

JEWETT, A., S. JONES, S. LUNEKE, AND S. ROBINSON. "Educational Change Through a Taxonomy for Writing Physical Education Objectives, *Quest*, 15 (January 1971), 32–38.

KNAPP, C., AND P. LEONHARD. *Teaching Physical Education in Secondary Schools*. New York: McGraw-Hill Book Company, 1968.

KRATHWOHL, D., B. BLOOM, AND B. MASIA. *Taxonomy of Educational Objectives: Handbook II: Affective Domain*. New York: David McKay Co., Inc., 1964.

KRYSPIN, W., AND J. FELDHUSEN. *Writing Behavior Objectives*. Minneapolis, Minn.: Burgess Publishing Co., 1974.

LEWIS, J. *Administering the Individualized Instruction Program*. W. Nyack, N.Y.: Parker Publishing Co., 1971.

MAGER, R. *Goal Analysis*. Belmont, Calif.: Fearon Publishers, 1972.

————, *Preparing Instructional Objectives*. Belmont, Calif.: Fearon Publishers, 1962.

MILLER, A., AND M. MASSEY. *Methods and Materials for Secondary Physical Education*. Englewood Cliffs, N.J.: Prentice-Hall, Inc., 1973.

National Education Association. "Performance Based Instruction." *Today's Education*. 61 (April 1972), 33–40.

RUSSELL, J., AND S. POSTLETHWAIT. *Modular Instruction*. Minneapolis, Minn.: Burgess Press, 1974.

SINGER, R., AND W. DICK. *Teaching Physical Education—A Systems Approach*. Boston: Houghton Mifflin Company, 1974.

6

The Delivery System: Getting The Picture

INSTRUCTIONAL UNIT FOR CHAPTER 6

Learner's Diagnosis

Directions: Read the questions below. Write out, discuss, or mentally review the answers. If you believe that you know the information, check the "yes" column. If you are not sure of the answer, check the "no" column. After reading the questions and deciding your knowledge, check the accuracy of your answers by reading the summary at the end of this chapter. If you answered a question incorrectly, change your answer to the appropriate column.

Can you

Yes	No	Questions
		1. Explain the use of delivery systems?
		2. Give major reasons for media alternatives?
		3. List four benefits of a delivery system?
		4. List six types of transmitting devices?
		5. Explain which types are best for beginners?
		6. Explain which types are best for advanced learners?
		7. List the three most desirable transmitting devices?
		8. Develop plans for production of media?
		9. Give two major sources of media information?
		10. List two delivery system management duties?

Suggested Prescription

Directions: Count the number of checks you have placed in the "yes" column. When the percentages are determined, you may increase your knowledge and skill by using the suggested Learning Program activities recommended in the Input and Practice columns. Input and practices not listed offer additional learning options.

Results	Input	Practice
More than 80%	#1, 8	#5
60% to 80%	#1, 3, 8	#1, 5
40% to 60%	#1, 2, 4 or 5, 6 or 7	#1, 2 or 3 or 4, 5
Less than 40%	#1, 2, 4 or 5, 6 or 7, 8	#1, 2, 3, 4

Learning Program

Directions: It is suggested that the reader attempt to follow any and all suggestions in this learning program. These are designed to increase knowledge and understanding of delivery systems for individualized instruction, and to improve skill in planning, operating, developing, and managing delivery systems.

Proposed Learning Objective: The learner will be able to develop and operate a delivery system for individualizing instruction in a selected physical education activity.

Input:

*1. Read Chapter 6 of this book.
2. Read Chapter 10 of Knapp and Leonard, *Teaching Physical Education in Secondary Schools.*
3. Read selected references at the end of this chapter.
4. Observe a learning center utilizing a delivery system.
5. Prepare a list of questions you have and arrange a conference with a media center staff member or a librarian to discuss these questions.
6. Visit a media center, go to a sound or camera shop, or attend a conference where delivery system software and hardware are displayed.
7. Discuss use of media with a faculty member who uses media extensively and with one who does not.
8. Browse through physical education activity books in your school bookstore or library.
9. Plan an input of your own.

*Highly recommended.

Practice:

1. Select a familiar school setting. Outline the equipment, media, and space that could be utilized to individualize instruction. Discuss the utilization, adequacy, and value of media with a colleague or the instructor in that school.

2. Select a physical education activity of your choice. Plan the production for some medium to transmit information concerning one possible learning program.

3. Operate any of the following transmitting devices: overhead projector, slide projector, loop film projector, audio-tape device.

4. Develop a collection of media catalogues and references.

5. Plan a practice of your own.

Evaluation: You will be able to plan an ideal delivery system for individualizing instruction for a sport of your choice, indicating the following:

1. Transmitting devices: hardware and software.

2. Plans for processing and managing the system.

The dynamic phase of the individualized humanistic system for facilitating physical education begins with the delivery system (means through which information is obtained). This consists of multi-media resource alternatives, so that information can be received in multiple ways by learners. In the past, media have been considered as supplementary to instruction through books, teacher explanations, and demonstrations. Teachers, as the sole source of demonstration and explanation, performed the role that technology can perform today through film and/ or audio-tape. Media can also provide a reference source whenever the student needs it. These alternative sources of instruction free the facilitator to interact with students and provide personal help to individualize learning.

Students, as was discussed earlier, have different perceptual strengths and weaknesses. Some learn easily by listening, others need visual experiences, and still others rely on tactile involvement. However, most learners acquire information through a combination of perceptual modalities. Learning occurs more easily and quickly when a greater number of senses are involved. The major reason for utilizing a variety of media is to pro-

VISUAL   AURAL   KINESTHETIC

SENSORY-BODY AWARENESS

vide the student with an opportunity to capitalize on his individual perceptual strengths through multiple sensory modalities. Media resource alternatives are included in learning modules or contracts to permit the learner to choose the media best suited to his or her perceptual strengths and needs.

Many other benefits can result from using media. Media serve to foster interest and self-direction. Attractive displays can clearly identify the needed information, creating a feeling of confidence and personal involvement which stimulate further pursuit of learning. The scope of information may be broadened to bring to the learner the exact motion, slow and stop action, expert performance, and combination of graphics, words, and sound. Filmed demonstrations performed by experts, peers, and even the learners themselves may be repeated at will through replay of loop films, slides, and video-tape. Interrelationships of parts to the complex whole can effectively be presented. It is possible to display each component skill or playing position coupled with an audio explanation. Furthermore, all of this may be retrieved and replayed as often as desired by the student. Retention of actual knowledge is enhanced by visualization of the whole and by overlearning through repetition. Chapter 3 discussed the teaching behaviors dealing with the source and direction of communication. Media serve as extra-extensions of teaching behaviors. Collectively, media options can serve the following teaching behaviors:

Clarifying
Answering questions
Offering information
Giving feedback
Confirming knowledge
Giving silent covert activity
Giving overt activity

The nonhuman conveyers or transmitters are deficient in providing accepting and judgmental behavior. Interaction and real-life experiences can be arranged to provide these behaviors. Effective individualized instruction is augmented by a well-planned delivery system.

TRANSMISSION VEHICLES

Delivery systems' conveyers of information fall into six major types: (1) printed words, (2) graphics, (3) projected graphics, words, and action, (4) recorded sounds, (5) real objects, and (6) human encounter. There is nothing magical or new about these transmitters. Each vehicle has developed several familiar models.

Printed Word. The printed word, of course, is most often presented in books, magazines, journals, and pamphlets. However, teachers frequently utilize the chalkboard and bulletin boards as additional sources of the printed word. Tradition, time, and money have encouraged widespread use of the printed word.

Graphics. Graphics are diagrams, pictures, lines, and designs. You may create your own graphics through photographs or drawings, or they may be purchased commercially. However, they are most frequently found in books, magazines, journals, and pamphlets.

Projected Graphics, Words, and Action.   Words, diagrams, pictures, and actions are transmitted through a variety of projective devices for slide, filmstrip and overhead transparencies, video-tape, movies, and the printed page graphic display. Projected information has the advantage of increasing the size of the information so that more than one person may view it at the same time. For example, a golf grip may be easily visible to an entire class if placed on a transparency for an overhead projector or slide.

Recorded Sounds.   Directions, explanation, music, and specific and random sounds may be recorded on audio-tapes, phonodiscs, film, and paper. They are reproduced through projectors, phonographs, and other playback devices. In addition, radio reproduces sounds, but is restricted to a single delivery. Exercise cadence, directions, and music cues can be put on audio-tape to free the teacher to assist learning.

Real Objects.   This vehicle is the most primary and simplistic. What better way can one understand the size of a ball or a field, the appearance of a net or racket, the feeling of water or speed, or the joy of activity than to be actually involved with the object?

Human Encounter.   In the school environment there is personal communication when the teacher explains and demonstrates to the class and when the student responds to the teacher. However, this kind of transmission must become broader, more flexible, and responsive to individual needs. The transmitter may need to make several deliveries and variations to several different students at differing times and places. The essence of individualized instruction is freeing both the student and teacher to obtain more personal communication when decided or desired. Conveying information extends beyond the teacher to peers, friends, experts, and community resources. Discussions, conferences, and inquiries are major transmitting human encounter sources.

The amount and type of transmission devices will be limited by availability, funds and feasibility. Nonetheless, it is necessary to structure the delivery system to include the most productive transmitters.

RECEPTION

Once the information is carried to the learner, it must be received or accepted. Providing media options for the student should help to ensure the most effective reception. Edgar Dale[1] has proposed a hierarchy of media preference which ranges from emphasis on concrete experiences to abstract experiences:

[1]*Audio-Visual Methods in Teaching* (New York: Holt, Rinehart, and Winston, Inc., 1969).

1. Real-life experiences (human encounter, real objectives)
2. Physical involvements with simulated experiences (models, etc.)
3. Direct perception or observation (real objects)
4. Indirect perception (projected, recorded)
5. Visual representation (projected, graphics)
6. Audio representation (recorded, radio)
7. Reading verbal reception (printed)
8. Hearing verbal reception (recorded, lecture)

It can be seen that most students are highly dependent upon direct experiences with materials, but that the more experienced learner can learn from media that are more abstract. Learning programs in which new concepts, skills, or terms are introduced should provide direct experience options to facilitate meaningful learning, concept differentiation, and generalization. Although there is evidence that most learners prefer a certain type of delivery system, it must be remembered that the individual approach requires provision for the atypical.

Reception may be facilitated by establishing certain transmission areas within or as near the learning laboratory as possible and by extending the scope of media sources beyond the school doors. Figure 6–1 represents the transmission areas that are needed in physical education learning centers, the desirable media, and possible extensions.

Laboratory Areas	Alternatives	Extended Range Areas
Reading	Books, rule books, magazines, chalkboards	Library, home
Viewing	Slides, films, loop films, projected graphics and print	Media centers, home, community
Listening	Audio-tapes, phonodiscs, radio, lectures	Workshops, home, radio, community
Interaction	Conferences, discussion	Anywhere, other staff
Practice	Transactions	Extracurricular, community clubs, private clubs

Figure 6–1

Media Provisions and Options

These areas are most useful when they can be established within the physical education learning environment. However, it may be possible to utilize nearby vacant rooms, corridors, storage and locker space as suitable areas.

IMPLEMENTATION

Although media is a vital tool to aid the process of individualizing instruction, a delivery system need not be extensive. Every effort should be made to secure a wide range of useful media—it may take several years to achieve a totally effective and efficient media system. However, the aim of a delivery system is to increase student achievement rather than to assemble an impressive display of gadgets. Developing an effective system requires three major functions: (1) procurement of hardware, (2) procurement of software, and (3) management of both.

Procurement of Hardware

Hardware refers to the equipment needed to reproduce sounds or projected graphics, words, and motion. It is recommended that selection be based on availability, potential for wide use, flexibility, feasibility, durability, and ease of operation and repair. Much of the following

equipment is commonly found in school media centers or other departments:

Loop film projectors
Slide projectors
Overhead projectors
Audio-tape playbacks
Phonographs
Movie projectors
Video-tape playbacks

Movie projectors are valuable, but have limited use because motion pictures are expensive if bought and restrictive in use if rented. Video-tape playback and recordings are extremely desirable, but expensive, difficult to maintain equipment, and technically complicated to operate.

Procurement of Software

Software is the material that is processed through the hardware: books, pamphlets, pictures, films, loop films, slides, audio-tapes, overhead transparencies, and video-tapes. Whereas hardware has a more or less permanent status, software can be worn out or outdated. It may be purchased commercially, rented, or produced by the facilitator, the school media center, or by the learners themselves.

The following criteria should be considered when you are deciding on media:

1. *Currency and accuracy.* It is difficult to undo incorrect input. Pictures should be in proper form and in the dress style of the day.
2. *Technical excellence.* Students are accustomed to quality audio-visuals, television shows, and radio presentations. As a result they are easily distracted by media that are poorly presented, lighted, or constructed.
3. *Feasibility.* The media should not be too difficult to operate or too ponderous and time-consuming to consult.
4. *Comprehensiveness.* The software should be available for all the various components of the course.
5. *Appropriateness.* The material should be well illustrated and in a vernacular and format that can be easily understood and followed.

There are two major sources of software: commercial productions and school productions. Commercially produced media have the advantages of technical excellence and experience. Their main disadvantage, that of cost, may be overcome by gradual acquisition of an adequate supply. Well-illustrated books and loop films are extremely effective transmitters of information and frequently used by learners.

General information about acquiring media may be obtained from your school librarian or media consultant. In addition, the various associations of the American Alliance for Health, Physical Education and Recreation produce an extensive list of rule books, pamphlets, books, journals, and audio-visual material. The *Journal* of the AAHPER carries articles as well as advertisements for a wide variety of media. Sport rule books published by the National Association for Girls' and Women's Sports contain extensive bibliography and audio-visual sections. You will be updated in media developments through exhibitions of products at professional workshops, conferences, and conventions. A resource section to give you further assistance is provided at the end of this chapter.

School-produced media have the advantage of precise tailoring to the dimensions of the course and the added advantage of possible use of peer performers as models. The process is time-consuming; however, many schools employ media developers or have other staff available for assistance. School-produced media should be guided by the following suggestions:

1. Plan the program content and production carefully.
2. Use closeups and other attention-getting means.
3. Arrange for adequate lighting.
4. Include titles wherever possible.

Overhead transparencies, slides, loop films, audio-tapes, graphics, and even video-tapes may be produced rather easily and economically.

Overhead Transparencies. Overhead transparencies may be created by drawing and printing with colored marking pens. Pictures may be printed through an infrared process such as a Thermofax machine. Transparencies can be easily filed in folders and labeled for ready access. They are inexpensive, durable, and flexible as means to transmit the printed word and graphics.

Slides. A slide series illustrating components of selected skills may be created by utilizing a 35 mm camera. The slides can be packaged for specific skills to help the student locate the exact help needed. They are relatively inexpensive and can be easily sequenced to illustrate cues, knowledge and exact techniques involved.

Loop Films. Super 8 mm movies may be taken of each skill or concept in a learning program. These movies can be processed in cartridges and used in loop-film projectors to serve as repetitive, potent transmitters of information. Experts, the facilitator, or talented students may be used as demonstrating performers.

Audio-Tapes. Cassette tapes are easily used audio devices. Directions and support information may be recorded to be used separately or in conjunction with visual or practice aids. Audio-tapes may accompany slide series, loop films, and transparencies. Directed skill practice can be effectively aided by audio-tapes. Cues, sequences, and explanations can be given to aid practicing skills in which timing is not an integral factor.

Graphics. Photographs, drawings, or copied printed illustrations may be arranged in sequences on bulletin boards, walls, or posters. Brief printed directions will serve to direct the learner's attention to crucial techniques.

Video-Tapes. Skills, rules, and game strategy segments can be video-taped for replay use. Each taped segment should be labeled, and directions given for ready access. The reproducing hardware is cumbersome and complicated, but this medium is desirable if the equipment and technical aid are available. It is not recommended that the facilitator serve as the technician because of the time required to operate the equipment. Verbal description, explanations, and direction can be recorded on the tape.

MANAGEMENT

Delivery system management duties include arrangement and use of the transmission areas, care of transmission equipment and supplies, and coordination of cooperating personnel.

Arrangement and Use of Transmission Areas.   Each reading, listening, viewing, and interaction area should be designated and each will need special arrangements. There should be a set of operational directions posted in each area so that the student can easily operate the hardware, find the media, and give proper care to their use. *Reading areas* require a table to display the materials and/or a bookcase in which to store them. If graphics are to be displayed in the same area, wall space or swinging boards can be used. *Listening areas* should be quiet places unless earphones are used. Tapes and phonodiscs should be labeled and easily retrieved. *Viewing areas* should be located where the equipment can be safeguarded and projected on screens or walls not affected by light. The media should be stored in boxes or shelves adjacent to the projector.

Space and storage of media may be reduced if your school has installed a dial access information retrieval system (DAIR). DAIR is an electronic system for transmitting audio and video media which are located remote from the learning setting. Physical education students may obtain access to materials in a designated area by dialing an assigned number for the program desired.

Care of Equipment and Supplies.   Regular inspection of equipment and media should be planned. Equipment that is not functioning properly frustrates and discourages the learner. Prolonged malfunctioning delivery systems will soon result in students' not seeking these learning aids. If the equipment and supplies cannot feasibly be stored or used in assigned areas, then they can be made portable by use of boxes and carts.

Coordination of Personnel.   Figure 6–2 illustrates the various personnel who may be involved in a delivery system and who will need coordination to ensure effective service to students.

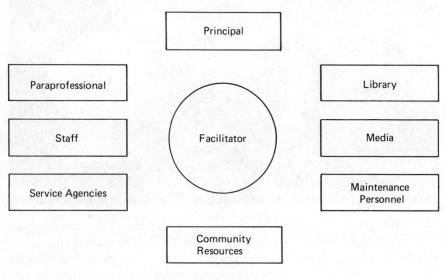

Figure 6–2

Delivery System Coordination

All educational institutions have different arrangements to enable the instructional staff to use media. Although the coordination needed is extensive, proper arrangements beforehand will decrease interruption and inefficient operation of the delivery system. Daily schedules need to be planned and communicated to extra personnel assigned to aid in the teaching-learning environment. The librarian, media consultant, and community resource agencies should be contacted prior to the beginning of the unit concerning the availability and possible demand for assistance. All hardware and software must be in perfect operational order.

Although the development and execution of a delivery system is complicated, it must be remembered that the aim of the system is to augment the influence of the facilitator in a variety of reception modalities so that students can acquire information. Once information is received, learners can proceed to apply the knowledge during practice conditions best suited to each of them to reinforce and integrate learning.

CASE STUDY

SETTING: Elementary school in urban community; 600 students, grades 1–6.

FACILITIES: One gym and a media center

PROGRAM: Grades 4, 5, and 6, composed of boys and girls, learning basic softball skills through twelve individualized instructional lessons

Physical education class sessions of 40 minutes every other day

Because the activity is outside and offered for only twelve lessons, the facilitator arranged with the media center to set up a display of informational sources available, and arranged for the classroom teachers to permit students to use the media center to learn more about softball skills. The students were made aware of the sources through reference to them in the learning modules prepared for each skill. These modules were attached to clipboards and placed by area markers in various locations when class was held outside. The media center provided the following hardware: 1 overhead projector, 2 loop-film projectors, 1 filmstrip projector, 3 audio-tape playbacks. The software available was as follows: 3 loop films (Batting, Throwing, Fielding), several well-illustrated softball books, 12 transparencies, 1 filmstrip on rules, and 1 audio-tape to be used with transparencies. The physical education facilitator developed the loop films, tapes, and transparencies with the help of the media center and art teacher. Of the eight classes totaling approximately 250 students, the media center director reported that the following use of the media was made by students for softball:

Loop films viewed	20
Filmstrips	13
Overhead transparencies	25
Books	50

SUMMARY

A delivery system consists of multi-media resources which are designed and made available so that information can be received in multiple ways. Multi-media resources are not merely supplements to instruction in the individualized humanistic approach but are essential transmitters. Their use frees the facilitator to provide personal help.

Students' perceptual modality preferences and dominance varies. The major reason for utilizing a variety of media is to provide the student with options to capitalize on their personal perceptual strengths. Media offer several benefits:

1. Foster interest and self-direction
2. Create confidence and motivation in learning
3. Broaden the scope of presentation
4. Permit repetitive demonstrations
5. Demonstrate interrelationships
6. Combine modalities
7. Perform many teaching functions

There are six types of transmitter systems: (1) printed words, (2) graphic illustrations, (3) projected graphics, words, and pictures, (4) recorded sounds, (5) real objects, and (6) human encounter. The extent and type of transmitting devices will be limited by funds, feasibility, and availability.

Media options ensure the most effective reception of information. Students tend to prefer concrete media such as real-life experiences and direct observation at the onset of complex learning. Once the concept is established, information can be gained from more abstract transmissions such as reading and listening. The teaching-learning environment must provide for easy and effective access to information. Areas need to be set aside and equipped to provide reading, viewing, listening, interaction, and practice.

Implementing an effective delivery system requires three major duties: (1) procurement of equipment (hardware), (2) procurement of media (software) and (3) management of the system. Equipment or hardware should be selected that has wide use, flexibility, and economic feasibility. Loop-film projectors, overhead projectors, audio-tape playback devices, and phonographs are considered essential hardware. Media or software refers to books, pamphlets, pictures, films, loop films, slides, filmstrips, audio-tapes, overhead transparencies, and video-tapes. Media are available through commercial venders, but can also be produced by the facilitator or others in the school. Media should be selected in keeping with the following criteria: (1) currency and accuracy, (2) technical excellency, (3) feasibility, (4) comprehensiveness, and (5) appropriateness. Overhead transparencies, slides, loop films, audio-tapes, graphics, and video-tapes are media that can be readily produced through facilitator direction within the school setting. Information about sources of media may be secured through school libraries, media centers, and the American Alliance for Health, Physical Education and Recreation.

Delivery system management duties include arrangement and use of transmission areas, care of equipment and supplies, and coordination of personnel.

MEDIA SOURCES

General:

American Alliance for Health, Physical Education and Recreation
1201 Sixteenth Street N.W.
Washington, D.C. 20036
(Filmstrips, rule books, pamphlets, high school textbooks, journals, books.)

American Library Association
50 East Huron Street
Chicago, Ill. 60611
(Annotated and comprehensive guides to educational media: films, filmstrips, kinescopes, phonodiscs, programmed instruction, slides, transparencies, video-tapes.)

Athletic Institute
805 Merchandise Mart
Chicago, Ill. 60654
(Loop films, booklets, movies, books.)

George Peabody College of Education
Nashville, Tenn. 37203
(Free and inexpensive learning materials.)

National Information Center for Educational Media
University of Southern California
Los Angeles, Calif. 90007
(Indexes available for 16mm films and 8mm cartridge filmstrips, phonodiscs, audio-tapes, video-tapes, overhead transparencies, programmed instruction.)

Westinghouse Learning Director
Westinghouse Learning Cooperative
100 Park Avenue
New York, N.Y. 10017
(Variety of sources and information on unique Sound-on-Page system.)

Rule Books:

> Amateur Athletic Union
> 233 Broadway
> New York, N.Y. 10007

> National Association for Girls and Women's Sports
> 1201 Sixteenth Street N.W.
> Washington, D.C. 20036

Sport Series:

These books are inexpensive, and available either as a series or singly, for specific sports. They are especially excellent for planning learning programs. Most are well illustrated.

> Allyn and Bacon, Inc.
> 470 Atlantic Avenue
> Boston, Mass. 02210

> Athletic Institute
> 805 Merchandise Mart
> Chicago, Ill. 60654

> W. B. Brown Publishers
> Dubuque, Iowa 52001

> Goodyear Publishing Company
> Pacific Palisades, Calif. 90272

> Prentice-Hall, Inc.
> Englewood Cliffs, N.J. 07636

Television:

> AAHPER Resource Center for Media in Physical Education
> Department of Physical Education
> Wayne State University
> Detroit, Mich. 48702

REFERENCES

BRIGGS, L., P. CAMPEAU, R. GAGNE', AND M. MAY, *Instructional Media.* Pittsburgh, Pa.: American Institute for Research, 1967.

CASSADY, R., AND S. CALDWELL. *Humanizing Physical Education, Methods for Secondary School Movement Programs.* Dubuque, Iowa: W. C. Brown Publishing Co., 1974.

DALE, E. *Audio-Visual Methods in Teaching.* New York: Holt, Rinehart, and Winston, Inc., 1969.

DUNN, R., AND K. DUNN. *Practical Approaches to Individualizing Instruction.* W. Nyack, New York: Parker Publishing Co., 1972.

FREDERICK, B. "The That's It Response!" *JOPHER.* Washington, D.C.: American Alliance for Health, Physical Education and Recreation (April 1973), pp. 30–33.

GERLACH, V., AND P. ELY. *Teaching and Media: A Systematic Approach.* Englewood Cliffs, N.J.: Prentice-Hall, Inc., 1971.

KLASEK, C. *Instructional Media in the Modern School.* Lincoln, Neb.: Professional Education Publications, Inc., 1972.

KNAPP, C., AND P. LEONARD. *Teaching Physical Education in Secondary Schools.* New York: McGraw-Hill Book Company, 1966.

LEWIS, J. *Administering the Individualized Instruction Program.* W. Nyack, N.Y.: Parker Publishing Co., 1971.

NOAR, G. *Individualizing Instruction.* New York: John Wiley & Sons, Inc., 1972.

PARSONS, L. "All You Ever Wanted to Know about Film-Loops But Were Afraid to ask," *JOPHER.* American Alliance for Health, Physical Education and Recreation, (April 1971), pp. 14–16.

RUSSELL, J., AND S. POSTLETHWAIT. *Modular Instruction.* Minneapolis, Minn:. Burgess Press, 1974.

SINGER, R., AND W. DICK. *Teaching Physical Education—A Systems Approach.* Boston: Houghton Mifflin Company, 1974.

WALKER, J., C. COWELL, H. SCHWEHN, AND A. MILLER. *Modern Methods in Secondary School Physical Education.* Boston: Allyn and Bacon, 1973.

7

Transactions: Practicing

INSTRUCTIONAL UNIT FOR CHAPTER 7

Learner's Diagnosis

Directions: Read the questions below. Write out, discuss, or mentally review your answers. If you believe that you know the information, check the "yes" column. If you are not sure of the answer, check the "no" column. After reading the questions and deciding your knowledge, check the accuracy of your answers by reading the summary at the end of this chapter. If you answered a question incorrectly change your answer to the appropriate column.

Can you

Yes	No	Questions
		1. Define a transaction?
		2. List four types of transactions?
		3. Define and explain each of the four types of transactions?
		4. Explain the value of each of the transactions?
		5. Construct a qualitative task?
		6. Construct a quantitative task?
		7. List the types of discovery tasks?
		8. Explain how discovery tasks differ?
		9. List five principles to follow when constructing transactions?
		10. Explain how transactions may be used?

Suggested Prescription

Directions: Count the number of checks you have placed in the "yes" column. When the percentages are determined, you may increase your knowledge and skill by using the suggested Learning Program activities recommended in the Input and Practice columns.

Results	Input	Practice
More than 80%	#1, 8	#4
60% to 80%	#1, 4, 8	#3
40% to 60%	#1, 2, 3	#2, 3
Less than 40%	#1, 2, 3, 5 or 6, 7	#1, 2, 3

Learning Program

Directions: It is suggested that the reader attempt to follow any and all suggestions in this learning program. These are designed to improve knowledge and understanding of practice procedures and skill in developing meaningful learning experiences to teach physical education.

Proposed Learning Objective: The learner will be able to construct learning transactions designed to teach a specific activity skill.

Input:

*1. Read Chapter 7 of this book.
2. Read Chapter 9 of M. Robb, *The Dynamics of Motor-Skill Acquisition.*
3. Read M. Mosston, *Teaching Physical Education,* Chapters 3 through 8.
4. Read selected references listed at the end of this chapter.
5. Select a learning task and attempt to follow it. Try to analyze your experience.
6. Observe a class being taught by transactions. Try to analyze the class involvement.
7. Select an independent learning packet in physical education and try to learn from it. What worked? What didn't?
8. Prepare an input of your own.

Practice:

1. Select a specific activity skill; sketch out components and develop qualitative and quantitative task differentiations.

*Highly recommended.

2. Administer a transactional task to a colleague. Discuss with colleague his or her feelings of satisfaction and dissatisfaction with the experience.

*3. Develop at least one transaction, which will be either a self-contained, interaction, or discovery task. Discuss the transaction with a friend or the instructor.

4. Plan a practice experience for learning about transactions.

Evaluation: You will be able to develop a transaction that will permit self-contained, interaction, and discovery practice and that will foster the achievement of a skill as evidenced by your student's performance of a terminal objective for a selected activity skill.

The transformation of the information gained through the various media from the cognitive domain to psychomotor action requires a catalytic element. In individualized instruction involvement experiences are crucial to arouse a spirit of inquiry and to provide sufficient rehearsing until the desired behavioral change is achieved. These involvement experiences or tasks are called transactions. The key to successful transactions is feedback facilitated by one or more goal-directed tasks. Since each learner is unique, activity alternatives within the transaction should be available for selection by the learner.[1]

Transactions or practice cycles are prepared in advance of the teaching-learning interaction and serve to free the facilitator for flexible, dynamic interaction with students on a one-to-one basis.

The use of transactions allows self-paced practice which is analyzed by a multitude of evaluation aids. The learners will have an opportunity to practice as much or as little as needed, they can repeat without penalty, and they can obtain tutorial assistance from the teacher, classmates, friends, or anyone whom they believe can help them to learn. The rationale for developing and selecting transactions is centered in the needs and interests of the learner rather than in those of the instructor. The crux of humanized individual instruction is the belief that the learner *does* want to learn and that self-motivation is a vital factor in retaining desired learning goals. Transactions encourage play, spontaneity, and individual creativity. They may be executed within or outside the school setting and should be always available to the student. Traditional edu-

*Highly recommended.
[1]Stuart Johnson and Rita Johnson, *Assuring Learning with Self-Instructional Packages* (Philippines: Self Instructional Packages, Inc., 1973), p. 49.

cators express concern that the more freedom a student is given, the more likely he will choose only what pleases him. Some humanists share this concern but point out it is the only way learning can begin. However, the system you are learning in this book suggests a balance between required and free activities. Disagreements regarding requirements versus freedom are mediated through structured transactions which provide a variety of practice opportunities.

TYPES OF TRANSACTIONS

Mosston[2] calls transactions "teaching styles" and contends that teaching styles progressively prepare the learner for more responsibility for learning. He proposed seven "styles" of teaching, from command to discovery. The relative position of each transaction along the continuum is determined by the number and types of decisions that a student may make concerning pre-class decisions, execution, and evaluation of the lesson. The shift from qne style to the next is characterized by the students' being allowed progressively more decision making. He theorized that each style increasingly develops the learner along four channels: intellectual, emotional, physical, and social. Research by Boschee[3] has failed to support this theory. Furthermore, he found that the decision to shift from one style to another is based on the teacher's perception of overall readiness of the class which, of course, does not allow for individual differences. *It is proposed that the selection of a style or transaction be determined by the preference and needs of each individual student.* The types of transaction proposed in this book may be classified into four categories: self-contained, interaction, discovery, and independent.

The *self-contained* transaction permits the learner to practice the skill or activity on his own. Practice conditions and precise quantitative and qualitative skill differentials specified are based upon the agreed learning goals. The student is free to decide the place and pace of practice.

The *interaction* transaction is characterized by cooperative practice with other students to provide feedback concerning the quality of performance as well as to perform teamwork skills. The qualitative judgments may be informal between the learners, or formalized by prescribed adherence to evaluative criteria supplied by the facilitator. The feedback is immediate and personal, and the conditions for practice are specified,

    [2]M. Mosston, *Teaching Physical Education* (Columbus, Ohio: Charles E. Merrill Publishing Company, 1966).
    [3]Floyd Boschee, "A comparison of the Effects of Command, Task and Individual Program Styles of Teaching on Four Developmental Channels" (Paper presented at National AAHPER Convention, Annaheim, California, May 1974).

except as to place and pace. Socialization is obviously a concomitant outcome of interaction transactions.

Guided discovery, problem-solving, and creative transactions are the three types of *discovery* transactions. These transactions are based on cognitive dissonance which is designed to lead to inquiry. There are variations in instruction, guidance, and goal identification given to the learner.

Independent program transactions may include self-contained tasks, interaction tasks, or discovery practice events. The program is planned by the facilitator and student. The directions are sufficient to permit the learner to proceed independently. Programmed learning, computer-assisted learning, and workbooks are examples of independent programs.

The construction of transactions must reflect procedures that will facilitate learning. The content should be meaningful and be selected in terms of the learner's aptitudes, physical needs, and personal aspirations. The practice should follow optimum serial order sequencing and reflect the proper whole-part presentation. Attention must be directed to important learning points and a schedule of events appropriate to the difficulty of the skill must be provided. Performance criteria should give the learner feedback to guide successive practice attempts. Although in physical education the major practice experience will be performing the skill itself, writing, drawing, and teaching others are also possible transactions.

GENERAL CONSTRUCTION PROCEDURES

The preparation of a transaction begins with the behavioral objective specified in the overall plan or prescription. From the objective, alternative media should be available for the student to gain performance information. The actual construction of the transactions should follow these steps:

1. Provide feedback by specifying quantitative and qualitative differentials, such as direction, duration, time, speed, distance, space, appearance, consistency, accuracy, and bio-mechanical performance variables. Analyze the components of the skill and the learning classification. This information will control the nature of the practice and prevailing conditions. Robb[4] has proposed a helpful procedure to assist with this step.

2. Plan clear, succinct, and complete practice directions. These directions should specify any constraints or contingencies. Choices should be available. You should specify where to practice, number of participants, number of trials, variations, and successful performance dimensions.

[4]M. Robb, *Dynamics of Motor Skill Acquisition* (Englewood Cliffs, N.J.: Prentice-Hall, Inc., 1972), pp. 138–46.

3. Facilitate ease in reading and in recording results. Include provisions for name, beginning and ending dates, and transaction identification. Each practice event should be underlined and space should be provided for recording trials and successes.

4. The purpose and utilization of the completed transactions should be indicated.

Self-Contained Transactions

Self-contained transactions may be performed in any learning domain—the verb in the specific taxonomy is the key to the type of experience to be practiced. Psychomotor tasks may use verbs like bat, bend, hit, throw, toss, run, kick, catch, and so forth. The sequence or progression of self-contained practice experiences should be from simple to complex. Careful analysis of the skill will help you to specify the appropriate sequence and combinations of movements to be practiced. In other words, using Jewett's psychomotor taxonomy (see Figure 5–1 in Chapter 5), the beginning self-contained tasks would use generic verbs which would promote perception, imitation, and patterning. More difficult tasks would use ordinative verbs which require organizing, adapting, and refining movement patterns. For example, the first task might be simply:

> Hit 10 underhand volleyball serves (the hit does not have to go over the net or inside the boundaries).

A trial is a successful hitting of the ball with the hand. The purpose of this generic self-contained task is to assist the learner to become aware of the space, time, dynamics, and feeling of the action through a transaction that stimulates sound, appearance, and external and internal feeling of the movement. A more difficult self-contained task would be:

> Serve 10 underhand volleyball serves that go over the net (the serve does not need to land within the boundaries of the opposite court).

In this task, distance is an added differential which will contribute toward repeating what is considered to be a desirable underhand volleyball serve. Defining a target area will add the dimension of accuracy to the skill:

> Serve 10 underhand serves over the net which land inside the opposite court boundaries.
>
> or
>
> Serve 10 underhand serves over the net which land in the left quadrant of the opposite court.

The number of trials or successful attempts may be specified. This variable is dependent on the skill, interest, and needs of the learner. A percentage or ratio of successes to trials may be specified:

> Serve at least 5 out of 10 underhand serves over the net which land in the opposite court.

The above task is more complex and would be used as the learner has moved from beginning or generic stages to the ordinative stage of adapting and refining the action. Another example might be:

> Serve 10 underhand serves. 60 percent must go over the net and land in the opposite court.

Directions for self-contained transactions should specify the practice conditions, the number of assistants, and/or whether the learner is free to set up the practice conditions. Figure 7–1 is an example of a self-contained transaction for practicing the high clear shot in badminton.

The major performance variables that supplied feedback to the learner in the example were distance and accuracy. If time is a crucial factor in a skill, then it should be specified as one of the conditions of the task. For example:

Secure a timer and run the fifty-yard dash. Record your
time _____

Run until you can reduce the time by _____ percent.

Record your additional trials until your goal has been
reached.

Date								
Times								

Qualitative differentials may be added to self-contained tasks by
asking the performers to observe certain criteria as they perform. If the
temporal patterning of the skill is too rapid for conscious application of
the criteria, the learner may augment the observation by arranging to be
video-taped or to have movies taken. Easily observable qualitative variables are precision, consistency, and the presence or absence of key bio-
mechanical factors. For example:

After running the 50-yard dash, it may be helpful in
your endeavor to reduce your time by observing that
these critical movements are being performed:

Task	*Comments*
1. *Takeoff.* Check your first step. It should be placed under the body and be less than a full stride.	
2. *Sprint.* Check your path. It should be straight.	
3. *Finish.* Check your speed. It should be all out.	

Self-contained tasks should provide qualitative and quantitative
feedback to the learner to guide subsequent activity toward planned
objectives. Feedback is usually more valuable if it can be immediate and
practice can be resumed close to the time of the analysis. Notice that the

CLEAR SHOTS

Self-Contained Transaction # 3

Name _____ Starting date _____

Purpose: The purpose of this task is to help you to learn to perform high deep clear shots so that you can constantly and effectively keep your opponent in a defensive position.

Directions: You should have an understanding of the high clear movement pattern secured by whatever media you selected. Courts 1 and 2 will be reserved for practicing this skill. Choose any student you wish to assist you. The clear shot may be attempted from either a tossed or served shuttle.

Note: If you need help, recheck your input source, see your instructor or someone who has completed this task.

Tasks	Attempted	Completed
#1. Hit 15 clears (any contact will count as a try).		
#2. Hit 10 clears that go over the net.		
#3. Hit 10 clears that go over the rope set up 4 feet from the rear doubles service line. The clears do not need to land inside the boundary lines.		
#4. Hit 10 clears as in #3 above but land them inside the sidelines of the opposite court.		
#5. Hit _____ of 10 clears as in #4 above.		
#6. Repeat any of the tasks 1 to 5, emphasizing practice with the weaker stroking side: forehand, backhand, overhead.	(indicate what you worked on)	

When you have completed this transaction, please submit this sheet to your instructor.

Figure 7-1

examples above provide a range from no options to maximum options, depending upon the interests and needs of the learner.

It will save you time if you produce your transaction in sufficient quantities for several similar courses. Self-contained transactions may be printed on index cards, on paper, in booklets, on posters, or on the blackboard. The results may be marked on the task card or recorded on a more centralized master sheet, either for the individual or for the class. Examples may be found in Chapter 14.

Interaction Transactions

The requirements of individualized instruction and the importance of human relations can be fostered through the use of interaction transactions. These may involve one or more paraprofessionals (adults, college students, student leaders), parent volunteers, one or more classmates, or cross-age helpers as well as the facilitator. The use of interaction transactions allows a proliferation of facilitator assistance through printed guidance. The process not only gives individual tutoring for the learner, but also is a reinforcing learning technique for the tutor. Furthermore, this kind of practice is often less threatening to the learner. Part of the success of interaction transactions comes from the pupil's feeling that someone really cares whether or not learning is occurring.

An interaction transaction uses a classmate or other helper selected by either the facilitator or student. One person performs while the other observes the performance. The observation is aided by applying criteria supplied by the facilitator or the learner to judge the quality of the performance. Since the transaction may be a learning experience for both

the performer and observer, interest in their success should be manifested to both. The small-group system is used when the practice events or game play require more than one performer and/or observer. Small groups may be formed on the basis of skill or role similarities or dissimilarities, friendship, or age. The decision should be based on which procedure will best aid learning.

The construction of interaction transactions follows previously mentioned basic steps. However, the focus is more qualitative than quantitative. The performer is given an involvement task but rather than focus being only on the success of the activity, emphasis is placed on the quality. The criteria for quality should be limited to no more than five to seven variables, since it is difficult for anyone to process more information than that at one time. After the observation, interaction takes place linking congruence of the performance variables with goal achievement. Remember that the interaction system if shared with another student is really a learning experience for all parties concerned. The non-performing partner is focusing on the cognitive aspect of the skill as well as increasing his observational ability. In addition, both are learning to receive assistance and criticism from peers. An example of an interaction qualitative transaction in baseball is as follows:

Directions for the doer:

Field a ground ball which is either hit or rolled directly to you from a distance of about 80 to 90 feet. Repeat practice 5 times. Secure someone to check whether you are following the suggestions below:

_____ Knees bent when picking up the ball

_____ Eyes on the ball

_____ Glove side foot in front of nonglove side foot about shoulder width apart

_____ Ball fielded off the glove side foot

_____ Ball secured by the throwing hand

Observer:

Look at the points above. Watch the performer field 5 ground balls. Check which suggestions above were followed.

Often a ranking of the degree of adherence to the criteria is requested. If such a ranking is desirable, then the directions should give guidance as to the basis of the ranking. An example of an interaction qualitative transaction in baseball is illustrated in Figure 7–2.

A small-group task is most often used for team sport skills requiring cooperation and teamwork. For example, a quantitative interaction task might be:

> During two quarters of play, your team must use a shifting man-to-man defense. The opposing team is to be limited to _____ points.

Note that this interaction transaction permits the team to decide upon the goal. An example of a small-group qualitative interaction transaction is as follows:

> During the game, those not playing are to analyze their team's performance based on the criteria given below. Tally a mark in the *Success* column for good examples and in the *Help* column for failures.

Performance	Successes	Help
Group defense position		
Individual defense		
Group offensive play		
Individual play		
Group encouragement		

Discovery Transactions

There are three types of discovery transactions: guided discovery, problem-solving, and creative. These transactions differ from each other in identified goals and facilitator directions. All students can use these transactions but they may be more helpful for the intermediate or advanced student whose psychomotor learning is at the stage of adapting,

FIELDING FORM

Softball #11

Doer _____   Observer _____

Purpose: The purpose of this transaction is to help you to improve your ability to field ground balls using good form.

Directions:

Doer: Get someone to bat or throw you ground balls from a distance of 80 to 90 feet for each task. Request that he observe each trial to determine how well the suggestions listed are being followed.

Observer: Observe his performance in terms of the listed suggestions below. Place a (+) after the item if it is completely followed, a (−) if partially followed or most often followed, and (0) if it is not followed.

Task	Trials					
	1	2	3	4	5	Comments
#1. Field a batted or thrown ball from 80 to 90 feet away for which you must move to your glove side to field. Look for: Knees bent when picking up ball						
Eyes on the ball						
Glove foot in front of non-glove foot about shoulder width apart						
Ball fielded off the glove foot side						
Ball secured by the throwing hand						
#2. Repeat #1 above, moving to your throwing hand side.						
Knees bent						
Eyes on the ball						
Glove foot forward						
Ball fielded off the glove foot						
Ball secured by the throwing hand						

Figure 7–2

refining, or creating. In addition to aiding psychomotor learning, this kind of transaction contributes heavily to the cognitive learning domain, tending to rely on the trial-and-error process.

Guided Discovery. The purpose of guided discovery is to allow the learners an opportunity to experience the consequences of various actions in any or all learning domains until they can discover the desirable procedures whch should be followed. The facilitator structures the questions or events from which the student may discover the successful procedure. An example of guided discovery is given in Figure 7–3.

As you can see, the learner is challenged to inquire, compare, draw conclusions, and make decisions. These activities are intellectually demanding and challenging. Finding the answer does not imply that new knowledge or skill will be uncovered for all the world but that new abilities will be uncovered for the learner. What is discovered may be principles, concepts, ideas, relationships, facts, skills, understandings, and so forth. As the facilitator, you may structure guided discovery by raising questions to the student to be answered by cognitive or motor activity. The student may learn through discovery in any learning domain. You assist the learner to find the knowledge or skill only through structured questions and activities. Informing the student of the answer before discovery destroys the need to investigate. Often you may feel uncomfortable utilizing this transaction in a group question-and-answer setting. For that reason, it may be helpful to use activity-type guided discovery tasks as in the example.

Although it may seem to be a time-consuming process when compared with simply telling the answer to the student, it should be remembered that the process of discovering is a powerful tool. People prefer a challenge, and the satisfaction of finding a solution is rewarding and thus reinforcing. Guided discovery is a basic foundation for individualized instruction. A guided discovery task may be structured as a self-contained or interaction transaction. The larger the group using guided discovery, the less the benefits for each individual since each student is starting from a different rung on the ladder.

When constructing guided discovery transactions, select activities or topics that are difficult to understand or are basically conceptual in nature. Next, sequence the activity and develop questions and cues that proceed from general to specific points. Questions should help the learner discriminate among multiple answers. For instance, in the softball-throwing example given, intervening questions and cues may be needed to achieve the stated purpose. These questions might be:

How far can you throw a ball with a straight line flight?
How far . . . with an arc?

THROWING

Softball Task #13

Name _____   Starting date _____

Purpose: The purpose of this practice is to improve distance in throwing a softball.

Directions: Get someone to help you, or find a blank wall to throw against.

Throw the ball about 10 feet to the target (wall or partner).
Repeat several times until you can answer the following questions.

1. What parts of the body were used?
   Wrist? Elbow? Upper arm? Back? Entire body? Legs?

2. How much was each used?

3. At what point was the ball released?
   Above your head? In front of you, head high? Shoulder high?

4. How did the ball flight appear?

Throw the ball from 20, 40, 60, 80, 100 feet.
Repeat several times from each distance until you can answer the questions above. Are there any differences as you get further from the target?

What conclusions would you make concerning desirable body action to throw a ball a great distance. Explain to a friend or write in space below. Ask the instructor for help if you are confused.

Figure 7-3

Which would take longer? Why?

What can you do to increase distance and speed?

Try out some of these ideas and find out.

Guided discovery transactions are intricate and difficult to develop. Careful analysis of the results obtained may help you to eventually structure more satisfactory tasks. The analysis should look at the clarity of the question, the connotation of words, the discriminatory power of the question, and the precision of the sequence. Guided discovery is dependent upon the student's expected responses to carefully structured questions and events designed to lead to preferred answers.

Problm-Solving.   Problem-solving transactions expect students to seek out answers on their own. The answers should conform to the criteria of the problem. In some instances the answer required would be specific or closed; in others it may be left open. Alternative solutions are encouraged to promote divergent thinking. A simple example of a problem-solving transaction might be:

Basketball Problem

Tomorrow's opponent is slow moving and shoots well from outside the key. Decide upon defensive and offensive procedures for yourself and make recommendations to ensure victory for the team.

As you can see, the process of discovery is still present. The students must inquire, explore, discover, and analyze results. Note, however, that the questions are missing and the response is guided only by two points: (1) the ability of the opponent and (2) the global goal—to win. The learner provides the ways to the goal.

When constructing problem-solving transactions, select topics that are broader in scope and that can best synthesize previous learnings for application to new solutions. If the solution is basically a cognitive decision, the transaction ought to provide opportunity to try out the solution and should call for an evaluation of its success with recommendations for improvement. There will be alternative solutions and the process of deciding preferences will elicit even more problems. The problem must not seek responses to the student, and the dimensions of the problem should be relevant to the readiness, experience, interests, and needs of the student.

Creative.   Astronaut David Scott said, "Through exploration comes discovery and through discovery we gain new knowledge." The creative discovery transaction permits complete freedom to the student. A global goal is identified but no criteria are given as to the solution since it must be created. An example of a creative experience is the Fosbury Flop in high jumping. Fosbury found that he could jump higher over the bar by using mechanically stronger muscles. He created a new way to high jump by going over the bar with his back facing the bar. A creative discovery transaction may be as follows:

> Given that you have tried known existing
> conventional and unconventional systems of
> putting, invent a new way to putt.

The genesis of this transaction should be from the student. He should ask the question and seek the answer. It is easier to imitate than to invent! It is one of the goals of individualized instruction to learn how to learn. Expert performers and coaches often caution against permitting deviations from "proven" form. Yet, observations of batting form have yielded a multitude of successful stances. The world of sports is constantly creating new movements, new games, and new rules to guide play.

Independent Transactions

Tasks within independent transactions may be self-contained, interactive, and/or discovery types. Sufficient information should be provided to allow the learner to proceed with minimum direction and assistance from the facilitator. Programmed instruction, computer-assisted learning, and workbooks provide action experiences as well as cognitive learning. Annarino's[5] *Individualized Instruction Programs* books are an example of a complete independent transaction.

Independent transactions may provide the inputs or delivery system and the terminal objectives. They may be based on single or multiple skills. Developers of independent transactions call them by different names. Some of these are:

Learning Activity Program (LAP), Nova System, Fort Lauderdale, Fla.

Physical Education Independent Study (PEIS), Ridgewood High School, Ridgewood, Ill.

Physical Activity Package (PhiPacs), Omaha School System, Omaha, Neb.

Teaching Learning Unit (TLU), Westinghouse Learning Corporation, Simmons Junior High School, Aurora, Ill.

Task-Contracts (TC), College of Health, Physical Education and Recreation, University of Illinois, Chicago Circle, Chicago, Ill.

Examples of these independent programs are presented in the last chapter of this book.

[5]Anthony Annarino, *Individualized Instruction Programs* (Englewood Cliffs, N.J.: Prentice-Hall, Inc., 1973).

STRUCTURE FOR PRESENTATION

Transactions are usually written as part of individualized programs but may be used separately in teacher-directed, class-centered instruction. The transaction may be printed as a single program in which progress is recorded, or on reusable index cards in which case progress is recorded on an individual record card or a mass record sheet. Some transactions may be put on posters and taped to the wall at various practice areas.

It is possible to use transactions as a part of a single course or unit of instruction or as a part of multi-course or units of instruction. In a single-activity unit, all the transactions are available for that activity and learners may progress from their respective entry points toward their final goals within a fixed or variable time schedule. In this situation usually one facilitator is assigned. Since practice may not need to be completed in the assigned learning laboratory (gymnasium) or under the surveillance of the facilitator, time may be extended until mastery is achieved, providing the imposed grading system will permit. In the multiple-activity system, several activities are available and several facilitators are assigned. Transactions are available for the various activities and the learners may select one or more activities to pursue. The process of planning and managing such systems has been discussed in previous chapters.

SUMMARY

Transactions are preplanned goal-centered practice events which are specified to permit the learner to try out the information gained from selected delivery systems. There are four types of transactions. The *self-contained* transactions tend to be quantitative in nature and manipulate carefully analyzed components of a psychomotor skill for practice in prescribed conditions of time, distance, accuracy, consistency, bio-mechanics, and space, in order to facilitate feedback. The *interaction* transactions tend to be more qualitative in nature and involve communication between the learner and other interested persons to ascertain the degree of congruence between actual and desired performance. The criteria that describe successful performance are presented for practice in specified conditions. Self-contained and interaction tasks are most useful in the generic stages of skill learning. The *discovery* transactions are more independent procedures which may contribute to learner independence or foster improved learning. There are three types of discovery transactions: guided discovery, problem-solving, and creative. They vary progressively from teacher-imposed constraints and goals to complete student control of the discovery process. Discovery transactional tasks are most useful for learners in the ordinative or inventive stages of learning. *Independent* transactions may include any or all of the above transactions which are personally prescribed or imposed on the group.

The construction of transactions requires adherence to the following procedures: (1) selection of the appropriate subject matter and amount of subject matter in terms of desired goals; (2) analysis of the skill components and sequence of practice; (3) specification of practice conditions; (4) provision for feedback concerning the progress toward the goal; (5) written or verbal directions that are clear and complete; (6)

communication concerning utilization of the transactions in verifying skill acquisition.

Transactions may be presented for single or multiple skills within single or multiple courses.

REFERENCES

ANNARINO, A. *Individualized Instruction Programs.* Englewood Cliffs, N.J.: Prentice-Hall, Inc., 1973.

BOSCHEE, F. "A Comparison of the Effects of Command, Task and Individual Program Styles of Teaching on Four Developmental Channels." Paper presented at National AAHPER Convention, Annaheim, California, May, 1974.

DEL REY, P. "Appropriate Feedback for Open and Closed Skill Acquisition," *Quest.* National Association for College Men and Women. Monograph 17:42 (1972).

DUNN, R., AND K. DUNN. *Practical Approaches to Individualize Instruction.* West Nyack, N.Y.: Parker Publishing Company, 1972.

FRYMIER, J. D. *A School for Tomorrow.* Berkeley, Calif.: McCutchan Publishing Company, 1973.

FRYMIER, J. D., AND C. M. GALLOWAY. "Individualized Learning in School for Tomorrow," *Theory into Practice.* College of Education, Ohio State University, 13:4 (1974), 65.

JOHNSON, R. B., AND S. R. JOHNSON. *Assuring Learning with Self Instructional Packages.* Philippines: Self Instructional Packages, Inc., 1973.

JOYCE, B., AND M. WEIL. *Models of Teaching.* Englewood Cliffs, N.J.: Prentice-Hall, Inc., 1972.

LEWIS, J. *Administrating the Individualized Instruction Program.* West Nyack, N.Y.: Parker Publishing Company, 1971.

MAGER, R. F., AND P. PEPE. *Analyzing Performance Problems.* Belmont, Calif.: Fearon Publishers, 1970.

MOSSTON, M. *Teaching Physical Education.* Columbus, Ohio: Charles E. Merrill Publishing Company, 1966.

NOAR, G. *Individualizing Instruction.* New York: John Wiley & Sons, Inc., 1972.

ROBB, M. *Dynamics of Motor Skill Acquisition.* Englewood Cliffs, N.J.: Prentice-Hall, Inc., 1972.

RUSSELL, J. D., AND S. POSTLETHWAIT. *Modular Instruction.* Minneapolis, Minn.: Burgess Press, 1974.

SINGER, R., AND W. DICK. *Teaching Physical Education—A Systems Approach.* Boston: Houghton Mifflin Company, 1974.

8

Evaluating
The
Goals

INSTRUCTIONAL UNIT FOR CHAPTER 8

Learner's Diagnosis

Directions: Read the questions below. Write out, discuss, or mentally review the answers. If you believe that you know the information, check the "yes" column. If you are not sure of the answer, check the "no" column. After reading the questions and deciding your knowledge, check the accuracy of your answers by reading the summary at the end of this chapter. If you answered a question incorrectly, change your answer to the appropriate column.

Can you

Yes	No	Questions
		1. Analyze why students should know beforehand what the goal is and the criteria upon which they are to be judged?
		2. Enumerate the purposes of evaluation?
		3. State how diagnostic goals can be evaluated?
		4. Differentiate between formative and summative evaluation?
		5. State the criteria for the selection of an observer to verify performance?
		6. Apply the purpose of formative diagnosis to how it would be operationalized in skill and knowledge acquisition?
		7. Synthesize how attitude and process-oriented instructional goals can be verified?
		8. Interpret how summative evaluation can be operationalized?
		9. Relate some misconceptions that can occur when students are graded immediately after instruction?
		10. Apply how methods of individualized instruction involve the student in goal setting?

Suggested Prescription

Directions: Count the number of checks you have placed in the "yes" column. When the percentages are determined, you may increase your knowledge and skill by using the suggested Learning Program activities recommended in the Input and Practice columns. Input and practices not listed offer additional learning options.

Results	Input	Practice
More than 80%	#1, 2	#1, 2 or 3, 7
60% to 80%	#1, 2, 6 or 7	#1, 2 or 3, 5, 7
40% to 60%	#1, 2, 4 or 5 or 6, 7	#1, 2 or 3, 4 or 9, 7
Less than 40%	#1, 2, 3, 5 or 7, 8	#1, 2 or 3, 4, 5, 9

Learning Program

Directions: It is suggested that the reader attempt to complete any or all suggestions in this learning program. These are designed to improve knowledge and understanding of how to evaluate the goals of learning and to explain the purposes of evaluating them.

Proposed Learning Objective: The learner will be able to develop formative and summative evaluation based on the purposes of these two types of evaluation.

Input:

*1. Read Chapter 8 of this book.
 2. Read M. J. Safrit, *Evaluation in Physical Education*, Chapters 1, 2, and 3.
 3. Read B. Bloom, et al., *Handbook on Formative and Summative Evaluation of Student Learning*, Chapters 1–12.
 4. Ask four or five students in the eighth grade and four or five sophomores in high school what the criteria were for their grades.

*Highly recommended.

5. Ask several students how "fair" they considered the grades they received.
6. Ask several students what they would consider "fair" criteria for evaluation.
7. Ask a teacher what means are used to determine the criteria for grades and how the students are informed of this criteria.
8. Ask one or two students how they would proceed in a class if they knew day by day how far they had to go to succeed.
9. Design an input of your own.

Practice:

1. Write an example of an evaluation to a parent of a student not working up to capacity, relating in humanistic fashion how well the student performed in the class.
2. John has selected tennis at the expert level. He is not achieving this level and seems disinterested. Develop a formative diagnostic evaluation with which you can identify what is wrong.
3. Mary, who has won the intramural tournament in tennis, has selected a beginner level of competency in instructional tennis, consistent with her diagnostic scores. How would you judge the diagnostic data?
4. Apply what is known about a student as revealed in formative diagnosis and identify the process for changing a non-productive learning program.
5. Identify a rule or technique concept. What would be the difference in phrasing the question to get a recall, understanding, or application answer?
6. Devise a performance grid format for the components of swimming and perceptual motor development, or other sport of your choice, to be used to plot a profile diagnosis.
7. Develop a formative diagnosis evaluation with alternate practice and error correction cues for two sports of your choice.
8. Devise criteria for summative evaluation in a sport and develop formative evaluation which would guide the student to master the criteria.
9. Identify three people who would be willing to learn a skill. Diagnose each of them as to their level of achievement. Ask them to identify how well they wish to learn the skill. Negotiate terminal behavioral objectives and summative evaluation. Develop learner objectives, practice agendas, and

formative diagnosis plans. Determine how many adjustments had to be made in the initial learning program to reach the goal in each case.

10. Develop a practice of your own.

Evaluation: You will be able to demonstrate the ability to construct formative evaluation which will effectively lead the student to success on summative evaluative criteria.

Before learners set out to learn something, they must have a clear idea of what is to be done. Each must get the fullest idea possible of the end goal: what it will look and feel like, how it can be reached, what can be done with it, and how to acquire it.

A goal is often multifaceted. The skill or knowledge to be learned is often paramount, but there are also supporting goals relating to process skills, perseverance, an enjoyment of the effort, increased self-esteem and concept, and sense of accomplishment. Students can be *trained* to perform a skill and often to perform it well, but it isn't *education* unless they understand the process of how they arrived at the skill, feel good in the learning act, and are pleased at having learned.

Individualized humanistic instruction has as its premise that the *whole* child must be satisfied. This whole includes the cognitive self, which governs thinking—wanting to know why and how; the physical self, which will be educated to perform in relative comfort, safety, ease, and efficiency; and the affective or emotional self, which judges what the *whole* of the activity has done for self-concept and how the learner feels about it. Thus, evaluation processes must be built in to determine if goals in each of these areas have been met.

In most school systems judgments are made regarding the degree of learning a student has acquired. The important fact to be remembered is that this evaluation should be something done *for* the student rather than *to* him. The only way a student can accept evaluation as being helpful is to know before the fact the criteria upon which the evaluation will be based.

Evaluation is used as an integral part of individualized humanistic instruction at every step along the way. It is the benchmark for the beginning, the signposts that mark progress, and the banner that signals arrival. It is the feedback that motivates and spurs the student on and is the signal that reflects symptoms of nonlearning or negative learning. If education is defined as modifying behavior in desirable ways, then the evaluation process should help determine whether or not behavior has been beneficially changed. For a student to wander aimlessly through a unit—perhaps with the mistaken hope that at the end he will be able to play the game with skill—not only is frustrating for that student, but is inhumane.

Chapter 1 stated some professional goals for physical education. These included understanding of oneself, facilitating socialization, development of skills, awareness of physical and psychological variables in the environment, and learning of process skills. Goals in each of these areas should be identified and transactions developed which will help the student reach these goals. Determination of where a student is at one point in time would be made in the diagnostic phase. Throughout the learning program the student should be aware of learning more about himself—his perseverance and ability to improve his capabilities—and of understanding why something is occurring. During the transaction phase he may learn about cooperation in the learning process and the need to cooperate to compete. The student should also be helped to develop independence and to seek reliance upon his own resources when appropriate. Sequential, realistic goals should be determined for enhancing skills, body awareness, coordination, strength, and endurance. The student's attention should be directed toward coping with the various physical and psychological phenomena that may affect performance. Through the learning act he should learn how to select appropriate objectives and learning modes, and to understand the mechanical and physiological principles governing actions. Education becomes dynamic when the student can move from being passive to being initiator of and his own facilitator for learning new skills when outside a formal school setting. Being part of the goal-setting process helps to focus the student's attention on this dynamic role in education rather than on being a static recipient of other-directed actions. At the conclusion of the time for learning the student should be involved in the evaluation of the end products. He becomes accountable for his own actions in the learning process, and thus is able to see his role in accepting the responsibility for his own learning.

Evaluation is based on measurement. Measurement refers to the process of determining how much of a given attribute a student has. In and of itself, it tells nothing but facts. Evaluation gives meaning to the measurement data. It interprets the data in relation to others or in relation to past records or desired goals. Hence, measurement supplies the data, and evaluation is the process of judgment concerning the meaning of the data. Educational measurement and evaluation processes and techniques are a study in themselves. The purpose of this chapter is merely to supplement this phase of teacher preparation to include adjustments peculiar to individualized instruction.

Goal evaluation is utilized in the three phases of instruction for different purposes: (1) for diagnostic evaluation validity, (2) for formative judgments during the learning program, and (3) for summative evaluation at the conclusion of the learning unit.

EVALUATING THE DIAGNOSTIC GOALS

The diagnostic step is used for three purposes: (1) to place students at appropriate entry points in the learning program, (2) to identify remedial areas affecting achievement, and (3) to identify appropriate modes of transmission of knowledge. It should enable you to make the judgments necessary to prescribe and begin instructional transactions. A unit can fail if the diagnosis does not yield correct data. As the learning program progresses it can become apparent whether or not the data attained in the diagnostic phase were correct or if all factors were seriously considered. The student may falsify diagnostic data if he does not understand that the goal of education is to seek self-actualization rather than a grade. Chapter 10 may be helpful in revealing decisions students may make that are not authentic. Chapter 9 will indicate how students are motivated to reach goals. In some instances a student may show low achievement in some of the component skills of the unit to be studied and, therefore, may be encouraged to select lesser goals; however, perseverance and desire to learn may cause the student to achieve higher goals than predicted. The converse can be true if the student's interest is not as high as you assumed.

The validity of the entry point determined in the diagnostic phase and the goals defined in the conference phase are periodically judged by you and the student. Throughout the learning program you must determine: Did the diagnosis do what was intended? Did it motivate the student to want to improve achievement? Did it give accurate data? Are the transactions that were selected appropriate for the student's ability and learning requirements? In some instances goals should be altered if they are proven to be unrealistic.

JUDGING LEARNING PROGRAM GOALS
THROUGH FORMATIVE EVALUATION

Formative evaluation measures the progress toward the mastery of learning. It occurs during the involvement or learning phase and is imbedded in the transactions in the learning module. Because it occurs during the formation of the learning, it is also useful in evaluating *process*. Thus, it should yield appropriate evidence to improve process as well as product. Means must be found to identify the most effective method of reporting the results. The effect of formative evaluation is lessened if it raises judgmental tensions related to grading. It should simply inform the student of how much he has mastered and how he can improve his mastery.

When a unit is identified for study, the scope and dimensions are defined. Global goals would be identified and the degree of mastery would be agreed upon. The global goal would be subdivided into learning modules with learning objectives identified which would structure the learning sequence and consistency of skill needed to perform at the chosen level.

As the transactions are developed they should follow the input needed for the student to master the goal. During the practice of the transaction, the components are identified as described in Chapter 7. The output is in terms of the behavior required for a fixed or flexible goal. When you first try this procedure for instruction you may have to make many adjustments in the learning program. You may begin at a trial-and-error level, but as you gain experience with a variety of students you will have more evidence upon which to base the original learning program, and you will be able to formulate a more valid program.

The learner's objective is to show mastery of a needed component of the skill or knowledge. The criteria for such mastery can be measures of accuracy, speed, consistency, form, or combinations of these items. In some instances you would determine how well the student should perform, and under what conditions, to be credited with attaining a given mastery level. The student could choose the level. If the sport or activity has several component skills the student may not desire to attain expert ability in all. Further, the time constraints or previous achievement may require that the student work in depth on a few and attempt other skills in a more cursory fashion. After entering the program, the student may discover that he or she has a greater facility in learning one skill than another, hence, may alter the mastery levels for selected skills.

Identifying standards of performance may begin as "guesstimates," guided by students' past achievements and perseverance records. Certainly each student must be encouraged to attain a level which assures more consistency than inconsistency if he or she is to enjoy the game. Hence, to pass beyond a beginning level it may be that at least 50 percent consistency under ideal circumstances would be reasonable. The student could then move to percents of consistency that would exceed a 50–50 chance. Formative evaluation and diagnosis should be directed toward improving the consistency levels.

Criteria for mastery in a given time specification or by competency would have some effect on forming learning modules and setting realistic goals. Chapter 10 explains these two grading references. The verification that the learning goal has been met can occur by a testimonial of the student, facilitator, peer, or a combination of these. This verification process is important because if the standards of performance are misread and the student assumes he has mastered the task and proceeds to the next level, he may be inhibited in his learning at the subsequent stage.

Achievement mastery can be easily verified when quantity is the goal. For instance, in an archery unit if the learner objective was to hit the target six out of ten tries, substantiation of this achievement is observable and objective; reporting of this accomplishment can be made by the student. However, qualitative judgments may require verification by an observer. When form is being judged, criteria must be identified upon which the quality can be assessed. The amount of criteria and the speed with which the skill is performed determine the degree of observational ability the observer must possess. If the performer were to do a simple front roll, beginning from a standing position, rolling in a straight line, and returning to a standing position, the performer and/or a relatively unskilled observer could verify the performance. However, if momemtum, shoulder and hand placement, synchronization of the tuck position, extension on the standup, absolute balance maintenance, and ending form were all to be judged, the observer would have to be more observant throughout the performance. Verification would have to be done by the facilitator or a skillful student trained to make the judgment. You should hold the verifier accountable for his testimony. It should be understood that once a skill has been attested to, you can ask the student to perform the task as proof that it has in fact been learned.

If the learner objective is not reached during the practice phase, the formative evaluation should be constructed to help identify the inhibiting factors. Locating the difficulties is important in motivating the student. Continual failure in the performance would cause the student to give up. Formative evaluation is a continual diagnosis for the student and in this regard should help to correct the inhibiting errors.

Formative evaluation should help students pace the learning. Frequent evaluations keep the students alert to how far they should have progressed at any given time in order to complete the unit. It also helps to give structure and sequence to the learning.

The degree to which the global goal is broken down into learner goals and specified practice transactions depends upon the nature of the learning needs of the student. For some students, perhaps those who have a strong inquiry desire, creative interest, achievement background, and independence motive, minimum designations are all that would be necessary. Others who have the opposite tendencies may feel more comfortable with a more structured learning program which is broken into smaller steps and more frequent feedback opportunities. Transactions can be used for formative evaluation. Figure 8–1 represents the aspects

FORMAT FOR FORMATIVE EVALUATION

Global goal (sum of the unit terminal objectives for the student in the realm of
    psychomotor, cognitive, and affective goals)
Learner goals per learning component and module

Module One
    Learner objective
    Input suggestions
    Formative practice
        Transaction selection directions
        Suggested trial repetitions
        Conditions of practice
        Accuracy and consistency
    Formative diagnosis
        Error correction
        How identified
        Alternate practice conditions
    Formative evaluation verification
        How verified
        By whom
        Method of recording results and verification testimony
Module Two

Figure 8–1

of the practice transaction that can be used as formative evaluation. If
the student is successful, the transaction was productive.

The number of steps to lead to the global goal can be specified or
left to the student to select according to his needs. Some students, knowing the global goal, can proceed with identifying their own practice program if they know the process of learning skills or knowledge. Figure 8–2
indicates a detailed learning transaction based on one learner objective.

Formative knowledge quizzes could be frequent and also should be
diagnostic. To be helpful in promoting mastery they should also have
directions for finding the answer. Answers should be supplied right after
the test is taken so the student can immediately grade the paper and
begin to understand the answers. Recall format tests should have the
reason for the answer available so the student doesn't just memorize on
a stimulus-response level. The answer and reason could be on the back,
question card or paper, or on another sheet.

Purpose of
Format

Formative
objective

Specifics level
of mastery

Verification

Formative
Practice

Formative
Diagnosis:
Is the student
alert to
visual and
kinesthetic
feedback?

Does the
student have
insight?
Was the goal
too high or
too low?

SERVING CONSISTENCY TRANSACTION

Learning objective: The student will be able to serve
with consistency in a practice situation.
Terminal behavioral objective: Hit _____ out of _____
overhand serves which land within 5 feet of the back
line in a practice situation.

Select practice transaction

Achieved _____ Attested by _____ . Begin program on
Serve Placement.
Not achieved _____ Check the cues below:
1. Review demonstration.
2. Reread explanation of skill.
3. Attempt more trials.
4. Select a different practice transaction

Error observation	Try
Flight of ball into net	Contact ball sooner on the downward follow-through.
Out of court over end line	Contact ball later on the downward follow-through.
Force of hit—not enough distance	Coordinate contact with transfer of weight from back to forward foot.
Lack of success	Ask a classmate to help. Review the loop film. Ask the teacher.

Why do you believe you are not successful?

How many successful overhand serves can you complete
out of _____ tries? _____

Figure 8–2

An Example of Formative Practice, Diagnosis and Evaluation

179

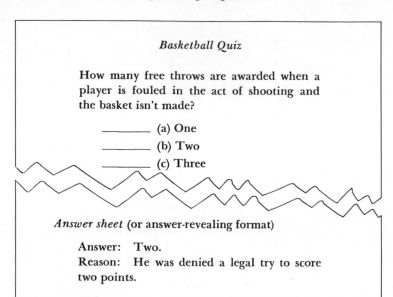

Basketball Quiz

How many free throws are awarded when a player is fouled in the act of shooting and the basket isn't made?

_____ (a) One
_____ (b) Two
_____ (c) Three

Answer sheet (or answer-revealing format)

Answer: Two.
Reason: He was denied a legal try to score two points.

The above recall question ensures only that the student knows the answer under certain circumstances. It does not imply that the student comprehends or can apply the knowledge to a variety of situations. Therefore, questions should be framed to measure how well the student can apply the knowledge. If he cannot apply the knowledge, the goal of understanding and applying knowledge has not been attained. Additional transactions would have to be designed to assure that the student was given practice and diagnostic conditions to help him reach the understanding level.

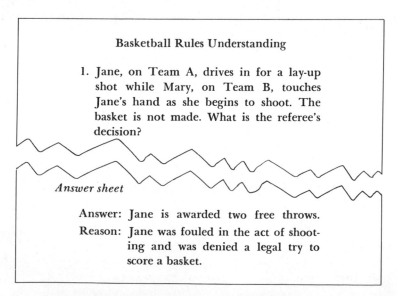

Basketball Rules Understanding

1. Jane, on Team A, drives in for a lay-up shot while Mary, on Team B, touches Jane's hand as she begins to shoot. The basket is not made. What is the referee's decision?

Answer sheet

Answer: Jane is awarded two free throws.

Reason: Jane was fouled in the act of shooting and was denied a legal try to score a basket.

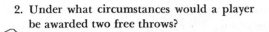

2. Under what circumstances would a player
be awarded two free throws?

Answer sheet

Answer: When the person attempting to
shoot for a basket was fouled in
the act of shooting and the basket
was not made.

Reason: The offensive team was illegally
denied an attempt to score a field
goal for two points.

Comprehension of concepts can be tested. For example:

A ball thrown in a flat plane from in front
of the basket and hit above the basket will:

_____ (a) rebound into the basket
_____ (b) rebound to the left
_____ (c) rebound in an identical
plane back to the point
of origin

Answer sheet

Answer: c

Reason: If an object is thrown toward a surface it will rebound at exactly the
same angle at which it was thrown
against the surface.

The tools used to evaluate the formative learning for knowledge or
skill must be such that they can give data at all levels and types of goals.
The complexity of the statements and conditions under which the knowledge and skill are to be demonstrated must be consistent with the student's vocabulary and experience level. Testing for cognitive knowledge
should not be limited to written form. Oral responses and explanations
help the student in his verbal growth, idea organization, and explanation
and communication skills.

Post-session attitude and interest opinionnaires or inventories can be given to determine the degree to which the student felt that the day's transactions were rewarding, satisfying, and productive. The student's reaction to the unit or learning program is caused by the impact of the subject matter and the events in which you engaged the student and should not be a criterion for grading the student. An example of a post-session reaction opinionnaire is represented in Figure 8–3. Various attitude scales or course-evaluation opinionnaires can also be used.

POST-SESSION REACTION OPINIONNAIRE

Name   (Optional)   Date _____

Directions: Your facilitator is interested in how the learning program you worked on today has helped you. Your answers will not affect your grade or standing in the class, and you have the option of signing this opinionnaire or remaining anonymous. Circle the answer that most reflects your feeling about the question. The results of the opinionnaire will help your facilitator improve learning programs.

1. How interested were you in the tasks?
   Not at all   Vaguely   Pretty well   Perfectly

2. How do you feel about your progress for the day?
   Not good   Poor   All right   Good   Excellent

3. How often did you feel the need to ask someone to help you?
   Never   A few times   Fairly often   Frequently   Always

4. How clearly did you understand the transaction?
   Not at all   Vaguely   Pretty well   Perfectly

5. How difficult is the task you are working on?
   Too simple   Fairly easy   Just right   Rather hard   Over my head

6. How satisfied are you with your accomplishments?
   Discouraged   Disappointed   Satisfied   Really delighted

Figure 8–3

Perhaps you had the following as an instructional objective for yourself:

> The students will develop a sense of pride in their accomplishments as demonstrated in their responses to how good they felt about their accomplishments.

Evaluation of how well you met these instructional objectives is important to the overall understanding of the student's complete growth in the unit.

An inventory of the student's activities can be made to determine the range of needs and the extent and variety of learning modes utilized. Figure 8–4 is an example of an activity inventory.

INVENTORY OF ACTIVITIES

Name   (Optional)   Date _____

Directions: Your facilitator is interested in knowing if you had enough aids to help you learn. Please circle the appropriate answer below that reflects your involvement during this session.

1. How many tasks did you work on today?
   1   2   3   4   5   6   _____

2. How many tasks did you complete?
   1   2   3   4   5   6   _____

3. Which delivery modes did you use?
   Written instructions   Audio-tape   Transparencies
   Loop films   Video-tape   Self-analysis   Classmate
   Facilitator   Other _____

4. How did you practice?
   Alone   With a partner   In a group   A little of each

5. Which mode of delivery was most helpful?

   _____

Figure 8–4

Profile sheets can be made to record progress which will give a graphic presentation of achievement. A profile sheet example is shown in Figure 8–5. In this example, the performance grid gives a profile of the student's strengths and weaknesses and can indicate to the student areas where more time should be spent. By reviewing the performance profile you can be alerted to major areas where the student is having difficulty. If several students are observed as having the same difficulty, you can then evaluate the learning programs or transactions that you have made available. Perhaps they are not providing the needed input. Hence, you can devise other transactions or delivery systems which may yield better results.

Process skill objectives can be evaluated by observation. You can see whether or not the student initiated questions, sought a variety of delivery systems, seemed pleased with his or her accomplishments and exhibited resourcefulness in seeking the goal decided upon. More formal evaluations can be obtained by asking the student about the structures followed in learning the skill. It can be determined to what extent the

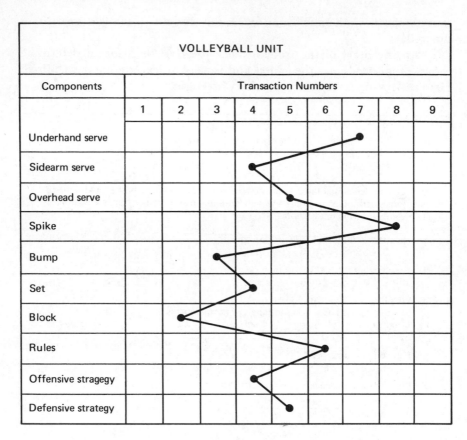

Figure 8–5

Achievement Profile Sheet

learner sought to gain a clear idea of the task to be performed, to attempt the whole, to perfect the parts and integrate the whole, to transfer knowledge, to judge success, to correct errors and be alert to kinesthetic as well as visual feedback. Students who are cognitively oriented may select tasks that would ask them to explain the goal of a task they have created, how the skill should look, where they can get input, what kinesthetic cues they should be "feeling," and what they will do if they do not succeed.

Formative evaluation specifically forms the succeeding learning experience. It is important to remember that it should be nonthreatening and should serve as a guide to improved practice and transaction selection.

SUMMATIVE EVALUATION GOALS

Evaluation occurring at the end of a unit, quarter, or semester is of a summative nature. It assesses how well the overall (global) objectives were reached and which quantitative and qualitative judgments are appropriate relative to the student's achievement of the global goal. It specifies where the student is at that final point in time, whereas the purpose of formative evaluation was to help focus upon the learning progress of the student.

Summative evaluation specifies the extent to which the student's terminal behavior is congruent with the stated unit goals. Furthermore, it is broad in scope, perhaps combining several concepts, skills, and knowledge components into an assessment of competency in an organic whole. It would occur after component skills, concepts and knowledge have been acquired and instruction in that unit has been completed.

Purpose of Summative Evaluation. Summative evaluation may have as its purpose to compare one student to another or to a norm. It may be to compare a learner's present state with the beginning state. It may be for grading purposes or to serve as a beginning point or qualification for a new learning series.

If the school requires a ranking of students, then the summative evaluation would be interpreted in relation to each student. Whichever students demonstrated the highest level of competency would be ranked "A," with the other students measured against the achievement of the best students. Norm-referenced evaluation may not reflect a competency level. It can only show that some students learned more and others learned less. If the grade is to indicate how competent the student is in the subject matter, then the summative evaluation or grade should be based on the level of mastery attained in regard to the total to be learned. This could be in relation to performance on established norms or identified standards of performance. Criterion-referenced grading need not rank students, and all could get an "A" if they achieved the criteria.

If the grade is used as a measure of the student's achievement potential and labels him as a "learner" or "nonlearner," either overtly or covertly, the summative evaluation must be conducted with tests that have content validity, reliability, and scoring objectivity. The weight of the various components of the tests must be congruent with the time spent on them, and emphasis must be given to the components during instruction.

Methods for Arriving at a Summative Evaluation. Many methods of arriving at a summative evaluation can be used. These could be: (1) giving skill tests and knowledge tests, and assessing the integration of the skills into a game or activity at the end of the unit, (2) concluding each component learning module with a skill and knowledge test and summating these at the end of the unit, (3) identifying levels of performance with assessed point values, which when completed give the student a point value relative to his or her accomplishments, and (4) selecting a percent of improvement from the entry point to the exit point, which would indicate the quantity and quality of achievement made in relation to the student's own performance.

Individualized humanistic instruction calls for an evaluation process that would give the student some latitude in how he wishes to be evaluated. If the student is to accept the responsibility for learning, he must establish appropriate goals, understand the constraints of imposed goals, and be accountable for all efforts made toward those goals. In this process he should be allowed to have input into the criteria by which he will be held accountable. Whichever technique is used, the student should know beforehand the dimensions of this evaluation. Within the constraints of the school policies the student can be given some latitude in how grades will be earned. If students are to be ranked with the ceiling on performance left open, they should be periodically informed of the progress of others if they wish to compete for the grade.

If mastery levels are identified, the student ought to be able to choose the level desired, and judgments should not be made relative to the worth of the student. In some activities a student may desire and possess the facility to attain a high mastery level and seek an "A." In other activities, because of interest or personal attributes, only a "C" level of competency may be desired. This level selection could occur before instruction begins. If, however, during the learning program the student becomes more interested or sees that accomplishment can be greater than predicted, the goals could be readjusted.

Consideration of the entry point can make a difference in the evaluation process. Rarely will all students enter at the same level. To penalize students because of past experience or achievement level makes the "race" for a grade fruitless for them. If the same criteria are identified for all students, those with higher entry points or better attributes for the activity have an advantage over those with less initial achievement. Personalizing the summative criteria can accommodate these differing entry points and talents.

Cratty suggests the following ways to neutralize varying entry levels.

> One of the more valid means of evaluating skill learning involves computing the percentage of possible gain by using one of the following formulas:
>
> 1. $$\frac{\text{sum of highest successive trials minus sum of first trials}}{\text{highest possible score minus sum of lowest scores}}$$
>
> 2. $$\frac{\text{sum of highest trials minus sum of first trials}}{\text{highest possible score minus sum of first trials}}$$
>
> 3. $$\frac{\text{sum of all trials minus sum of first trials}}{\text{highest possible score minus sum of first trials}}$$

These formulas do not unnecessarily penalize individuals who start with high initial scores as contrasted to those who have low initial scores. ... Thus, with these "percentage of possible gain" formulas, more valid and equitable comparisons may be made among numerous individuals in a class exposed to a given skill, some of whom evidence high initial score and others of whom evidence relatively little previous exposure to the task at hand.[1]

As was indicated in the formative evaluation section, a learning module may have standards of performance specified. The student may select the components and indicate the level of mastery desired. Summative evaluation can be accomplished by adding up the number of learning modules mastered or the levels of mastery acquired. Figure 8–6 is an abbreviated example of a student's evaluation contract. Other methods could be similarly formulated with percents of improvement required over the entry level. In reporting grades to parents or students the evaluation contract could be presented for clarification of the grade's meaning. Furthermore, these evaluation sheets can be filed as a diagnosis for the next level of instruction in the activity.

Evaluation Cautions.   Often success on a summative test can give the student or teacher a false sense of achievement gain. When summative evaluation is directed solely to specific quantities of knowledge or skill it may be evaluating incomplete learning.

The results of one's learning are not always immediately visible. Conversely, achievement gains may be impermanent or artificial. When achievement is evaluated immediately after instruction you do not know how much is attributable to memorization. It does not tell the permanency of the knowledge or how well the need or desire to know has been inculcated. If the learning program taught solely specific or specialized skills with little carry-over or process skills, terminal training rather than dynamic education has been learned.

Immediate testing has some value in measuring short-term objectives and some insight can be gained regarding the incubation of long-term concepts. Since student gain must be in reference to the stated objectives or goals, care must be exercised that all goals are stated and evaluated. These include not only the substance of the knowledge and the extent of the skill, but also process and attitudinal goals. The latter goals are measures of the effectiveness of you, the facilitator. If students are lost in the process or are noninvolved, you must review your methods and transactions, rather than having the students bear the stigma that there is something wrong with them because they aren't interested.

When the objectives are based on performance criteria, the instruc-

[1]B. J. Cratty, *Teaching Physical Skills.* p. 52.

BEGINNING TENNIS UNIT

Name _____   Date _____

Serving Component

Student's Choice	Level	Criteria	Points	Grade	Completed
_____	1	Serve with 50% accuracy	10	C	_____
_____	2	Serve with 60% accuracy	20	B	_____
_____	3	Serve with 70% accuracy	30	A	_____

Forehand Stroke Component

_____	1	Place 5 out of 10 forehand strokes 3 feet above the net and landing within 10 feet of the baseline.	10	C	_____
_____	2	Place 7 out of 10 forehand strokes 3 feet above the net and landing within 5 feet of the baseline.	20	B	_____
_____	3	Return balls stroked to you. Use a forehand stroke and place 5 out of 10 within 5 feet above the net and landing within 8 feet of base line.	30	A	_____

Grade contracted _____   Points contracted _____

Readjusted grade _____   Readjusted points _____

Contract completed _____ Grade _____ Points _____

Point value for grade
 0-25 points = F   51-75 = C   86-100 = A
26-50 points = D   75-85 = B

Figure 8–6

Abbreviated Example of Summative Evaluation Allowing the Student to
Select Grade or Points from Options

tional goals can be easily quantified and qualified on an objective basis. It should, however, be cautioned that the narrower the objective or goal, the more trivial it becomes, while, on the other hand, the broader it is the less objective measurability it has.

A successful facilitator can help students establish realistic and sequentially challenging goals and enable the student to reach the goals. You should be able to employ the student's resources to help the student move toward a goal. These process goals should also be evaluated.

Some open-ended goals should be established. If every goal is quantified and qualified it may stifle expectations beyond the set objective. In some cases not knowing the expectations may cause students to discover knowledge or acquire skills not originally conceived.

The extent to which the evaluation can follow all the suggestions in this chapter will depend upon time, format for recording results, and resources available. The overriding consideration should be: what is fair to the student. Some schools have computer assistance available, others have paraprofessional help. All schools have students who can be educated to assist with the process. The depth to which you evaluate each goal is, of course, dependent upon time. But slighting certain areas in the interest of "saving time" totally belies the intent of valid assessment of students. When reliable evaluation can be made in the light of congruence with pre-established goals, the impact of learning can be assessed.

CASE STUDY

SETTING:	Urban middle school
CLASS:	Fifth grade, 16 boys and 15 girls
PROGRAM:	Unit in object reception and propulsion, ten lessons
STAFF:	One teacher
FACILITIES:	One gymnasium, 70 × 50 and one outdoor blacktop playground

The unit objectives are to increase the students' ability to throw, kick, and catch or trap a variety of balls for the purpose of improving hand-eye and eye-foot coordination, visual tracking, and spatial awareness. Orientation to the unit content and procedures occurred in the first lesson.

The first two days were used to diagnose the students. Stations were set up where the student could perform the task. Criteria were established for each area which would indicate the level of ability. Students worked in pairs and recorded their own scores. The facilitator threw the balls for the catching tasks, but also observed the general ability of the students who were testing themselves so a check could be made as to the general accuracy of the recorded data. The facilitator tabulated the scores to obtain a general profile of the students' general ability. The following is this tabulation for throwing.

Students selected their learning goals and desired level of competence above the essential prescribed level. With their entry points established, their learning programs were determined.

One boy who was at the advanced football throw level elected transactions to help others improve football throwing. The interaction transactions contained cues for observation of critical points in performing the skills and suggestions for how to correct the errors that might occur. The four girls and two boys with whom he worked moved from the beginner to advanced beginner skills. It could be assumed that the interaction transactions were adequate for assisting him to help others. In addition he worked on his own skill improvement in other areas.

Another boy, who was a beginner in the discus throw, elected to work for the intermediate level in this skill. Several preliminary trials for distance and accuracy proved too difficult, so he changed to more elementary transactions which broke the skill down into practice trials on parts. He also reviewed the loop film for the footwork on the discus

DIAGNOSTIC SCORES

Throwing

	Distance						Accuracy						Mechanical Form					
	Beg.		Int.		Adv.		Beg.		Int.		Adv.		Beg.		Int.		Adv.	
Skill	B	G	B	G	B	G	B	G	B	G	B	G	B	G	B	G	B	G
Softball throw	1	8	5	4	10	3	3	6	5	6	8	3	2	9	4	3	10	3
Basketball throw	7	9	6	4	3	2	5	8	6	5	5	2	4	7	5	7	6	1
Football throw	4	10	10	5	2	0	10	7	7	3	3	2	5	10	7	3	4	2
Soccer ball throw	6	8	7	6	3	1	8	5	5	6	4	1	6	9	5	3	5	3
Discus	9	11	6	3	1	1	12	3	3	1	3	1	9	11	6	3	1	1
Shot put	11	13	5	2	0	0							10	12	5	2	1	1

throw. These alternate transactions proved helpful, but he renegotiated his original expected level of competency to the advanced beginner level.

Scores on student satisfaction inventories and achievement gain indicated that the entry points suggested by the diagnostic data were accurate. All students accomplished the "C" or essential level of competency in their respective classifications and 20 students reached a "B" level, with 6 reaching the "A" level. Hence, it could be assumed that the transactions were effective in helping the students learn.

Three girls achieved the "C" level and expressed disinterest in gaining higher competency because the ball skills were mostly "boys' " games. This feeling on their part alerted the facilitator to a greater need to minimize the sex role in sports and encourage the learning for the coordination value.

Two students did not achieve minimal level because of excessive absences. Since this unit was viewed as fundamental to succeeding game units, times were designated for these students to continue their work in this unit.

SUMMARY

If the student is to be held accountable for attaining a goal, the dimensions of that goal must be known before instruction begins. The student must know what he is to do, how he can accomplish it, and the criteria upon which his mastery of the goal will be judged. If education is to be dynamic, more than static skills and knowledge should be evaluated. Measurable goals should be set for learning *process* as well as *product*. The student's enjoyment, perseverance, and personal growth should be evaluated. These goals are instructional ones rather than specifically learner's objectives, so the results of the evaluation of these objectives should be the facilitator's "grade."

Evaluation is used to determine whether the intents of the instruction are being met. It can be used to determine diagnostic evaluation validity, to judge formative tasks and make diagnoses during the learning program, and for summative evaluation at the end of the unit.

Diagnostic goals can be evaluated during the learning sequence by observing whether the data obtained placed the student at the correct entry point, identified remedial areas so transactions could be designed to remedy these problems, and suggested appropriate delivery system options. Furthermore, the motivational value of the diagnosis should be evaluated.

Formative evaluation is built into the transactions and serves to pace the learning, sequence the subject matter, diagnose the inhibiting learning factors, and adjust the standards of performance. It lets the student know where he is in his pursuit of his goal. As feedback it forms the succeeding learning modules or transactions. It should not be threatening to the student, but should encourage him to continue.

Verification of the formative evaluation can be attested to by the student, a peer, or the facilitator. The complexity of the observation gives some insight as to who has to do it. Most quantitative objectives are easily observable. However, a task that is complex and requires constant observation of a series of actions requires an observer with a higher degree of ability.

The format for formative evaluation would include the global unit goal relative to the instructional component, the learner's objectives, input suggestions, formative practice conditions, formative diagnosis provisions, and formative evaluation verification.

Formative evaluation for knowledge acquisition would be in the form of frequent quizzes which would be graded instantly with reasons for the correct answer given. Knowledge questions should help the student comprehend, analyze, and apply the knowledge.

Post-session attitude opinionnaires can help you get a feel for the effect the day's transactions had on the students. Profile sheets or performance grids can help identify areas of strengths or weaknesses in the learning program, and readjustments can be made if indicated. Process goals can be evaluated by observation of the number of questions the students ask, the resources they seek, and the progress they are making. Providing some open-ended tasks can challenge the cognitively or creatively oriented student to apply process to learning a skill.

Summative evaluation occurs at the end of a unit, quarter, or semester. It assesses the end product. It may compare one student with another or to a norm (norm-referenced), may compare student's present achievement with his initial achievement, or may be based on levels of mastery or standards of performance achieved (criterion-referenced). It may be used to assign a grade or verify competency, and it may also serve as a diagnosis for the next level of instruction. The summative grade could be arrived at by summative tests given following each learning module, or by giving a final test at the end of the unit. Students may contract for a grade by selecting levels of mastery or transactions upon which point or grade values have been placed; a summation of these scores would yield the grade. It should be cautioned that summative grading immediately after a unit of study does not give data on the permanency of the knowledge. The grade may be earned solely on memorization or mimicry which may be forgotten in time. Also, the utility of the skill or knowledge for future activity cannot be accurately assessed.

Individualized humanistic instruction calls for the student to know the standards by which he will be judged, and to be a participant in the process of selecting criteria. The student would select a level of mastery consistent with his or her interests or natural attributes. This process should be free of judgmental inference as to the worth of the student.

To encourage creativity, students should be allowed to design some tasks and assessment criteria on their own. If all the dimensions are precisely identified, the student's quest for excellence beyond a predicted level may be stifled.

REFERENCES

BLOOM, B. S. "Learning for Mastery," *Education Comment*, I, no. 2 (1968), 1–8.

BLOOM, B. S., J. T. HASTINGS, AND G. F. MADAUS. *Handbook on Formative and Summative Evaluation of Student Learning.* New York: McGraw-Hill Book Company, 1971.

CRATTY, B. J. *Teaching Motor Skills.* Englewood Cliffs, N.J.: Prentice-Hall, Inc., 1973, Chap. 3.

GLASER, R., AND A. J. NITKO. "Measurement in Learning and Instruction," in *Educational Measurement*, ed. R. L. Thorndike. Washington, D.C.: American Council on Education, 1971.

JOHNSON, J. M. "A Look at Grades," *College Physical Education*, ed. H. M. Heitmann. Washington, D.C.: American Alliance for Health, Physical Education and Recreation, 1973, pp. 78–84.

KRATHWOHL, D. R., AND D. A. PAYNE. "Defining and Assessing Educational Objectives," in *Educational Measurement*, ed. R. L. Thorndike. Washington, D.C.: American Council on Education, 1971.

MOOD, D. "Grading Systems," *College Physical Education*, ed. H. M. Heitmann. Washington, D.C.: American Alliance for Health, Physical Education and Recreation, 1973, pp. 65–72.

POPHAM, W. J., AND T. R. HUSEK. "Implications of Criterion-Referenced Measurement," *Journal of Educational Measurement*, VI, no. 1 (1969), 1–9.

SAFRIT, M. J. *Evaluation in Physical Education.* Englewood Cliffs, N.J.: Prentice-Hall, Inc., 1973.

————. "Formative and Summative Evaluation in Physical Education," *College Physical Education*, ed. H. M. Heitmann. Washington, D.C.: American Alliance for Health, Physical Education and Recreation, 1973, pp. 73–77.

PART III

GETTING
IT
DONE

9

Motivation: Activating The Student

INSTRUCTIONAL UNIT FOR CHAPTER 9

Learner's Diagnosis

Directions: Read the questions below. Write out, discuss, or mentally review the answers. If you believe that you know the information, check the "yes" column. If you are not sure of the answer, check the "no" column. After reading the questions and deciding your knowledge, check the accuracy of your answers by reading the summary at the end of this chapter. If you answered a question incorrectly, change your answer to the appropriate column.

Can you

Yes	No	Questions
		1. Describe a motivated student?
		2. Explain two theories of motivation?
		3. List four sources of motivation?
		4. Explain the role of ability in motivation?
		5. Give examples of achievement motives?
		6. Give examples of affiliative motives?
		7. Explain intrinsic incentives?
		8. Give examples of extrinsic incentive?
		9. Explain the role of success experiences in motivation?
		10. Plan a motivational program for a student?

Suggested Prescription

Directions: Count the number of checks you have placed in the "yes" column. When the percentages are determined, you may increase your knowledge and skill by using the suggested Learning Program activities recommended in the Input and Practice columns.

Results	Input	Practice
More than 80%	#1, 8	#5
60% to 80%	#1, 2, 7, 8	#1, 5
40% to 60%	#1, 2, 4 or 5, 6	#1, 2, 3 or 4
Less than 40%	#1, 2, 3, 4 or 5, 6, 7	#1, 2, 3, 4

Learning Program

Directions: It is suggested that the reader attempt to follow any or all suggestions in this learning program. These are designed to improve ability to motivate students for individualized instruction.

Proposed Learning Objective: The learner will be able to motivate a student to learn an activity skill of his choice at the level of learning desired.

Input:

*1. Read Chapter 9 of this book.
2. Read selected references in the bibliography.
3. Discuss with several students their goals and expectations in a physical education class.
4. Complete the *Neumann Physical Education Like-Dislike Inventory* which is provided in the Appendix.
5. Read the story *Lost at Sea* in the Appendix. Follow the directions provided. What implications do you believe your values have on you as an educator?
6. Prepare a list of questions and concerns that you may have concerning motivation. Discuss your list with at least two teachers.
7. Complete the Challenge Task which is provided in the Appendix.
8. Plan an input of your own.

*Highly recommended.

Practice:

1. Select a student whom you are teaching who has only casual interest in an activity. Apply the motivation formula. Achieve 70 percent of your mutually agreed upon goal.

2. Teach a skilled student a new skill. Discuss with the student the procedures that were used that gave direction to him and intensity to the learning of the skill.

3. Plan an extrinsic incentive system. Teach a class or student utilizing the system. Analyze the results in terms of the behavioral objectives.

4. Plan an intrinsic system and follow the procedures described in number 3.

5. Plan a practice of your own.

Evaluation: You will be able to select a learning program, or an outline of a previously developed unit plan, and identify contributions that the components can make to motivate the students, with their various differences, in the potential class.

Behavior change will occur if the learner has desire or motivation to be involved in the learning process. Indeed, you can bring to the student all the well-laid plans, delivery systems, and transactions, but if the student is not "turned on," little activity toward learning will result. How do you get learners to participate? What if the student chooses to do nothing? These are all legitimate questions and concerns. The answers lie in the rationale for this book. Motivation is the basis of this whole approach.

DEFINITION

Motivation is the desire of the organism to act and, once aroused, to sustain and direct that action. It is behavior that has been stimulated to be ready or activated in a given direction and at a given intensity. You will note that motivation is an intangible which is inferred from behavior. The word *direction* means that a choice has been made from several options or goals. *Intensity* implies that motivation, like an accelerator, can be regulated in terms of the degree of energy or effort released.

The basic goal of individualized instruction is to help the student to learn how to learn. According to Jack Frymier:

Learning how to learn ... is meaningless if students have not learned to want to learn. In other words learning to want to learn is an educational objective.[1]

Motivation involves valuing, and values are learned behaviors. It may, therefore, be presumed that motivation can be taught. The key to facilitating motivation is the process of shaping values.

THEORIES

Two major theories of motivation are held by psychologists: behavioral or hedonistic theory, and the cognitive or self-actualization theory. The theories differ regarding motive, arousal, and type of behavior.

Behavioral or Hedonistic Theory.   This theory holds that organisms will act in a way to maximize pleasure and to minimize pain. This position sees living organisms as reacting to their environment. The tenets are based on the need-drive incentive idea and thus hedonistic theory is closely tied to behavior learning theory. Motives may be conscious or unconscious, and primary or secondary. A primary motive is considered a basic physiological need and a secondary motive is one that has been associated with a primary motive and can now stand in its place. For example, money is associated with reducing physiological needs and can stand in place of the primary motive.

Cognitive or Self-Actualizing Theory.   Human beings are motivated to the extent that they recognize their goals and can therefore make clear plans toward them, guided by expectations and the assessment of risks involved. Rogers, a proponent of this theory, sees a properly motivated individual as reaching for self-enhancement. The self-actualization approach seeks to understand actions of people from *their own* point of view. One's perception of reality is the crucial determinant of the individual's behavior rather than an environment stimulus.

In keeping with the functional theory of learning, it is proposed that you understand what is involved in motivating people and make multiple pathways available in the hope that learners will be able to accept and move forward toward their learning goals.

PROCESS

The process of providing learning experiences that will motivate students involves four major sources of effect: ability or capability, mo-

[1]"Motivation: The Mainspring and Gyroscope of Learning." *Theory into Practice*, (Columbus, Ohio: College of Education, Ohio State University, 1970), Vol. IX, No. 1, 25.

tive, incentive, and expectancy of success. Some theorists[2] have proposed a formula which would combine these sources to predict the likelihood of goal-directed, appropriately sustained action:

> Motivation = Ability × Motive ×
> Incentive × Expectancy of Success

Note that the sources are multiplied, indicating the interrelationships of each component. Therefore, if one source is a bit weak, a stronger source may offset this deficiency.

Ability or Capability. This is the extent to which a particular stimulus selection makes available a particular source of action. The present and past contribute to its availability. What is proposed here is that the task to be performed must be within the person's capability. Capability is flexible and may vary from task to task. Many individual differences which were cited earlier operate to influence capability: physical, intellectual, social, and experiential and self-conceptual. You have little control over these differences; however, you do have an opportunity to help students define goals that are attainable and challenging. Learning programs should be adjusted to provide for an appropriate learning rate and style. Diagnosis will provide some insight to ascertain the learner's capability. The decision may be only a calculated estimate derived by the learner and the facilitator. Nonetheless, no action will occur if a student does not have the ability to perform the task. For example, if

ABILITY   MOTIVE   INCENTIVE   EXPECTANCY

[2]James Atkinson and David McClelland, "Motivation and Behavior," in George H. Litwin and R. Stringer, eds., *Motivation and Organization Climate* (Cambridge, Mass.: Division of Research, Graduate School of Business Administration, Harvard University, 1968).

the task is to shoot an arrow with a 24-pound draw bow which the learner does not have the strength to draw, it may be concluded that the student is not able to perform the task. Another example would be to encourage a transaction that would require speed on the basis that the performer has the physiological potential to perform the act.

You may examine your own personal physical education activity preferences and wonder how much a part of these preferences are based on the match between your ability and the requirements of the activity. Maybe this match had to do with your ability to learn through the imposed teaching styles and practice cycle. We often hear learners lament, "I know I could have learned it better but the way the teacher...!" Motivation is facilitated through providing options that will foster congruence with the student's ability to perform and to learn.

Motive. Motives are modifiers of incentives. They have been defined as something that incites the organism to action. That "something" may be called needs, goals, urges, and desires. These were discussed in Chapter 2. Some researchers claim that motives fall into two categories: the need for achievement and the need for affiliation. Figure 9-1 is an illustration of possible motives involved in these categories.

Self-actualization belongs on both lists since it seems to cut across both types of motives. It has been referred to frequently throughout this book as the primary goal of education. It is postulated here as a primary motive of human beings. Self-actualization has been defined as "being open to change and continuing to learn." Combs and Snygg[3] refer to it as maintenance and enhancement of the self, and indicate that it is all-inclusive and motivates all behavior. As such, then the self-actualization

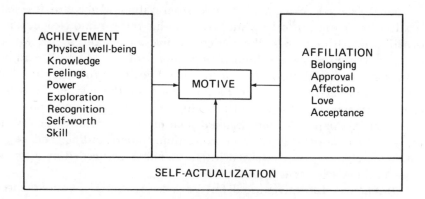

Figure 9-1

[3]Arthur Combs and Donald Snygg, *Individual Behavior: A Perceptual Approach to Behavior* (New York: Harper & Row, Publishers, 1959).

motive would include both a need for achievement and a need for affiliation.

How are students turned on? They must feel that at least one or more of their personally desired needs could be satisfied in the teaching-learning environment. When a student is activated toward some learning goal, he strives to reduce that drive by achieving it. For example, if you were teaching a class outside and it started to rain, students would feel a need for shelter and be driven to reduce that drive by finding shelter. No educator would fail to provide for the physical well-being needs. However, the concern all too often stops at that point.

As an effective motivator, you must attempt to make it possible for each student to achieve any or all of the achievement, affiliation, or self-actualizing goals that he may value. The desire to learn must be generated within the student. All students need to be helped to define and clarify their goals and to have the subject matter constraints widened to permit entry wherever it seems possible for them to achieve. Students should be initiators of what is worthwhile to learn. More energy is expended when satisfaction is the goal.

Does it matter if a boy wishes to master a hook shot in basketball and therefore chooses to master it while ignoring other skills? If hook-shooting is his goal and represents a particular challenge for him, then that is where the learning must begin. Maybe skill in hook-shooting is more satisfying than mediocrity in other basketball skills. Kneer conducted research and determined that when students' goals were assessed and when the teachers were informed of these goals, learning improved and the students were significantly more satisfied with the experience than when this was not the case.[4]

Goals, desires, or motives evolve from values which are learned. As a facilitator you try to help students to value certain knowledge, skill, or beliefs which may assist the student to live an enhanced life. Much has been written about the humanizing impact of self-worth. Providing options and a climate for a student to achieve goals is probably the most complimentary activity that can be performed for the learner. It is behavior that expresses trust, understanding, and cooperation. You may recall that in Chapter 3, interpersonal relations were cited as the "wellspring of motivation." Trust, communication, understanding, and cooperation were given as the essential interpersonal skills needed by a facilitator. A person behaves as he sees himself.

Incentive. Incentives are defined as need reducers or consequences of action. If the consequence results in approaching or avoiding a goal,

---

[4]M. E. Kneer, "Influence of Selected Factors and Techniques on Student Satisfaction with a Physical Education Experience" (Doctoral dissertation, University of Michigan, 1972).

it has incentive value. Thus, incentives have positive and negative value. Food, water, interesting stimuli, novelty, success, and social interaction are types of positive incentives. Pain, failure, social isolation, and inadequate reward can be usually considered to have negative incentive value. Whether positive or negative, incentives determine the strength of the tendency to act.

Incentives influence individuals differently and this variability is what makes incentives complex. They are rooted in a person's values. Values can be taught, but are more often caught. You must begin where your students are by accepting them as worthwhile people. Consequences are differentially perceived depending upon the needs of the learner. The "Challenge Task" in the Appendix is designed to help you understand about incentives and consequences. This practice suggests that students be asked to select one of three challenges ranging from simple to almost impossible. Rewards are attached. Which task is selected will depend upon the student's expectancy of success and his need for the reward. By varying the reward, you will be able to effect a change in the selection of the challenge. Generally, to motivate a student to attempt a task not perceived to be achievable will need an incentive that is tangibly or intangibly valued.

Achieving skill in football may have approach consequences for one student, but for another it may have avoidance consequences. Both learners may have the ability to perform the skill, but if the consequences are dissimilarly perceived, the desire to learn will differ. Praise is normally considered a positive incentive. However, if praise results in embarrassment or leads to other negative consequences for the recipient, it is not valuable. Some students pursue a skill goal for enjoyment, some for recognition, others to be with friends, and others for personal self-worth.

Incentives are often referred to as intrinsic, coming from within; and extrinsic, coming from outside. Humanistic educators contend that intrinsic incentives—self-actualization, happiness, and personal satisfaction—are longer lasting and more fulfilling. However, extrinsic incentives such as trophies, rewards, grades, or penalties seem to result in more immediate positive consequences and therefore tend to be used more often by teachers. As a matter of fact, it often appears that grades are the *only* incentives offered. It is no wonder that so many physical education students become disenchanted with participation in psychomotor behavior when the goals or outcomes differ from what they perceive to be valuable and attainable. Although intrinsic motivation is considered more desirable, it may be necessary to resort to extrinsic incentives to at least move the student to act. Once the learning is started, it can be sustained by success experiences; students will begin to turn inward as they enjoy better personal relationships and satisfaction in learning.

Physical education teachers often rely on competition as the other "great motivator." But for every winner, there is a loser. What is needed is personal concern for students, and actions by the facilitator that will cater to each student's uniqueness so that every learner can be a winner!

Expectancy. Expectancy refers to the anticipation that the action will be directed toward the goal or consequence with the probability of its being achieved. Atkinson[5] has theorized that success-oriented people prefer tasks that offer them a 50/50 chance of succeeding, and that those who fear failure will select tasks at either of the extremes. This theory has implications for setting the level of qualitative and quantitative goals. A task that is too difficult or too easy will not arouse or challenge a success-oriented person. On the other hand, those students who are anxious about failure will choose either a task that they can succeed at or a task that nobody expects them to accomplish. Failing a complex task is not as embarrassing as failing a less difficult one.

The background of success and failure experiences will influence the tendency of students to pursue or to avoid physical education activity. Nothing succeeds like success. Every terminal objective must be perceived as achievable; thus, your role is to provide individual help to ensure achievement. Success will contribute to the learners' self-confidence and encourage them to be effective decision makers about their learning. Success experiences are predictable if you diagnose accurately and are able to provide "steps" that are of interest, are of proper size, and allow sufficient time for mastery.

ROLE OF SELF-CONCEPT

The key to turning students on in a humanistically oriented educational setting is the student's concept of self. Everything that you do with the student must contribute toward the student's believing that he or she is capable, worthy, trusted, loved, and accepted. Donald Hamachek says:

> If we, as teachers, are to facilitate motivation and learning through self-concept enhancement, we must . . .
>
> 1. Understand that we teach what we are, not just what we say. We teach our own self-concept far more often than we teach our subject matter.
> 2. Understand that anything we do or say could significantly change a student's attitude about himself for better or for worse.
> 3. Understand that students, like us, behave in terms of what seems to be true.

[5]Atkinson and McClelland, "Motivation and Behavior," p. 616.

4. Be willing not to teach subject matter, but to deal with what the subject matter means to different students.

5. Understand that we are not likely to get results simply by telling someone he is worthy. Rather, we imply it through trust and the establishment of an atmosphere of mutual respect.

6. Understand that teacher behavior which is distant, cold and rejecting is far less likely to enhance self-concept, motivation, and learning than behavior which is warm, accepting and discriminating.[6]

"Accentuating the positive and eliminating the negative," as an old song suggests, points to the way to build positive self-concepts. Figure 9–2 illustrates the results obtained by Hurlock in an experiment with four matched arithmetic classes. After each lesson, regardless of how well they actually did, one class was praised, one blamed, and one ignored.[7]

Since learning is personal, the self is involved. Self-concept becomes central to learning since it determines relevancy, openness, and adequacy.

GAINS MADE BY FOURTH AND SIXTH GRADE PUPILS
UNDER DIFFERENT INCENTIVE CONDITIONS

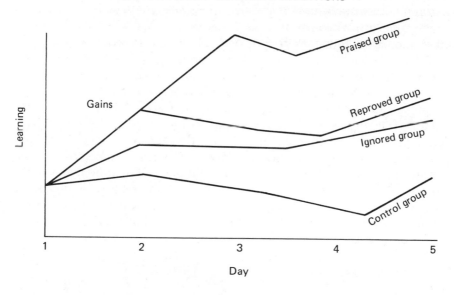

Figure 9–2

[6]*Motivation in Teaching and Learning* (Washington, D.C.: National Education Association, 1968), p. 8.

[7]E. Hurlock, "An Evaluation of Certain Incentives Used in School Work," *Journal of Educational Psychology*, (1925), XVI, 145–59.

IMPLICATIONS

Motivating students is really attending to their needs. The interactions of all the major variables that influence people result in an infinite number of patterns of behavior. To motivate students then, you must provide alternatives and help the students to find the proper combination of incentives and goals which will meet their needs and which they are capable of reaching. Their activities will be sustained by valued incentives and the prospect of success. The whole effort is re-energized by linking series of these experiences.

Now this is how it all fits together. Suppose you have a student who does not seem to want to participate. The causes for the lack of motivation may be found in the answers to these questions:

1. Is the student capable of learning the skills?
2. Does the student have a motive to learn the skills?
3. What are the student incentives? Can they work?
4. Can the student expect to succeed at learning the skill or playing the game?

A "no" answer to any of the above questions will lessen the student's motivation to participate. If a "no" answer is given to questions 1 or 4, then the nature of the problem is the involvement experience. A simpler task may be the solution. A "no" answer to questions 2 or 3 requires further discussion with the student because the solutions will be more complex. Explore what the student's needs seem to be—friends, power, approval, acceptance, recognition, security, and so on. The incentive question is crucial since the consequences of participation will either activate or deactivate the motive. Some incentives that may be considered are: encouragement, a reward (candy, favor, privilege), punishment, and praise. Thus, maybe the student needs a simpler task that he may be able to do and can perceive a chance to complete successfully, or maybe he needs encouragement and support. Only you, working and interacting with the learner, can determine the procedures that would be helpful, based on your knowledge of the student.

CASE STUDY

SETTING: Junior high school of 1,000 students in small suburban community

CLASS: 7th grade boys and girls (80 girls and 70 boys) with previous experience in individualized instruction

PROGRAM: Tumbling, square dance, wrestling, and volleyball
STAFF: Four teachers (two women and two men)
FACILITIES: One large gym, one balcony space, one stage

The facilitators developed a team approach to individual instruction in the four activities on a multi-unit basis. Except for wrestling, all activities were coeducational. Each teacher prepared the learning program for one activity. The activities were offered on a daily basis for six weeks. Students could select one or more activities depending upon the time it took them to achieve their goals. Activities selected by the boys and the girls at the beginning and approximately midway through the time block were as follows:

Activity	Beginning	Midway
Volleyball	25 girls, 10 boys	30 girls, 17 boys
Square Dance	30 girls, 8 boys	30 girls, 18 boys
Wrestling	35 boys	25 boys
Tumbling	25 girls, 17 boys	20 girls, 10 boys

Approximately half of the students changed activities between the third and fifth weeks. Students who changed activities started at their diagnosed entry levels. Learning modules were available, to give direction to the students concerning how to perform the skills and how to practice them, and to determine the level of achievement sought. Some students spent the entire time on one activity, and some less than half of the time. How much time was spent depended upon student interest and achievement. Changing activities was contingent upon mutual agreement between the facilitator and the student.

An analysis of the learning activity observed for one lesson is as follows:

Skill Development (all students at one time or other)

Working on self-contained tasks	20%	(high need for achievement)
Working on interaction tasks	35%	(high need for affiliation)
Working on discovery tasks	10%	(exploration motive)
Working on independent tasks	5%	(high need for achievement) (low need for affiliation)

Game play involvement Almost all students
No obvious activity About 10% of the students

SUMMARY

Motivation is the desire to act and to sustain and direct that action. This means that student actions are directed by choice and sustained in varied degrees of intensity. The actions are regulated by values. Since values can be taught, the key to motivating is the process of teaching or facilitating value learning.

Two theories of motivation are: hedonistic or behavioral, and cognitive or self-actualizing. Hedonistic theory holds that a person reacts to his environment to maximize pleasure and minimize pain. Cognitive theory stresses that the person's perception of environment helps to recognize goals. Plans are then made in terms of the expectations of success or failure based on an assessment of risks involved. The self-actualization approach defines the ultimate goal to be self-enhancement.

Four major sources of effect provide motivational learning experiences: ability, motive, incentive, and expectancy of success or failure. *Ability* refers to what a person can do or is able to do. You must help students to define goals which are attainable and challenging for their level of capability. *Motives* are needs, goals, urges, or desires. They serve to incite a person to action and fall into two categories: achievement and affiliation. Achievement motives include physical well-being, knowledge, skill, feelings, power, recognition, and self-worth. Affiliation motives are belonging, approval, affection, love, and acceptance. Self-actualization includes both an achievement and an affiliation motive and is seen by most humanistic educators as the major motivator. Turning students "on" requires that they be involved in an activity that meets their personal achievement and/or affiliative needs. *Incentives* are need reducers which have positive or negative values. Pleasure, success, and social interaction are positive incentives, while pain, failure, and inadequate rewards are negative incentives. They determine the strength of the tendency to act. Incentives influence people differently because they are rooted in a person's value structure. Humanistic educators tend to favor intrinsic incentives, those coming from within, because they believe that such incentives contribute heavily to the development of self-actualization. Extrinsic incentives, those coming from outside, are believed to be more ephemeral, but they have value as "starters." Once action has commenced, it is hoped that less reliance on grades and more reliance on the satisfaction of success will sustain activity. *Expectancy* refers to the judgment whether a given activity is likely to achieve the desired outcomes. Success-oriented people favor 50/50 chances, whereas those who fear failure prefer either extreme of the continuum. Facilitators must recognize the value of success experiences and plan options that can be successfully completed by the learner.

Student self-concept is considered to be the most important key to motivate learning. Your actions in providing individualized humanistic instruction must contribute meaningfully to the learners to enhance their sense of self-worth.

REFERENCES

ATKINSON, J., AND D. MCCLELLAND. "Motivation and Behavior," in George H. Litwin and R. Stringer, eds. *Motivation and Organization Climate.* Cambridge, Mass.: Division of Research, Graduate School of Business Administration, Harvard University, 1968.

BIRCH, D., AND J. VEROFF. *Motivation: A Study of Action.* Belmont, Calif.: Brooks/Cole Publishing Company, 1966.

CLARK, F. "Psychology, Education and the Concept of Motivation," *Theory into Practice.* Columbus, Ohio: College of Education, Ohio State University, Vol. IX, no. 1, 1970.

COMBS, A., AND D. SNYGG. *Individual Behavior: A Perceptual Approach to Behavior.* New York: Harper & Row, Publishers, 1959.

CRATTY, BRYANT. *Psychology and Physical Activity.* Englewood Cliffs, N.J.: Prentice-Hall, Inc., 1968.

FRYMIER, J. "Motivation: The Mainspring and Gyroscope of Learning," *Theory into Practice.* Columbus, Ohio: College of Education, Ohio State University, Vol. IX, no. 1, 1970.

HAMACHEK, D. *Motivation in Teaching and Learning.* Washington, D.C.: NEA, 1968.

HILGARD, E., AND R. ATKINSON. *Introduction to Psychology.* New York: Harcourt Brace Jovanovich, Inc., 1967.

HURLOCK, E. "An Evaluation of Certain Incentives Used in School Work," *Journal of Educational Psychology,* 16 (1925), 145–59.

KNEER, M. "Influence of Selected Factors and Techniques on Student Satisfaction with a Physical Education Experience." Unpublished Doctoral dissertation, Ann Arbor: University of Michigan, 1972.

MASLOW, A. *Motivation and Personality.* New York: David McKay Co., Inc., 1954.

MURPHY, G. "Motivation: The Key to Changing Educational Tone," *Theory into Practice.* Columbus, Ohio, College of Education, Ohio State University, Vol. IX, no. 1, 1970.

PATTERSON, C. *Humanistic Education.* Englewood Cliffs, N.J.: Prentice-Hall, Inc., 1970.

STROM, R., AND E. TORRANCE, eds. *Education for Affective Achievement.* Chicago: Rand McNally & Company, 1973.

WAETJEN, W. "The Teacher and Motivation," *Theory into Practice.* Columbus, Ohio: College of Education, Ohio State University, Vol. IX, no. 1, 1970.

10

Decisions
For
Learning

INSTRUCTIONAL UNIT FOR CHAPTER 10
Learner's Diagnosis

Directions: Read the questions below. Write out, discuss, or mentally review the answers. If you believe that you know the information, check the "yes" column. If you are not sure of the answer, check the "no" column. After reading the questions and deciding your knowledge, check the accuracy of your answers by reading the summary at the end of this chapter. If you answered a question incorrectly, change your answer to the appropriate column.

Can you

Yes	No	Questions
		1. State why a facilitator is responsible for making decisions about the student's learning?
		2. State why a student should be responsible for making decisions about his learning?
		3. Define absolute (essential) knowledge versus knowledge, activities, or skills that are relative?
		4. Indicate which attributes the facilitator must regard as absolute within the student?
		5. Identify which would be relative for the student?
		6. Analyze the pre-decisions the facilitator must make?
		7. Explain the decisions the facilitator must make regarding the diagnostic phase?
		8. Identify which things the facilitator must take into consideration in establishing criteria for the diagnostic decisions?
		9. Indicate the decisions and their purposes which are necessary during the learning program?
		10. Determine criteria you would use to make the decisions for the learning program?

Yes	No	Questions
		11. Identify the means which will help to make ongoing decisions regarding the effectiveness of the learning program?
		12. State how formative and summative evaluation affects or assists the decision-making process?
		13. State a benefit of permitting the student involvement in making decisions about his learning program?
		14. Differentiate how individualized humanistic instruction differs from traditional (class-centered teacher-controlled) in regard to decision-making?
		15. Indicate how the conference phase helps to humanize the succeeding learning program?

Suggested Prescription

Directions: Count the number of checks you have placed in the "yes" column. When the percentages are determined, you may increase your knowledge and skill by using the suggested Learning Program activities recommended in the Input and Practice columns. Input and practices not listed offer additional learning options.

Results	Input	Practice
More than 80%	#1, 5	#2, 3, 6
60% to 80%	#1, 5, 10	#2, 3 or 4, 6, 7
40% to 60%	#1, 2, 5, 8	#2, 3 or 4, 6, 7 or 8, 9 or 10
Less than 40%	#1, 2, 5, 7 or 8, 9	#2, 3 or 4, 5 or 6, 7, 8, 10

Learning Program

Directions: It is suggested that the reader attempt to complete any or all of the following Input and Practice suggestions. These are de-

214

signed to improve knowledge and understanding of the decisions to be made to facilitate learning, and to guide appropriate selection of criteria upon which the decision is based.

Proposed Learning Objective: The learner will be able to state the process for establishing an individualized humanistic instructional unit by being able to identify the decisions the facilitator and students will have to make for each integral phase of the system.

Input:

*1. Read Chapter 10 of this book.
2. Read Chapters 3, 4, and 7 in Jack Frymier, *A School for Tomorrow.*
3. Read Chapter 3 in Rath, Louis, et al., *Values and Teaching.*
4. Select other readings from the bibliography.
5. Review several individualized instruction units and try to identify all the decisions the facilitator had to make.
6. Watch a traditional class (class-oriented teacher-directed) and count how often the student gets to make decisions.
7. Interview a student who has had input into the decisions relative to his learning. Contrast his comments with statements from a student who was teacher-directed. How did each feel about the relevancy of the learning and the process?
8. Interview three or four students and ask, if they had had an opportunity to make decisions about their learning, how they would change what the teacher did.
9. Develop an input of your own.

Practice:

1. Indicate how you would redirect the thinking of a child who selects easy goals.
2. Identify the essential skills and knowledge needed in a sport of your choice just to play the game.
3. For the sport chosen in question 2, list more advanced skills in sequential order.
4. Develop a list of relatives (optional skills or knowledge) in learning an activity. Which absolutes are needed to learn these relatives?

*Highly recommended.

5. Contrast the decisions you would have to make regarding the diagnosis, for a class you had had before versus one you had not had.
6. Contrast the differences in decisions you would have to make if the class was co-ed versus one sex.
7. What decisions would you have to make if you had 32 students in a class of heterogeneous ability and wished to provide time for working on skills and playing the game each session?
8. Contrast the decisions you would have to make and the criteria you would use to make the decisions in structuring the learning programs for a class of 10-year-olds versus high school juniors.
9. How could you engage students in learning the process of learning through decision making?
10. Develop a practice of your own.

Evaluation: You will be able to enumerate the decision options you and the students will have to make for each phase of the learning unit and select criteria for making the appropriate decision.

Decisions regarding what is to be learned, how much is to be learned, and how it is to be learned are shared responsibilities between the facilitator and the student, each with a distinct role to play. Since the student is the center of learning, the focus should be not on the *teaching*, but rather on the *learning*. The teacher can only facilitate learning and only the student can learn.

Traditionally all the overt decisions were made by the teacher. The student made covert decisions whether to persevere or drop out at some level. The facilitator, in an attempt to make the student's perseverance more constant, engages the student in many of the overt decisions regarding his learning program. The student thereby learns the *process* of education as well as the *product* of learning.

Teachers are employed to maintain the integrity of the subject matter, societal values, and standards of mastery of the subject matter. They are also charged with inducing learning; hence, they should seek to reduce the conflict that may occur among the teacher's goals, the student's goals, and other students' goals. Also paramount should be the facilitation of an appropriate and conducive learning environment in which each student can learn.

EDUCATIONAL DEMANDS IN DECISION MAKING

Schools and teachers must make decisions about what is essential for the student to learn in order for society to continue productively and for the student to function effectively and lead a self-fulfilling life. The physical education profession has identified some basic knowledges and skills which are essential for a child to learn, along with the educational circumstances in which this learning should take place. These essentials, which were identified in Chapter 1, relate to the basic activities needed for development and maintenance of organic vigor, neuromuscular coordination, and recreational competency. Certainly these basic physiological, neurological, intellectual, and emotional integrations could take place outside of the school. However, in today's society, opportunities for physical exploration and integration may be curtailed; hence, education of and through the physical is a bona fide educational experience in the context of school education.

ABSOLUTE AND RELATIVE CONCERNS
IN DECISION MAKING

The basic needs for perceptual-motor integration, neuromuscular coordination, movement patterns, and organic efficiency are among the primary goals for physical education. These essentials, or *absolutes*, can be learned through a variety of activities, sports, dances, and aquatic media. The choice concerning these activities can be *relative* (related to nonessential needs).

The learning of basic movement and coordination may be sequentially dependent. Thus, professional knowledge may be needed to order the sequence so a progression of mastery can be established. Some basic fundamentals may be unrelated to learning other fundamentals. An identification of the relationship of one fundamental to another is needed. Some combinations of skills are not essential, but might be nice to possess. Sport learning may be essential for recreational competency; however, a specific sport is not necessarily essential, nor are sports sequentially dependent one upon another in their adult, culturalized form. One's learning to play basketball is not dependent upon the person's first learning volleyball, and one may have adequate recreational competency without ever having played baseball. However, within any culturalized sport exists certain basic movement skills which must be mastered before one can engage in the sport.

Within each student there are absolutes and relatives. The student's unique physical, intellectual, and emotional characteristics as well as his learning mode are his own absolutes. Given these absolutes, how they are served can be relative.

FACILITATOR DECISIONS AND STUDENT DECISIONS

The facilitator's initial decision in the learning process is to assess within the body of knowledge what is absolute and what is relative. Once the decision is made on what the absolutes or essentials are, decisions regarding the relative must be made, such as, the level mastery, mode of delivery, and sequence of learning. Also within these decisions there are absolutes operative in the student, as well as certain things that may be relative.

When the teacher makes the decision regarding the absolutes, the student makes the decisions about the relative. In the relative area of subject matter and learning, the student may change the specific game or activity, the mode and transactions needed for learning, and the level of competency desired.

The student's characteristics are his or her absolutes. However, relative decisions can be made by the facilitator concerning how the absolutes will be attended. For instance, a girl may be highly visually oriented —this is an absolute. What she looks at—a still picture, loop film, movie, transparency, or live demonstration—may be relative. Here you can make the decision according to which visual transmission vehicles are feasible in the facility setting. If it were possible to provide every visual tool, then the student could select.

Thus, some decisions may fall clearly within your domain and some within that of the student. In most instances, an interaction must occur: information regarding the absolutes and relatives must pass from the facilitator to the student and from the student to the facilitator during the conference or link-up stage. The initiation of this information sharing can come from either. In other words, you should not be the sole initiator of questions or giver of information. The student should be encouraged to ask questions of you or to feel free to give you information. Schematically this can be represented as follows:

It is necessary to combine the right static learning modules or transactions pre-decided upon by you with the static entities of the student to make the process dynamic. This interaction link is one of the main differences between traditional class-centered, teacher-directed education and individualized humanistic education. It further contributes to a more valid process of decision making. Figure 10–1 represents this process. Figure 10–2 illustrates its application to basketball skills.

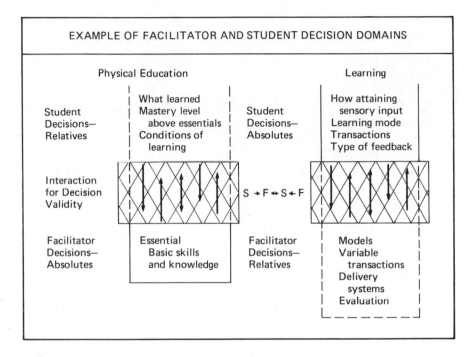

Figure 10–1

Within each choice the student makes there would be absolutes necessary regarding the skills, knowledge, and learning environment that the student would need in order to be successful. For instance, if the student chooses basketball there are certain absolutes he must be able to do and understand in order to play the game. But he has some relative learning options that would be operative also. How well does he want to play? How many types of shooting patterns does he want or need? If he wants to learn the hook shot he must do certain things in order to learn it.

Figures 10–3, 10–4, and 10–5 indicate examples of decisions regarding the facilitation of the learning and the student's preferences for learning modes, transactions, and affective environment.

ABSOLUTES AND RELATIVES IN SPORT SELECTION BASKETBALL			
Beginning ⟶	Intermediate ⟶		Advanced
Absolutes	Relative	(How well?	How many?)
Dribbling	Right hand, left hand, either hand, side, behind, speed, combined with running agility, peripheral vision		
Shooting	Lay-up, free throw, hook shot, set, jump		
Passing	One-hand, two-hand, underhand, chest, overhead, bounce		
Guarding	Body, hands, facing		
Offense	Weave, give and go, fast break, set		
Defense	Person-to-person, zone, shifting zone		
Rules	Essential, more intricate		
Coaching	Offensive, defensive, skills (shooting, guarding, strategy, training)		
Officiating	Leading offical, trailing official, timer, scorer		

Figure 10–2

PRE-DECISIONS

Before instruction begins you must make extensive plans relative to the probable learning needs of the students: identification of the possible subject matter, time requirements, possible levels of aspiration and achievement of the students, diagnostic measures, delivery systems, transactions, and evaluation processes. You must bring to this pre-planning all the professional knowledge you have relative to the subject matter and how students may learn it.

Many of the pre-decisions have constraints put upon them. These can be school policies, legal liability, space, equipment, as well as the nature of the specific students. Within these constraints you identify all the options possible. Materials are prepared and the options are identified before the teacher meets the "class." Each student is then engaged in pre-decisions of his own. Figure 10–6 identifies some pre-decisions. As the student becomes oriented to the possible dimensions of the unit, modes of learning, and transactions, he communicates to you his preference for the options. Some of these decisions can be easily made by the

MODE OF LEARNING DECISIONS
(Perceptual Media for Maximum Receptivity)

Student's Learning Mode Absolutes	Facilitator Decisions Mode Absolutes	Student Decisions Relative to His Absolutes
Visual	Models to see	Types of demonstrations Pictures Loop films Movies

	Instructions to be read
	Visual discrimination
	Visual display or dis-
	    tracting factor
	    tolerance
		Vocabulary level
		Intricateness
		Whole-part-whole
		Parts, whole
		Multi-visual display
		Solitary display

Auditory	Oral explanations Auditory discrimination Auditory distraction factors	Person explaining Audio-tapes Whole-part-whole Whole, parts Noise tolerance Sound determination
Tactile (feeling) Kinesthetic	Propioceptives stimulation	Mental imagery Selective perception Manual assistance Feedback mode Practice repetitions

Cognitive	Principles
	Concepts
	Problems to solve
	Clarification of
	    relationships
		How many
		How intricate
		Inquiry-desire
		Background in other
		    subjects

Combinations	All modes	How many How often How intricate

Figure 10–3

student because of past knowledge. Other decisions may be hard to make because of lack of knowledge about himself or the subject matter. Diagnostic testing can give the student this needed knowledge. Furthermore, it can identify with greater precision where each student is on the continuum of needs.

TRANSACTIONAL DECISIONS

Learning Transactions	Facilitator Decisions Absolutes	Student Decisions Relative to His Absolutes
Self-contained	Can be completed by one person	Pace Level Place
Interaction	Another person or persons	Friend—any, particular Classmate Older student Other student Peer ability student Skillful student Teacher Paraprofessional Homogeneous group Heterogeneous group
Discovery	Cognitive dissonance	
Guided	Cues End product identified	Visual, written, auditory, person
Problem-solving	Statement of problem Sources	place pace
Creative	Criteria Permissive environment	Intricateness End product
Independent	All tasks and trans- actions, feedback, and evaluation written or visual. Directions for entry and decisions	Place Pace Intricateness

Figure 10–4

DIAGNOSIS DECISIONS

Decisions to be made in the diagnostic phase relate to (1) the purpose of the diagnosis, (2) how much time can be spent on the phase, (3) the manner in which the diagnosis is to be organized and conducted. The diagnostic phase should not be viewed as noninstructional time; elements of instruction should be built in. It should be a time when the students learn more about themselves and when you learn more about your students' needs and current achievement levels.

Purpose Decisions. The diagnostic phase can serve many purposes,

DECISIONS REGARDING AFFECTIVE ENVIRONMENT

Need Absolutes	Facilitator Decisions Absolutes	Student Decisions Relative to His Absolutes
Physical Comfort	Optimum heat and cold tolerance Provisions for water, toilets, showers	Temperature tolerance Fatigue levels
Safety	Protective equipment Load tolerance of equipment Supportive assistance Safety rules	Degree of risk desired Degree of protective equipment necessary Degree of support assistance
Belonging	Oral acknowledgment Nonverbal acknowledgment School policy regarding gang identity	Degree desired To what: team, partner, teacher, class, school, club, gang
Esteem	Rewards: verbal, monetary, grades, symbols, intrinsic Presentation methods	By whom: approval by peer, teacher, parent, school Self-achievement
Self-actualization	Allowance for optimum development Integration of all domains	Level desired

Figure 10–5

and you must have the purposes clearly in mind in order to utilize this time in the most efficient manner. Also you must know the dimensions of the unit to be learned so that the diagnosis is relevant to the intended learning program. The diagnosis could then evaluate the pre-ability of the students in specific knowledge and skill areas required for the intended unit, through either standardized or facilitator-made tests. The tests may begin at a simple level and get more complex until the student can no longer score adequately, or you may start the student at a higher or more complex level and work downward. Once the degree of skill and knowledge is measured, you must decide whether to accept the data at face value or whether other factors which may have been present have influenced the results. If the student cannot perform at a given level, more specific testing may be necessary to determine the inhibiting factors.

Facilitator's Pre-decisions	Modifiers	
	Operational	Student

Units of Study	Space available
	  in school: fixed
	  outside school: open
	Equipment available
	Level of mastery
		Interests
		Achievement level
		Potential

Maximum Amount
of Time
	School day, period,
	  grading period
	Number of students
		Tolerance
		Massed or distributed
		  practice
		Level of mastery
		Interest
		Experience

Subject Matter
Sequence
	Requirements for
	  mastery level
	Uni-sequence
	  vertical, horizontal
	Parallel sequence
	  vertical, horizontal
	Age of student
		Receptivity level
		Learning pace
		Learning plateaus

Transactions and
Delivery Systems
	Development of resources
	  tasks
	  media
	  feedback devices and
	    criteria
	  formative evaluation
	  motivation
		Learning modes
		Learning transactions
		Personal characteristics

Evaluation	School requirements
	Grades, norm- or
	  criterion-referenced
	Verifying program
	  effectiveness
		Interest
		Achievement needs
		Certification
		Requirements

Student
Decisions
	Maturity of students
	Legal requirements
	Individual versus
	  others' freedom
		Seriousness of intent
		Past experience in
		  decision making
		Social development

Figure 10–6

Care must be exercised to identify the correct inhibiting factors; incorrect assumptions can result in incorrect learning programs.

In some cases fundamental movements needed for the skill may be poorly developed or the student may have some physical problem which inhibits his mastery. For instance, a student may fail at hitting a pitched softball because the bat is too heavy or long, or the student's depth perception or visual tracking ability may be at fault. It may also be lack of experience in the activity if the other factors prove to be no problem. Also, diagnosing primary and middle school children should include maturation and readiness factors, whereas for high school students, interest may be more important.

You may decide to use the diagnosis for motivational purposes. It can serve to whet the student's interest in what is to be learned or it can call attention to the progress he has already made. Often we forget our beginning points, looking only at the small daily gains, and can become discouraged because they seem so insignificant. Having records of achievement from a longer perspective can heighten motivation. A boy reviewing his previous records may be encouraged to continue his efforts if he sees that originally he did only 3 curl-ups and can now do 15. You may decide to have their longitudinal records available or perhaps the student would like to know how well he or she is doing in relation to other children of the same age. Then scores could be checked against norms collected within that school or from a more global population.

Another purpose may be to show the student what is to be learned and what the end products will be. It can help to speed learning if he knows the full dimensions of what he will be able to do upon mastering the unit.

You must decide the use of the data collected. Will it be to establish the entry point or to determine remedial areas, or will it also be used as the benchmark for establishing grades? Will the student's grade be based on progress from this entry point? If this is so, certain decisions have to be made regarding how reliable and valid this entry point is. The data could also be used to group students by ability, or identify those with similar achievement or remedial problems for which group transactions could be designed.

Other factors can be assessed in the diagnosis, such as the amount of stress the student can tolerate or will need to improve performance, as well as the degree of intricacy the student can handle. In some instances the type of learning modes can be assessed, which will help determine the learning transactions that should be provided. You will have to decide how best these purposes can be diagnosed. Thus, the purposes of a diagnosis may be varied and you must decide how many and which purposes are to be accommodated.

Time-Factor Decisions. You may view the diagnostic phase as too cumbersome for the number of students you have or for the time constraints on the unit. Obviously you must make decisions about how to reconcile these difficulties.

When you establish how long a unit should be, you should select time modules that can adequately accommodate the learning requirements. Realistically, if you do not know what the students can already do and how they can learn best, you can waste time in the teaching-learning process; while some students are repeating what they already know, some have to attempt skills beyond their present potential, and some are locked into learning modes that are nonproductive. Thus, while diagnosing takes time, a more productive learning program can make up for this time.

Decisions on how much time need be spent depends upon how well you already know the students and how new the activity is to them. When you have students for the first time, more extensive diagnosis may be necessary than in subsequent sessions. If records move with the students, their past achievement is already known. Other teachers can also give some insight into a student's learning mode, interests, and perseverance under a variety of settings. For instance, vocabulary and reading levels for children can be obtained from the reading teachers.

Decisions to conduct the diagnosis in an orientation session at the beginning of the year may suffice for gross diagnosis data, with follow-up sessions prior to special units to test for competency in specific skills. Pre-school testing sessions are often conducted on a school-wide basis. If reading, I.Q., placement, hearing, and vision tests are given before the school year begins, you may decide to conduct the diagnostic tests during this time.

Organization and Conduct Decisions for Diagnosis

You must decide how this phase can be conducted and organized to yield a maximum of valid data with the minimum amount of confusion and time. How it will be conducted is dependent upon whether you must do all the testing (which is rare) or if the students can test themselves or their peers. Perhaps there are adult paraprofessional or lay teachers available to assist.

Decisions must be made as to how the data will be recorded. Cards can be used, as well as contract-type assessment sheets. How it is to be recorded is somewhat dependent upon the nature of the tests and who is to do the recording. If students are to do the recording and testing, decisions must be made as to how the integrity of the assessment can be maintained. Control of cheating must be undertaken and ways to encourage appropriate attitudes must be attended to.

You must determine how best the students can have their interest heightened in the diagnostic process. Young children may have a game made out of the diagnosis while older children may enjoy challenge or an approach designed to encourage them to know their present abilities better. If a peer group or older children are to be used in the testing process, decisions must be made as to how they can be oriented to what is expected of them. If the students do the testing you must observe the process and judge the accuracy of the results.

CONFERENCE DECISIONS

As the conference stage is to set the proposed learning program, decisions must be made as to how it will be conducted. The student should be motivated to select appropriate goals and should be made to feel free to discuss his or her concerns and desires with you. Communication channels must be two-way, but you must be prepared to provide leadership in the selection of the goals for the learning program. The student must see the purpose of the learning in order to wholeheartedly accept the responsibility of learning.

It is possible that the student may select skills that are at too low a level. You have to determine whether the student just wishes to avoid working harder or whether there is fear of nonsuccess. Lack of knowledge on the part of students may cause them to fear trying something new. You must decide how best to present what is to be learned so the student knows the end product and how to reach it sequentially. Students must understand that there are some minimum standards of performance and minimum varieties of skills and knowledge that must be learned. From this base they can build toward the greater perfection of certain goals or select a wider variety of skills.

You must decide how many open tasks (tasks or transactions designed by the student) the student can propose versus the amount of fixed tasks which the transactions propose. This will depend upon the amount of self-directedness the student possesses. Since self-fulfillment is an aim of individualized humanistic instruction, esthetic and creative goals and methods of satisfying the student's inquiry desires must be encouraged. Allowing some open-ended transactions or standards of performance may encourage the student to seek achievement beyond either the facilitator's or student's expectations.

During this conference phase the individualization of the learning programs occur. Students select from the many options, the transactions which most meet their needs. Also, students should understand that no decision is irrevocable. The goals can be renegotiated if they are too easy or truly nonreachable.

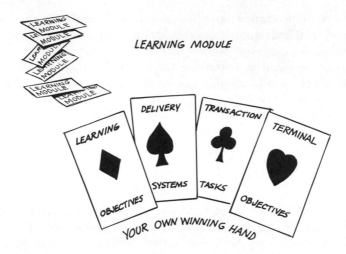

Thus, in the conference stage you set the minimum or absolutes which students must learn, and the students may select transactions they need to reach the goals. They will also be making decisions about the content and the standards of performance they wish above the essential level. The final decisions about the initial learning program are made by the communication between you and the student.

LEARNING PROGRAM DECISIONS

Decisions involving the learning program cover a range from the subject matter to the types of transactions, tasks, media, and evaluation. Criteria for making judgments depend upon the student's characteristics, interests, goals, perseverance, and pacing requirements. You must decide if you have made available the appropriate spread of tasks, adequate degrees of difficulty in the subject matter, and a sufficient variety of media in the delivery system to accommodate the student's needs.

Decisions can be made as to how the material will be presented or learned. You can decide which part of the subject matter can be learned in a large group, which in a small group interaction session, which with a partner, which by tutoring, and which as an independent study project. The AAHPER book *Organizational Patterns for Instruction in Physical Education* gives ideas for what can be taught in these settings.

Your professional knowledge and sensitivity are essential for deciding when a transaction is being nonproductive. You must decide when to switch the transactions and which alternative practice mode is needed. Furthermore, you must decide the content and intricacy for the transactions (self-contained, interaction, discovery, independent) that would be desirable for the age and maturation level, as well as when each should be used and for whom. Which media are necessary—textbooks, workbooks, programmed material, and visual, auditory, or kinesthetic aids—for whom and when?

Decisions have to be made regarding how long a student would engage in a transaction. These decisions can be based on motor learning. Beginning a new skill is more fatiguing than practicing ones already known. Hence, short distributed practice sessions may be more suitable for the beginner, whereas massed practice time could be better for a more skilled student. If the student isn't skilled or used to working independently, short and easily completed transactions that bring success quickly should be chosen. If the purpose of an interaction transaction is competition between teams, the transaction should be designed so appropriate levels of competition can be generated. If a discovery transaction is to be done, decisions have to be made as to how all cues and resources for engaging in the discovery can be present.

Decisions about number of trials and levels of mastery are dependent upon the speed with which the student gains consistency and the level of the student's aspiration. Chapter 11 gives assistance in making these decisions. Usually the student can decide when a program is nonproductive or becomes uninteresting and will naturally select another mode or transaction.

The degree to which the student needs a strong interpersonal support system must be evaluated. If the student seems to withdraw from participation or rejects involvement, you must move to assist the student or devise groups in which the student can find the needed security. For some students you must play the traditional teacher role, at least initially until the student can become self-motivating. This need for an other-directed environment may not be a constant for all activities. A boy may be self-motivated and secure in basketball, although in swimming he may need your support. As you observe the student in the learning environment, the art of facilitating becomes evident if you can decide when to provide a more personal support system and when to leave the student to his or her own discoveries. Students whose social development is less than their peers, or who are reticent to seek peer help because of fear of rebuff, must be given structured ways in which they can be helped to enter into peer interaction. In all cases each student should be helped toward the end of self-actualization.

FORMATIVE EVALUATION DECISIONS

The ongoing formative evaluation helps to identify the areas of difficulty and can suggest alternate learning resources or modes to be used.

You are free during the transaction phase to observe the students and provide a support environment and, by observation, make formative evaluation judgments. You should decide if you should use concrete as well as abstract illustrations or cues, use approval or reinforcement techniques, make suggestions or facilitate other modes or styles. Your support role can be adjusted as you see which techniques work best with each student.

During the formative evaluation stage the students are provided with feedback which will alert them to their degree of productivity. All formative evaluations should have material to guide the student in decision making. The "ifs" should be present. For example, "If you can succeed at this level of competency, proceed to the next task." Or, "If you do not succeed: check _____; review the model; ask someone to help you; return to the preceding step; try another mode for input"; and so on. As students believe they have accomplished the task, they should be encouraged to have someone else verify their beliefs. This could be another student or the facilitator. When other students are asked, their own observation and evaluation powers are being sharpened. Criteria should be identified to help the assisting student make decisions about the accuracy of the doer's performance.

SUMMATIVE EVALUATION DECISIONS

The final or summative evaluation decisions include: Should a grade be given, reflecting the degree of mastery the student has attained or the number of objectives accomplished? Should this grade be in relation to the student's goal, his entry point, other students? Should it be pass-fail, or should it be in narrative form? Should a point value be assigned to tasks? Should the summative evaluation be recorded as a diagnosis for a new entry point?

The individualized humanistic approach emphasizes that the student must know *beforehand* how judgments will be made regarding his productivity and progress in the unit. Accountability is not counter to humanistic treatment. Judgment of our acts is part of daily living, its acceptance is part of our self-development process. It is important that you carefully identify all the factors being learned and weigh the asssessment of these factors according to the objectives and time or emphasis placed on their mastery.

Both you and the student should be involved in this decision making. If the school policies permit, it would certainly seem to foster continued learning to have the students decide what is most helpful to them. Does a girl want to know how well she has done relative to a specific population, her current distance from her own entry point, or what seemed to inhibit her from complete mastery of the material? Perhaps you and the student could decide that all these needs could be met. A series of grades could be offered:

Type of Grade	Grade	Reason
Course grade	B	School policy
Normative grade	C	Class standing
Own progress	A	Entry and exit distance
Narrative	Weak in visual perception; basket shooting	Diagnosis for future work

The student should be encouraged to evaluate his or her own progress, perhaps by self-analyzing the achievement in regard to the learning mode, transactions, goals, interest, and so forth. This engages the learner in understanding the strengths and weaknesses and helps to focus attention on the *process* of education rather than solely on the *product*. A student could say: "Okay, I failed the behavioral objective in basket shooting because time ran out. Why didn't I succeed? The criteria for success were too high for my entry point for the amount of time I had, or I didn't use as many kinds of media as I could have. I waited too long to ask for help. I lost interest when I didn't succeed instantly." He can then postulate how he will do it another time.

A critical decision has to be made regarding (1) whether learning is to be judged as that which has occurred in a fixed amount of time (holding time constant for all) or (2) whether learning for mastery is important regardless of time. In the first case the student's success is dependent upon the speed with which the learning takes place. The student's optimal learning potential is not measured. If time is to be a factor, decisions have to be made regarding how much time is reasonable for each student. Lack of learning in a fixed time may be a manifestation of a wrong learning program being inflicted on the student or the time allotted may be unrealistically short.

The second case implies that mastery of the learning module is paramount and the attainment of the standards of performance, regardless of time, is most important. If it is determined that certain standards of performance (criterion-referenced evaluation) are necessary for competency, then these standards should be the reference point for termination of instruction rather than artificial designations of time. Decisions concerning variable standards of performance could be based on initial starting points. Figure 10–7 represents graphically the differences in summative evalution in these two cases.

Student 1 in the fixed-time designation would mark time waiting for the unit to end, whereas Student 3's learning is interrupted at an incomplete level. It could be said that Student 1 could continue to improve or have additional time to play the game, thereby improving his or her grade; but Student 3, who is having trouble for perhaps a variety of

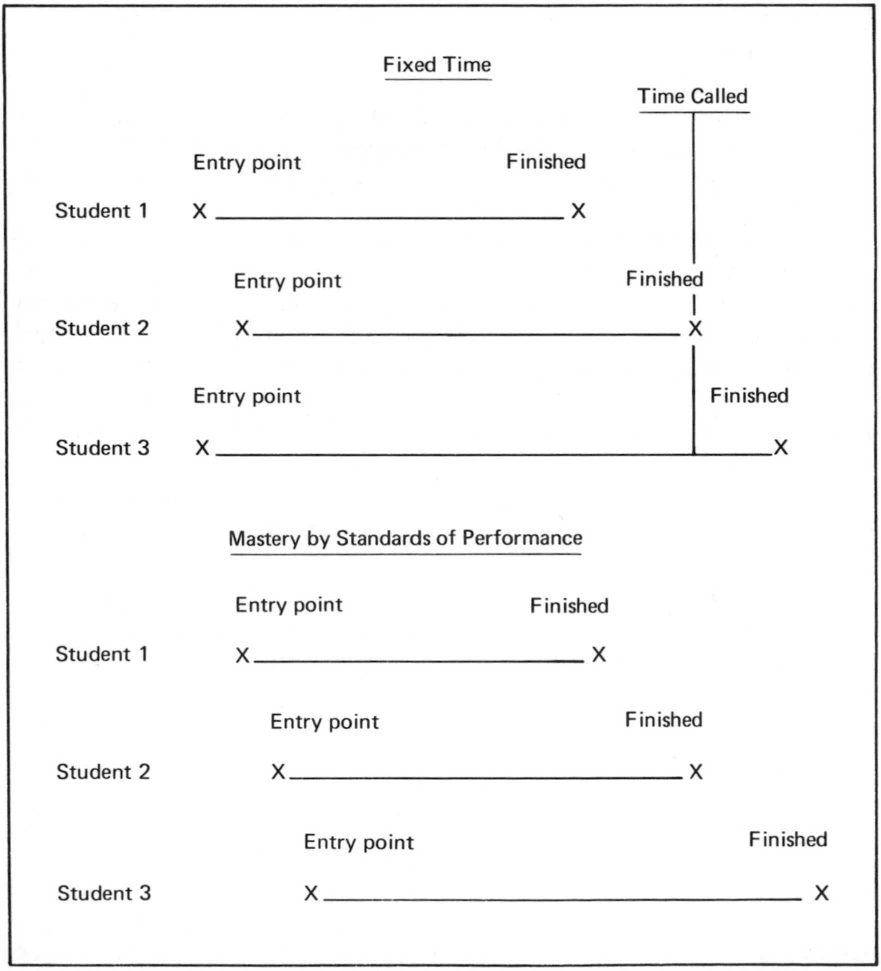

Figure 10–7

Effects on Student Evaluation by Time or Standards of Performance

reasons which may or may not be solely the student's fault, doesn't know that Student 1 by going on has raised the grading curve.

Fixed-time criteria for grading is compatible with the normal curve of grade distribution. The principle of the normal curve relegates some students to the lower end of the curve. By its very nature it says that some students must fail or get a "D." The only assumption that can be made from this form of grading (norm-referenced) based on time is that X amount of students either learned quickly, were congruent with the teaching mode, or may have had higher entry points into the learning program. Students at the lower end of the curve may have needed a different learning mode, entered at a lower level of achievement, were slower in their physiological maturation, or needed more time to master the material.

Much knowledge and many skills are sequentially dependent upon each other. If a given level is not mastered, the learning of the next phase will probably be inhibited. To merely assign a student a failing grade and then proceed on to the next phase leaves those students who have not learned with handicaps for future learning. This is not to discount failure as being an alternative for those students who fail to seriously try to learn. All students must be accountable for their efforts. However, you must make decisions as to how to parcel out the student's intentional disinvolvement from other inhibiting factors which may have been operative.

Therefore, decisions must be made regarding how time versus mastery can be accommodated. Realistically an ending time must be identified, but valid decisions must be made relative to how long it would take the student to master the skill. Unless students can be administratively placed in classes according to their learning speed, some accommodation for this variable factor should be made within each class.

Solutions to this dilemma may be many. One may be to assign grades on the basis of differentiated mastery based on accurate entry levels. For instance, if the student is diagnosed as performing at a specific level, the terminal standard of performance might be, say, 25 percent improvement. (Keep in mind here that greater raw gains are made at the lower end of the learning curve and smaller gains are made by those at the upper end.) Another solution might be to count the number of agreed-upon goals that were attained. Still another may be to allow an incomplete grade if time has elapsed and the student has shown bona fide involvement and met minimal criteria; in this case the grade would be deferred while the student worked on the skills independently until the standards of performance were met. Consider, also, setting the minimal or essential levels as a "D" or "C" and then allowing the student to select additional skills, knowledge, or competency to earn a "B" or "A". The fluid time block accommodates this dilemma quite nicely. Rather than having an absolute time cutoff, a period of time could be inserted between units that could be used in a variety of ways.

Unit I	Fluid Time	Unit 2

Those completing Unit 1 could engage in enriching game opportunities, unique sports, or special skills—perhaps unrelated to the unit or compatible with it, or to help those who are not achieving as quickly. Those not completing their work could continue into the fluid time to complete their mastery. Another accommodation may be to have multi-activities available. A student who completes the essential module would move on to a higher level or could enter another activity.

FACILITATOR'S GUIDANCE IN STUDENT DECISIONS

When students are allowed to participate in the decision-making process, you must be able to guide the student to valid choices. A wrong decision on the part of the student isn't any less a deterrent to negative affective learning than if you make the wrong choice. Students may impose wrong criteria for making a decision. They may seek lower standards than what they are capable of, or may select skills beyond their capabilities because they wish to be with certain friends. Motivation toward good decisions must be constant on your part. Also, consequences of the selected decisions should be pointed out to the student.

The student must come to accept the responsibility of his or her own decisions in regard to the consequences. You, in establishing the climate and limits of decision making, should take into consideration the student's maturity, seriousness of purpose, and experience in decision making. In a very positive manner the facilitator must help students to learn the *process* of decision making in terms of productive outcomes.

CASE STUDY

SETTING: High school of 2,500 students in a suburban setting
CLASS: 63 students selecting tennis instruction in the third
                    period
PROGRAM: Unit duration: daily for 6 weeks in the spring

STAFF: Two teachers assigned to tennis

FACILITIES: Five tennis courts; one black top area with a rebound wall, two indoor stations in one gymnasium 80 × 60; one rebound net; one ball-throwing machine; two cartridge loop film projectors; one overhead projector, two audio-tape players; bulletin board; loop films; transparencies showing grip, serve form, court markings, rules, ball contact, and trajectory for various strokes

Subject Matter Decisions: The essential and relative skills and knowledge of tennis were identified and sequentially ordered according to independence, interdependence, and difficulty level. Terminal behavioral objectives were specified which would indicate essential levels of competency in the skills for the beginner, advanced beginner, intermediate, and advanced players.

Diagnostic Decisions: Diagnostic forms were developed which would permit student self-appraisal or peer appraisal of ability by skill and knowledge tests. Students who had instruction in previous tennis units could retrieve their past records, which would become their starting point. Those who had achieved at least a B grade in the beginning unit would enter the intermediate level. This diagnostic phase would be conducted during the first three to four class sessions. Knowledge diagnostic tests were to be taken in the instructional media center during the students' study or unassigned time.

Delivery System Decisions: Books, photographs, and movies on tennis were placed in the media center. In addition, single-concept 8 mm cartridge films on various aspects of tennis, as well as transparencies and instructional audio-tapes, were placed in the gymnasium for ready access during transactional practice. Some intermediate and advanced players selected student teaching transactions, and special tme was arranged to instruct and certify them to assist other students.

Transactions Decisions: Learning modules with transactions were developed, prepared in appropriate format, labeled according to degree of difficulty, and placed in a sturdy box for easy access. A resource box was developed for the transactions. Included were the media resources, i.e. pictures, transparencies, notations for where to use them or to procure other resources such as audio-tapes, books, or human assistance. There were also written explanations and rules.

Space and Material Management Decisions: A folder was developed for each student in which would be placed the diagnosis sheets, learning program, and completed modules. These were placed in another box in numerical order corresponding to the student's identification number. (Students can file better by number than by alphabet.) Time and space designations were made for rally, skill practice, and game or tournament play. At least twenty students could be accommodated in each facility.

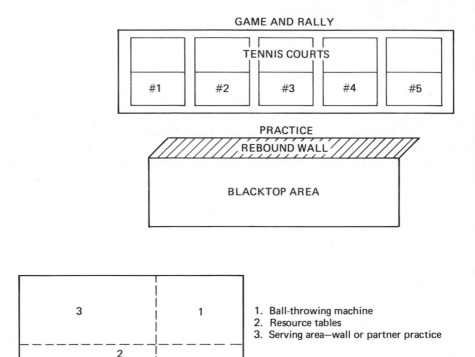

Community tennis courts were identified and students informed of the locations so they could augment their class time practice after school.

Implementation: During the first lesson the students were oriented; they were given a composite sheet of essential and relative activities, behavioral objectives, and the evaluation criteria. At the second lesson students were diagnosed. As the diagnosis was completed, conferences were held with each student or with a small group of students who had similar diagnoses. Essential levels were identified and explained, and the students contracted for specific transactions and levels of competency which were relative to the interests of each. The learner's objectives and terminal behavior objectives were identified, and transactions selected which would specify input and practice activities leading to the terminal behavioral objective.

DIAGNOSTIC RESULTS	
Number of Students	*Level*
25	Beginning
4	Advanced beginners
19	Intermediate
15	Advanced
63	

Evaluation was criterion-referenced and grades were assigned on the basis of the total point value given to each standard of performance within each competency level.

SUMMARY

The decisions to be made regarding the learning act are shared by you (the facilitator) and the student (the learner). The facilitator is charged with the responsibility of making decisions which will foster learning because of his or her professional knowledge of the subject matter and learning requirements. The student shares in the responsibility because he is to be affected by the learning. The involvement of the student must be taken seriously and not as a token involvement role. He must know the dimensions of his choices, and they must be broad enough to make the choices valid reflections of his needs, interests, and understanding.

There are certain *absolute* (essential) things which must be learned. The facilitator identifies and makes pre-decisions regarding these absolutes. This may be the sequence of skills and knowledge, the essential level of mastery necessary, as well as certain essential steps, materials, and conditions in the environment which must be available.

The student makes decisions regarding things which extend beyond the absolutes—those that are *relative*: the sport to be learned, degree of mastery beyond the essential level, learning mode, transactions, pace, and the like. Within each student there are absolutes which you must recognize: the student's learning characteristics, past achievement, physical and temperament attributes, social needs or desires, and interests. However, there are relatives within these absolutes, since there are many ways in which the student's absolutes can be accommodated. Furthermore, when a student decides to master a specific skill, there are attendant absolutes for doing so. Thus, from out of absolutes can arise relatives, and out of relatives can arise absolutes.

Before instruction begins you must make some pre-decisions considering facilities, time, school policies, and the like. You must anticipate the maturation and interest levels, achievement, learning characteristics, and personal attributes of the students you will have. You must prepare material which will serve for motivation, diagnosis, and evaluation purposes, encompassing many types of transactions and perceptual learning modes.

Diagnosing the student before instruction sets entry points for the student, should heighten interest in the material to be learned, and can also guide decisions about selecting the learning program. You must decide the purpose of the diagnosis, how much time needs to be spent on it, and how it will be conducted and organized, and whether it will be a simple or sophisticated procedure.

Considering the data, the facilitator's and the student's decisions are mediated in the conference or link-up stage. Herein you must decide how to open communication, orient the student to the learning possibilities, give a clear picture of the end product, and seek to guide the student to make valid choices. The student must fully understand the constraints placed upon him or her, and must also seriously consider all options and make thoughtful decisions.

Learning program decisions may deal with whether the subject matter lends itself to large group, small group, independent study, or tutorial arrangement, perceptual input needs of the student, types of transactions that will be appropriate, need for feedback, and pacing. You must also decide if you have prepared sufficient variety and types of transactions and levels of attainment.

Formative evaluation built into the transactions can allow for midcourse corrections to adjust the parts of the program which are nonproductive.

Final evaluation (*summative*) decisions include the purpose of determining the end result. Should the grade be norm-referenced (in relation to others in the class), or criterion-referenced, or in relation to the student's beginning and ending points? Should it be narrative or numerical? Should it be a diagnosis for future work? Should it include how well the student learned process as well as product? Decisions must be made regarding whether the evaluation is to be time-referenced (what has been achieved in a fixed amount of time) or mastery-referenced (learning is judged when a bona fide standard of performance is accomplished). Time-referenced learning can penalize those with slower pacing requirements, lower entry points, or nonproductive learning programs. It is essential that the constraints of time and learning mastery be mediated. A fluid time block could exist between units, during which those who have not finished may do so, and those who have may be allowed enrichment activities.

It is the essence of humanistic evaluation that the student know beforehand what is expected of him and how he will be judged. He also should have some say in how far he can progress and be given the ground rules as to what the consequences will be of his noninvolvement. Facilitators must constantly guide the student in the decision-making process. Students should understand all the options open to them and the possible consequences of their decisions. They must also be helped to accept the responsibility of their decisions in regard to the consequences of their selections.

REFERENCES

BIRCH, D., AND J. VEROFF. *Motivation: A Study of Action.* Belmont, Calif.: Brooks/Cole Publishing Company, 1966.

CASSIDY, R., AND S. F. CALDWELL. *Humanizing Physical Education.* Dubuque, Iowa: Wm. C. Brown Company, Publishers, 1974.

FRYMIER, J. R. *A School for Tomorrow.* Berkeley, Calif.: McCutchan Publishing Corporation, 1973.

GORDON, L. D., M. M. THOMPSON, J. W. ALSPAUGH. "The Relative Importance of Various Physical Education Objectives for Grades K-12," *Research Quarterly*, 44:2 (May 1973), 192–96.

HAWKINS, D. E., AND D. A. VINTON. *The Environmental Classroom.* Englewood Cliffs, N.J.: Prentice-Hall, Inc., 1973.

MAGER, R. E. *Developing Attitude Toward Learning.* Palo Alto, Calif.: Fearon Publishers, 1966.

NOAR, G. *Individualized Instruction: Every Child a Winner.* New York: John Wiley & Sons, Inc., 1972.

POPHAM, W. J., AND E. L. BAKER. *Establishing Instructional Goals.* Englewood Cliffs, N.J.: Prentice-Hall, Inc., 1970.

RATH, L. E., et al. *Values and Teaching.* Columbus, Ohio: Charles E. Merrill Publishing Company, 1966.

SMITH, B., AND H. LERCH. "Contract Grading," *The Physical Educator.* Vol. 29, no. 2 (May 1972).

STROM, R. D., AND E. P. TORRANCE. *Education for Affective Achievement.* Chicago: Rand McNally & Company, 1973.

11

Guiding: Helping Learners

INSTRUCTIONAL UNIT FOR CHAPTER 11

Learner's Diagnosis

Directions: Read the questions below. Write out, discuss, or mentally review the answer. If you believe that you know the information, check the "yes" column. If you are not sure of the answer, check the "no" column. After reading the questions and deciding your knowledge, check the accuracy of your answers by reading the summary at the end of this chapter. If you answered a question incorrectly, change your answer to the appropriate column.

Can you

Yes	No	Questions
		1. Define three areas where guidance will be needed by learners?
		2. Explain the use of an orientation learning module?
		3. List possible topics for discussion at a conference for preparing the learner for individualized instruction?
		4. List at least three important phases of guiding the learning of the student?
		5. List two sources of information about student progress?
		6. Explain three effective methods of communicating error correction to students?
		7. Give and evaluate two types of practice?
		8. Develop a practice schedule for beginners trying to learn a complex skill?
		9. Specify which portion of a skill should be given extra practice: initial, middle, final?
		10. Explain the speed-accuracy trade-off problem?
		11. List three values of feedback?

Yes	No	Questions
		12. Identify two types of feedback?
		13. List three common problems of individualized humanistic physical education?
		14. Explain how discipline problems should be handled?
		15. Give three possible means of skill assessment?

Suggested Prescription

Directions: Count the number of checks that you have placed in the "yes" column. When the percentages are determined, you may increase your knowledge and skill by using the suggested Learning Program activities recommended in the Input and Practice columns.

Results	Input	Practice
More than 80%	#1, 7	#6
60% to 80%	#1, 3, 7	#1 or 2 or 3 or 4 or 5, 6
40% to 60%	#1, 2, 4 or 5	#1, 2 or 3, 4 or 5
Less than 40%	#1, 2, 3, 4 or 5, 6	#1, 2, 3, 4, 5

Learning Program

Directions: It is suggested that the reader attempt to follow any and all suggestions in this learning program. These are designed to improve knowledge and understanding of guiding the learner during individualized physical education.

Proposed Learning Objectives: The learner will be able to guide students to learn during individualized physical education as evidenced by successful completion of learning modules.

Input:
    *1. Read Chapter 11 of this book.
    2. Read Margaret Robb, *Dynamics of Motor Skill Acquisition.*

*Highly recommended.

3. Read selected references given at the end of this chapter.

4. Prepare a list of questions that you may have about guiding student learning. Interview two teachers to secure answers.

5. Observe a teacher guiding student learning. Look for modes of communication and types of feedback.

6. Observe a student attempting to learn a skill. Notice errors being made, attempts to correct the errors, and the perseverance of the learner.

7. Plan an input of your own.

Practice:

1. Conduct a conference with a student to plan a learning program.

2. Observe the skill practice of two students. Analyze their errors and identify corrections needed.

3. Give manual and verbal assistance to two students needing instruction while practicing a skill.

4. Attempt to augment feedback to three students who are involved in learning a sport skill.

5. Develop a plan which will accommodate during one class hour, a game of basketball as well as individualized skill or knowledge instruction. You have 24 students and a gymnasium the size of one standard basketball court.

6. Plan a practice of your own.

Evaluation: You will be able to guide a student to master a skill with which he is having difficulty so that he can complete the prescribed assessment in a learning module.

The learning resulting from the *process* of instruction is one of the major goals of individualized humanistic physical education. It is the process which not only allows the learner to achieve personal goals, but also fosters the development of a more autonomous and self-actualizing human being. Responsibility for this process of learning is shared by the student and the facilitator. Although learning programs provide directions for acquiring and practicing the knowledge and skill desired, effective application of this prescriptive approach will need the guidance of the facilitator. Learners will vary as to the locus, extent, and kind of assistance needed.

The dynamic conditions illustrated in the individualized humanistic instruction model in Chapter 4 were presented as a circular and interacting process. A prescription is a suggested program of study which specifies learning programs that are designed to involve students in experiences to bring about a behavior change (Figure 11–1). Guidance by the facilitator will be needed (1) to orient the student to the process, (2) to interpret the diagnosis so that the student will be able to select a meaningful prescription, (3) to execute the program, and (4) to solve operational problems.

Figure 11–1

ORIENTING THE STUDENT

Students are often confused and insecure at the onset of an individualized approach. An orientation learning module is valuable to introduce the learner to the course and operational procedures. Information may be developed for the students via filmstrips, slides, pamphlets, discussions, and audio-tapes. The content should include an overview of the course, contents, process, use of media, the role of transaction or tasks, the grading process, terms, availability of assistance, the student's role, and the general operational plan of the system. Figure 11–2 is a sample of an orientation learning module.

Initial units of instruction should be simply structured and verbalized at the appropriate reading level, language, and interest span, and be made possible to complete at the available time for the course. Complexity may be added as the student learns the process. It is often helpful to role-play a student utilizing the process. Attempt to give the student an understanding of the entire process and its goals. Patience will be

ORIENTATION

Topic: Beginning Basketball
(5 merits)

Name _____ Starting date _____

Instructional Objective: All of the students will understand the class procedures and objectives. All of the students will be able to identify needs and plan a meaningful learning program.

	Attempted	Completed
A. INPUT (1, 3 and 4 required)		
1. Listen to talk by the facilitator.		
2. Observe a basketball game.		
3. Browse through some basketball books; make note of what you feel you need to learn.		
4. Read the course direction sheet.		
B. PRACTICE		
1. Look over the basketball learning modules. Check on your prescription programs that interest you.		
2. Complete the Diagnosis section of your Planning Sheet.		

C. ASSESSMENT

The student will be able to:

1. Plan prescription with assistance of the facilitator.

2. Be able to utilize the instructional process to complete the prescription.

Secure signature of facilitator when you have both agreed upon your planned prescription for learning in this class.

_____ Date _____
Facilitator

_____ Date _____
Student

Figure 11–2

245

needed early in the unit as each student learns not only the content of the course but also the process for learning it. It may take a few minutes of each lesson for several class meetings to correct and guide students to fully understand both the "what" and the "how." Failure to communicate properly at this stage will almost ensure failure to achieve the anticipated advantages of the system.

CONFERENCE

Problems or misunderstandings can be solved with the initial and subsequent conferences, which may be held with individuals or a small group. The initial conference should be held after the diagnosis and orientation. It is designed to help the student to understand the implication of the diagnosis and to interpret the available alternatives in light of the student's unique self and goals. The conference may be held while students are engaging in practice or game play. A time schedule may be posted along with directions. If an orientation learning module is used, it may be the basis for the first conference.

Begin the conference with a brief discussion of the student's concerns, questions, interests, and goals. Compare the responses given with the information obtained from the diagnostic tests. Inconsistencies should be discussed and advice given to the student; however, it is wise to permit the learner's wishes to prevail. Flexibility should be exercised in the

pursuit of the learning goals. No prescriptive decision should be irrevocable. Many questions will surface during the initial conference. Often learners will have difficulty in arriving at decisions concerning their learning, usually because of concern about success or failure. They will be delighted to be given an opportunity to make choices, but will need a commitment from you that success is possible and that assistance will be available. After the prescription is agreed upon, you should try to determine if the student understands how to proceed. Instruction may be necessary to instigate initial activity. If an orientation learning module is a part of the program, end the conference by acknowledging the completion of the first module.

Additional conferences may be spontaneous or planned and may be conducted on an individual or group basis. These conferences may deal with the student's progress, class actions, problems, or concerns. Communication channels must be open, trusting, and filled with genuine concern for the good of the learner. Call the students by name as much as possible. Some students will need considerable assistance to persist at involvement in learning experiences, whereas others will need little or no help.

EXECUTING THE PROGRAM

Filling the prescription is the heart of the instructional component of individualized humanistic instruction. The facilitator's role will be (1) to observe and analyze student progress during play and practice, (2) to communicate additional information verbally, visually, and kinesthetically, (3) to adjust practice in order to foster learning, and (4) to provide feedback in order to reinforce learning responses and thus sustain student perseverance. All of these activities may occur in any one class meeting; it will seldom be possible to preplan them. Since each student knows how to proceed to pursue learning, you, as the facilitator, will now have time to work with students on a one-to-one or small-group basis. The execution of these duties in a personal and caring manner is crucial to the attainment of the learning objectives.

The early stages in guiding students to learn independence of the teacher are complex. Often you may feel useless and less important than when leading group drills and practice. Older students tend to turn to peers, extra helpers, and media before seeking help from you.

Observation and Analysis. It is wise at this time to observe activity, give positive feedback, and attempt to put the learners in touch with possible learning aids. Personal discipline is often needed for you to notice the extent of involvement of each student during play, at practice, or in acquiring information. Information about student progress and satisfaction may also be acquired by checking the learners' records and by casual discussion with them.

Each learning program may be differently perceived and interpreted by learners. Furthermore, the varying levels of basic motor ability of the students will result in many imprecise attempts to learn skills. You must have a thorough knowledge and understanding of the components of the various skills to be learned, so you can compare the observed performance with the intended performance. The observation should be focused not only upon the results of the action, but also on the causes of the result, the key elements of the task, or as Robb[1] explains, "the critical components." Attention must be given to the proper sequence and timing of the activity. The analysis must be made rapidly, and for that reason, several repetitions may be needed to confirm the nature of the problem. Generally, it is agreed that sequential problems should supersede timing problems. If the skill is one in which only the performer is moving, emphasis may be initially placed on the sequence. For example, the sequential pattern for a golf swing may be:

> From the address position:
>> Forward press of the hands
>> Backward movement of the club, hands, and weight
>> Cocking of the wrists
>> Forward movement of the hands
>> Uncocking of the wrists
>> Follow-through of the club, hands, and weight

Obviously there is a timing pattern for each component, but it is not as critical as the sequential pattern. However, if both the performer and the object are moving, as in tennis, then the temporal pattern becomes equally important.

Communication.   Once the decision is made concerning the needed treatment or guidance to help the learner, this information must be given to the student. The learner's attention may be directed to the problem by verbal directions. These directions may be a simple explanation of the task and its components. Additional techniques may be (1) to have the learner imitate the model, (2) to touch the part which must strike the object or be corrected, and/or (3) to place the body in the proper position. If the quality of the skill is to be explained, then perhaps the use of "effort-shape" words proposed by Kleinman[2] would be helpful. The

[1]Margaret Robb, *Dynamics of Motor Skill Acquisition* (Englewood Cliffs, N.J.: Prentice-Hall, Inc., 1972), pp. 132–42.

[2]Seymour Kleinman, "Effort-Shape for Physical Educators," *Journal of Health, Physical Education & Recreation*, Vol. 45, No. 7 (September, 1974), 21.

system encourages the use of terms that describe the quality of movement such as:

Move *freely*
Feel *energy*
Remain *light*
Move *gently*
Lay it up *softly*

If a problem is sequential in nature, then visual input should be used. Demonstrations performed by you, by other students, or through media will be helpful. On the other hand, if timing is the problem, verbal assistance is of more value. Cueing the crucial time by directing the students to "swing," "move," "release," or "shoot" can help the learner to correct timing errors. Kinesthetic awareness may help learners to focus attention on the specific problem if they are manually guided through the sequence and get the "feeling" of the action. For example, the arm may be held and guided through the forehand drive action several times. Manual assistance is most beneficial after the learner has had an opportunity to practice.

Communication may be promoted by means of transfer. Transfer is the ability to learn from previous related experiences. Thus, it is helpful to recognize that the overhand volleyball serve is similar to a previously learned skill such as an overhand throw. Making an old response (throwing) in a new situation (overhand serve) is called positive transfer and is helpful to the learner. Conversely, a negative transfer situation, such as making a new response to a similar stimulus, interferes with the learner. An example of negative transfer is learning to swing vertically when executing a golf stroke as opposed to swinging horizontally in batting a softball. The stimulus is identical (an object that is to be struck with an implement), but the response is different. Of course, if the stimulus and response are completely unrelated, then neither positive nor negative transfer will operate. The learner's attention must be drawn to similarities when positive transfer can occur, and should be made aware of differences in negative transfer situations. Helpful positive transfer statements may be:

"Swat a fly."
"Rotate like a wheel."
"Catch a water balloon."
"Glide like a fish."

It is imperative that you be aware of the aiding influences of transfer and guide the learner's practice accordingly.

Practice.   Sometimes the nature of the practice may impede as well as enhance learning. Practice in physical education may be physical or mental. Physical practice embraces most of the skill-learning involvement and without doubt is the most productive type of practice. The potency of physical practice is influenced by the following factors: schedules, repetition, serial order, and trade-off.

Individualized instruction permits each learner to work at the most desirable and productive pace. However, failure to learn may be due to the amount of time available to practice. Usually the learner will switch to another skill if satiated, bored, or fatigued. Simple skills can be practiced until mastered, but more difficult skills, especially those requiring concentration or accuracy, may need frequent diversions. Learners should be given this knowledge and encouraged to follow their instincts as well as wisdom in persevering. Sometimes, simply suggesting that the learner practice another skill for a while may remove frustration feelings or permit time for mental integration of the knowledge and skill needed for proper execution. Generally, the learning of a difficult skill is aided by short, interrupted practices, whereas simpler skills or learning by experts may need to be mass practiced until mastery is achieved.

Research is inconclusive as to whether the entire skill or part of a skill should be practiced. However, the most successful approach seems to be to practice the entire skill first, to learn the sequence, and then concentrate on particular components. Skills have a natural order of execution, so that fragmenting practice interferes with the flow and carry-over of one component to the next. If the skill is fairly independent of sequence and flow, or extremely complex, it may be useful to practice the parts first. For example, in driving in for a lay-up shot in basketball, the components of driving and shooting may be practiced as parts and then combined as a whole. Here the whole skill really has two relatively independent parts and would be quite complex to practice as a whole.

Once the skill is learned it should be repeated to about 150 percent above learning level to fix the sequence and timing in the learner's memory. Because motor skills are frequently overlearned, there is less tendency to forget them than would be the case with cognitive learning. For example, when a learner has finally mastered a lay-up shot, practice should be encouraged until proper execution with good form and accuracy is consistently performed.

Another influence on practice effectiveness is the serial order or position of the task components in the sequence. Research has shown that the first and last parts of a skill are more readily remembered than the middle portions. This phenomenon is thought to be related to the amount of rehearsal time and to interference. A sequence may be to serve a tennis ball, move to ready position, and hit the return. In this case the student often forgets to move into position. The first part of the sequence is often overlearned since it is frequently repeated, and the final portion has little interference, but the middle part has less repetition and suffers from both retroactive interference (serving) and proactive interference (hitting the ball). Another example might be the learning of a badminton clear. In this case, the backswing and follow-through will be learned readily but the wrist snap may be forgotten. Special wrist snap practice may guide the student beyond this possible error in performance of the task. A wise facilitator will encourage the learner to give additional practice time to the middle portion of a skill.

A final aspect of practice is the speed-accuracy trade-off problem. The question is often asked as to whether speed or accuracy should be practiced first. Learning motor skills is very specific to the task. Thus if speed or accuracy or both are singled out and practiced, whatever is emphasized is learned. The consequence of the trade-off is powerful. Failure to be accurate usually brings the most undesirable results; therefore, learners prefer to trade speed for accuracy. Thus, if speed is most essential to the skill, it will need encouragement and early emphasis. If both speed and accuracy are important to the successful performance, then each aspect should be stressed equally.

Mental practice or reviewing the sequence, timing, or feeling of a skill can aid the learner. Learners should be encouraged to think through the skill before performing. Tasks such as bowling, diving, and golfing are most often aided by mental practice. Obviously a basketball player has little time to mentally rehearse a fake before driving in for a lay-up shot. Mental practice may be augmented by verbal assistance through the recitation of the sequence or timing. A mental review of the sequences can be effective guidance. Golf, for example, could be reviewed as follows:

Checking the grip
Feet shoulder-distance apart
Knees relaxed
Arms free of the body
Slight bend in the waist
Eyes on the ball

The human mind has difficulty processing more than seven variables; therefore, care should be taken that mental practice does not overload the brain's channel capacity.

Feedback.   Practice without feedback is worthless. Feedback is the information that a learner receives from internal and external sources that assists the learner in attempting to regulate or control actions in order to approach as close as possible the intended goal. In addition, feedback may motivate and reinforce behavior. Fortunately, as long as the learner has sensory input channels, it is almost impossible for practice to be pursued without some form of error information or feedback to be supplied. Studies have shown that learning proceeds best when the learner is given a time schedule permitting self-practice and assisted practice.

Perceived compatible or almost compatible actions cause the learner to repeat those actions, thus reinforcing them. When the learner attempts to alter incompatible actions, they are not consistently repeated, and therefore, not reinforced. The satisfaction derived from progress toward desired goals and success experiences is extremely motivating. The important factor in any practice is the remembered reference pattern for the desired action. You, while guiding practice, must be certain that the student has a reasonably accurate reference pattern in mind. Asking the student to verbalize the action protocol may provide some insight into the quality of the perceived goal. Help may be given by a brief explanation, demonstration, or suggestion to review the learning program, filmstrip, and/or other available input materials. Reference patterns should be perceived as attainable, and external goals should not be set too high. A tennis sequence of goals might be as follows:

1. Number of contacts made with the ball
2. Number of shots that went over the net
3. Number of shots that landed inside the boundary lines
4. Number of shots that accomplished numbers 2 and 3 above and achieved the desired trajectory
5. Number of shots that landed near certain targets

The correct movement response may be perceived as attainable if classmates who have mastered the skill are asked to demonstrate. Your ability to demonstrate and analyze reference patterns are essential to help the learner to correct his errors.

There are two types of feedback: *concurrent and terminal.* Concurrent feedback is supplied mainly from the proprioceptors. It is always present and is often referred to by physical educators as kinesthetic sense. External concurrent feedback may be supplied by the facilitator in the form of verbal directions during practice. Directions must be succinct and direct, such as:

Weight back
Swing
Move forward
Jump
Hurry
Slower

Too many directions or other interfering stimuli are called "noise." It is important that the learner be able to concentrate to properly receive feedback. Another form of external concurrent feedback is devices such as wrist bands, grippers, and electronic sensors which serve as reminders to execute certain actions. When concurrent feedback is received, alterations are attempted almost instantaneously. Depending on the nature of the activity, some substantial changes are made while the activity is in progress. Most often the learner "senses" the error and attempts to correct the mistake on the next trial. No doubt you have sensed in your own performance when you were off balance while performing a skill, but could not change before it was too late.

Terminal feedback is the appraisal of the quality of the completed performance. This appraisal may be apparent, as when viewing where the arrow hit, how many pins were knocked down, or whether the ball went through the basket, escaped the fielders, or went between the goal posts. When the result of the performance is not apparent, an observer such as a classmate or the facilitator will be needed to give succinct directions for correcting the mistake. Too much or too little information will inhibit or retard the learner's ability to improve performance. You should avoid reporting apparent results or detailed mechanical explanations. Simply inform the learner what to do to correct the error. Be generous with approval, in comments and gestures. Failure to give augmented feedback, either concurrent or terminal, often results in the learner's becoming disinterested or bored.

PROBLEMS

As in any teaching-learning situation, problems will develop. These problems often center around the self-discipline of the learner, progression in the learning program, game play, verification of learning, the persistent need for additional instructional assistance, and management of the program.

Discipline. Facilitators are often concerned whether learners will be able to be self-directed. Most experienced facilitators report little or no problem with discipline because students do have an opportunity to find an outlet for meeting their needs. When nonparticipation or behavioral problems occur, they must be handled as in a more controlled teaching situation. Students should be consulted concerning the reasons for their behavior. If their response has implications for the nature and conduct of the course, then steps should be taken to correct the problem. If, on the other hand, the problem is a desire to merely "play" or refrain from any activity, then the students need to be reminded that they do have responsibility to reach the goals that they have set. It is suggested that students be questioned concerning what they are doing, whether their actions are helping them or the class, and what they can do to help themselves. Wait for a response to each of these questions. Be aware of good learner behavior and reward it with an immediate compliment. Failure to respond to fair and firm treatment should result in the learners' receiving whatever consequences have been defined. Humanistic educators wish to avoid such confrontations and depend upon the quality of the process to diminish the probability of discipline problems.

Progression.   Some learners will practice learning programs that are too difficult in the early stages of learning because they seem more attractive or challenging. Although logical progression is important to learning, it is fruitless if the student is not ready or interested to pursue skills in the order recommended. Suggest, but not require the order in which skills should be practiced. Students will usually not persist in tasks in which they fail. If the problem does continue, discuss the problem at a conference.

Game Play.   Most learning is task specific. That is, we learn by involvement in the real experience. You should attempt to manage the time and space to provide some game play experience at each lesson. Failure to make such a provision will seriously hamper student learning, which depends upon personal satisfaction, social interaction enjoyment, and involvement in the "whole" for which the "parts" are being pursued. No practice can really approach the multi-variant experience of playing the game. If space is limited, it is suggested that game modifications be made such as playing games with smaller boundaries, releasing students from class to visit the media center, or giving credit for game play experience gained elsewhere.

Verifying Learning.   Chapter 8 discussed many of the dimensions of evaluation. It will be almost impossible for you to guide individual learning if time is preempted to assess each student's terminal performance. Alternatives might be self, peer, or paraprofessional assessment. In these cases, concern may arise about the credibility of the assessment. One solution to this problem is to remind learners that they are accountable to you. You should periodically check reported learning module completions against performance indicators during practice or play. Failure of a student to perform as reported may result in revocation of the completed module. Completely eradicating dishonesty in assessment procedures is a continual problem in any teaching-learning act. Honesty is what should be taught, and firmness with trust can contribute to fostering it.

Sufficient Instructional Assistance.   Many of the problems in implementing instruction may be avoided if you have sufficient help. Class size and class ability may dictate how much help is required. You may

wish to make use of student leaders, parent helpers, and/or paraprofessionals. Differentiated staffing to provide the specific expertise and mode of instructional guidance is desirable. Temporary specific skill-ability grouping may efficiently utilize staff to assist learners. At the same time, tutoring by talented peers or other staff may be needed for some students. If extra help is utilized, in-service training is essential to ensure quality assistance to the learner.

Management. Managing an individualized instructional program has many logistical problems centering around setting up and striking support equipment and supplies. Rotating assignments may be arranged with students in the class. Just as in any teaching-learning setting, students may need to learn how to care for the media and equipment. Time should be allotted and planned for this training. Another problem is the maintaining of records. Although students, aides, or you, the facilitator, are usually involved in keeping track of the overall progress of the student, you should be aware that computers can be used to record accomplishments, diagnose needs, and prescribe remedies.

CASE STUDY

SETTING:	Inner city high school, senior girls, basically beginners
CLASS SIZE:	34 (average of 30 present)
ACTIVITY:	Beginning badminton
FACILITIES:	Three singles-width courts; three feet of space between walls and end line
EQUIPMENT:	Seventeen racquets, thirteen badminton shuttlecocks
NUMBER OF LESSONS:	Fifteen

The instructor taped ten poster boards on the wall. Each poster was a learning module for a particular badminton skill. Each module gave three suggestions for learning how to perform the skill: (1) study the pictures which were posted below the directions on the module, (2) check the chart to locate a student who has mastered the skill and arrange for help, and/or (3) see the instructor and/or attend the demonstration and explanation scheduled on a specified date. In addition, practice procedures and assessment of performance were written on the poster.

Since space was limited, the class had been divided into three groups of about ten each. Each group rotated every twelve minutes to a different phase of the learning experiences: (1) practicing skills on court 1, (2) reading modules and learning about skills, rules, and strategy, and (3) playing the game or rallying on courts 2 and 3. The instructor in a space of about twelve minutes was observed guiding learning as follows:

Manually assisting a student with a low short serve (2 students)

Cueing temporal patterns by saying: "drop-hit" (3 students)

Suggesting timing, sequence, and execution corrections (3 students)

Answering questions (4 students)

Solving equipment problems

Assessing skills (2 students)

Helping a doubles team to improve defensive positions

Checking the student progress chart and then seeking out two students to determine their progress.

In addition, students were observed in the following activities:

Discussing rules (group of 3)
Giving advice to classmate on a skill (group of 2)
Giving manual assistance (group of 2)
Evaluating the skill attained on a learning module (3 groups of 3)

SUMMARY

Responsibility for learning through the process of individualized instruction is shared by the facilitator and the student. Although learning modules provide a map for the student to pursue learning, guidance from the facilitator is imperative. Learners will vary as to their need for assistance in understanding the process, interpreting the diagnosis for deciding the prescription, and executing the learning program.

If the students have had little or no previous experience with learning on an individual basis, they will need to learn the process. The learner can be introduced to the course and operational procedures through an orientation module, using media and formal instructions.

The conference is useful to interpret the diagnosis and to assist the learner with process concerns. If an orientation learning module is used, it should be the basis of the initial conference. No prescriptive decision should be irrevocable. Students should be assured that it is possible for them to complete their learning program successfully and that assistance will be given to them.

The facilitator will need to observe and analyze student progress, to communicate needed information, to adjust practice procedures, and to provide feedback concerning performance. Since each student is directed to pursue learning, you have time to guide individual student learning.

Students' progress needs to be monitored from observation of their performance and from written records. You must have a thorough knowledge of the skill, in order to properly analyze the quality of the execution, to determine performance errors, and to give precise directions for corrections. Sequential patterns should be corrected before working with timing problems.

Once the analysis is made, a meaningful mode of communication must be selected to call to the learner's attention the nature of the problem. Verbal directions, imitation of a model, touching the crucial surface, and manual placement of the body parts may be helpful. Verbal directions are most helpful for timing problems, whereas visual guidance such as demonstrations are more potent for sequential pattern errors. Communication is facilitated though the use of transferring like elements of a previous learned skill pattern.

Practice in physical education may be physical or mental. Physical practice is always the more productive type. Although individualized instruction permits learners to determine their practice schedule, it may be necessary to assist them with pacing. Beginners at a skill and those learning complex skills will need distributed practice time, whereas experts and those learning simple skills will need massed practice time. Similarly, simpler skills may be practiced in their entirety, and complex skills should be practiced as parts after a concept of the whole skill has been given. Once a skill has been learned, it should be overlearned to reduce forgetting. You should encourage extra practice for the middle portion of a skill since it is most easily forgotten in a serial order of the execution plan. Learners usually trade off speed for accuracy, so if speed is more important it should be given early attention. When both speed and accuracy are a part of a skill, both should receive equal emphasis. Mental practice, or viewing the sequence, timing, or "feeling" of a skill, can aid the learner. Mental practice may be carried out by the learner's thinking through the sequence and timing of the skill before action is initiated.

Feedback is the information that a learner receives from internal and external sources to regulate actions to approximate the perceived reference pattern. Feedback also serves to reinforce action and to motivate performance. Concurrent feedback is received while the action is in progress, from kinesthetic sources or from succinct and precise verbal directions from the facilitator. Terminal feedback is received from the appraisal of the result of the action at the completion of the skill.

Problems in individualized humanistic instruction could center around discipline or self-motivation, progression, game play, verification of assessment, and the need for additional instructional help. Discipline problems are normally lessened under the individualized process, but when student behavior is not satisfactory, it must be handled firmly and fairly. Responsibility to learn is fostered by invoking the *a priori* defined consequences. Although logical progression of skill learning is desirable, it is not essential. Advice should be given to the student concerning possible learning difficulties. Most learning is task specific; therefore, game play is essential to provide the multi-variant experiences to integrate the skills as well as to promote enjoyment and satisfaction. Game play should be provided as part of each lesson, if possible. If verification of assessment is left solely to you, little time will be available to guide the learner. Therefore, assessment may also be verified by the learner, classmates, or extra helpers. If extra instructional help is needed, student leaders, parents, or paraprofessionals may be secured, but each should receive specific training.

REFERENCES

BELL, V. *Sensorimotor Learning*. Pacific Palisades, Calif.: Goodyear Publishing Co., 1970.

CRATTY, B. *Movement Behavior and Motor Learning*. Philadelphia, Pa.: Lea & Febiger, 1964.

——. *Psychology and Physical Activity*. Englewood Cliffs, N.J.: Prentice-Hall, Inc., 1968.

DEL RAY, P. "Appropriate Feedback for Open and Closed Skill Acquisition," *Quest*. National Association for Physical Education of College Women and National College Physical Education Association for Men, Monograph 17, Winter 1972.

DUNN, R., AND K. DUNN. *Practical Approaches to Individualize Instruction*. West Nyack, N.Y.: Parker Publishing Company, 1972.

FITTS, P., AND M. POSNER. *Human Performance*. Belmont, Calif.: Brooks/Cole Publishing Company, 1967.

KLEINMAN, S. "Effort-Shape for Physical Educators," *JOPHER*. Washington, D.C.: American Alliance for Health, Physical Education and Recreation, September 1974.

LAWTHER, J. *The Learning of Physical Skills*. Englewood Cliffs, N.J.: Prentice-Hall, Inc., 1968.

LEWIS, J. *Administrating the Individualized Instruction Program*. West Nyack, N.Y.: Parker Publishing Co., 1971.

MAGER, R., AND P. PIPE. *Analyzing Performance Problems*. Belmont, Calif.: Fearon Publishers, 1970.

MOSSTON, M. *Teaching Physical Education*. Columbus, Ohio: Charles E. Merrill Publishing Company, 1966.

NOAR, G. *Individualized Instruction*. New York, N.Y.: John Wiley & Sons, Inc., 1972.

OXENDINE, J. *Psychology of Motor Learning*. New York: Appleton-Century-Crofts, 1968.

ROBB, M. *Dynamics of Motor-Skill Acquisition*. Englewood Cliffs, N.J.: Prentice-Hall, Inc., 1972.

SINGER, R. *Motor Learning and Human Performance*. New York: The Macmillan Company, 1968.

SINGER, R., AND W. DICK. *Teaching Physical Education, A Systems Approach*. Boston, Mass.: Houghton Mifflin Company, 1974.

STALLINGS, M. *Motor Skills*. Dubuque, Iowa: W. C. Brown Co., 1973.

"Student Orientation Pamphlet for the New Physical Education," *Physical Education Newsletter*. Old Saybrook, Conn.: Physical Education Publications, September 15, 1974.

12

Accountability:
Did I Do It?

INSTRUCTIONAL UNIT FOR CHAPTER 12

Learner's Diagnosis

Directions: Read the questions below. Write out, discuss, or mentally review the answers. If you believe that you know the information, check the "yes" column. If you are not sure of the answer, check the "no" column. After reading the questions and deciding your knowledge, check the accuracy of your answers by reading the summary at the end of this chapter. If you answered a question incorrectly, change your answer to the appropriate column.

Can you

Yes	No	Questions
		1. Explain why accountability is important after instruction?
		2. State the aspects of the program which should be evaluated?
		3. State two or three procedures which will obtain data to assess the process employed?
		4. State two or three procedures which will obtain data to assess the attainment of the objectives?
		5. List influences on learnability?
		6. Tell which populations should be involved in the evaluation process?
		7. Tell why setting target dates can be useful?
		8. Explain to whom the evaluation assessment should be communicated?
		9. State components of the evaluation report?
		10. Identify possible constraints on pursuing assessment procedures?

Suggested Prescription

Directions: Count the number of checks you have placed in the "yes" column. When the percentages are determined, you may increase your knowledge and skill by using the suggested Learning Program activities recommended in the Input and Practice columns. Inputs and Practices not listed offer additional learning options.

Results	Input	Practice
More than 80%	#1, 2	#1, 6
60% to 80%	#1, 2, 5	#1, 3, 6
40% to 60%	#1, 2, 5, 7	#1, 3 or 4, 5, 6
Less than 40%	#1, 2, 3, 5, 7, 8	#1, 3 or 4, 5, 6, 7

Learning Program

Directions: It is suggested that the reader attempt to complete any or all of the suggestions in this learning program. These are designed to improve knowledge and understanding of the role program assessment plays in accountability and improvement of learning programs.

Proposed Learning Objective: The learner will be able to understand the need for evaluating the instructional program, and the operational processes involved.

Input:

    *1. Read Chapter 12 of this book.

    2. Read C. Avedisian, "Planning Programming Budget Systems."

    3. Read D. Field, "Accountability for the Physical Educator."

    4. Select additional readings from the bibliography.

    5. Discuss with a principal what he or she and the Board of Education expect from physical education instruction. Does this differ from what they expect from other disciplines?

    6. Discuss with a physical education teacher how he or she evaluates the program and reports the results.

*Highly recommended.

7. Ask several parents if they can state the objectives of their children's physical education program.
8. Develop an input of your own.

Practice:

1. Administer a questionnaire to determine the value various groups place on physical education objectives.
2. Develop an agenda for a plan of action to accomplish your objectives with target dates for implementation.
3. Develop a presentation to the Board of Education relative to the accomplished goals and the intended goals if more money could be allocated for resources.
4. If the community were to cut educational programs, support your belief for retention of your program with facts, figures, and appropriate judgments relative to the accomplishments and value of physical education.
5. Develop a plan for program accountability if time is limited.
6. Interpret results of the unit as to probable causes for success and failure.
7. Develop a practice of your own.

Evaluation: You will be able to explain with supporting data the causal relationship between the intended product and process objective and actual outcome.

Now that the component steps for an individualized humanistic approach to facilitating the learning of physical education have been identified and, hopefully, practiced, it becomes imperative that you judge the success of your efforts. A humanistic facilitator must ask, "What have I done for my students and how can I improve for future students?" The onus of accountability for learning has traditionally been placed on the student. However, humanistic instruction requires that anyone directing the learning in a gymnasium or classroom share the burden of accountability for learning.

Teachers have more or less considered themselves not subject to evaluation. However, no teacher, curriculum, or lesson has ever escaped evaluation. You as a teacher may sense acceptance or rejection of the lesson. But often your sensing is colored by what you want to believe, hence you overlook dissonance on the part of the students or attribute it to the wrong reasons. Yet the students know the effect that you, the curriculum, and the lesson had on them.

No business would leave the effectiveness of its product to chance. Private enterprise has built-in quality checks at all points of production and marketing. It is not implied here that education and business are synonymous in intent and function. Education is dealing with the most precious of resources—human beings. Errors in judgment must be minimized and the "marketing" of human beings must be soundly based, because imperfect "products" cannot be recalled for repair or be thrown away when they do not function. Professional physical educators who care about their students and their profession must be accountable for the educational program they institute and take the responsibility for ensuring that the goals are fulfilled.

The complete plan detailed in this chapter is extensive and perhaps ideal. You will have to determine how extensive an evaluation you can realistically make, based upon the time and assistance available to you. With clerical or computer assistance, a total evaluation can easily be conducted. Accountability gives you authentic direction: it requires that you accept responsibility for the results, but also enables you to explain the results. Both of these functions are important. The more facts you have and the more valid judgments you can make, the more persuasive you can be in selling your program to your principal, Board of Education, and taxpayers. Your understanding of the results of your instructional program and your ability to communicate this can help to improve the conditions under which you are asked to facilitate learning. Furthermore, you will have better guidelines with which you can develop future units of instruction.

SCOPE OF ACCOUNTABILITY

Accountability is pertinent to areas extending from goal selection and attainment, curricular validity, and instructional methods, to fiscal responsibility for wise use of tax funds per student and instructional activity, and expenditure of student and teacher time. Deciding on the curricular content is an important task of the facilitator. Selection of the appropriate curriculum based on maturation and interest is not within the scope of this book, and curriculum evaluation is included only as part of the instructional evaluation process.

The focus of this chapter is on the assessment of the components of the individualized humanistic approach with the general purpose of determining the extent to which the objectives were valid and were met. In other words, "Did I do it?"

Assessment of the program must include *process* as well as *product* evaluation, as described in Chapter 8. However, the evaluation cannot stop there. It extends into the range of diagnosing causes. It helps in the decision-making process for short- and long-range program improvement to determine the cause-and-effect relationship between success and failure of the instructional program. It serves no purpose to merely know that 57 percent of the students achieved their stated objectives; you must know why these students succeeded and why the other 43 percent did not. It is important to make a careful analysis, to parcel out all possible causes. Any measure of effectiveness that cannot make a causal connection between what is measured and what caused its existence is an exercise in futility.

Assessment must follow a sequential plan, dealing first with the determination of goals and then with the management of the resources to attain these goals. Assessment is the analyzing of the purposes of the objectives, and developing a plan of action with a schedule aimed at accomplishing the objectives. The overall evaluation includes judgments on how valuable was the product and how effective was the process. This analysis gives rise to new input for succeeding units.

Brownell[1] suggests a management plan that can be schematically represented as follows:

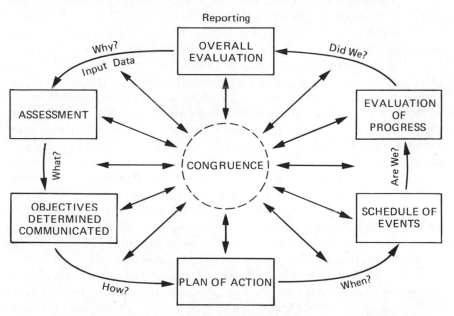

[1]John A. Brownell, "Planning and Evaluating Within the Hawaii Curriculum Center," *Educational Perspectives*, October 1967, p. 24.

JUDGING OBJECTIVES

There are two criteria for judging the determined objectives. One is the students' terminal behavior assessed against the intended objectives. The second is data describing the values placed on the objectives by the various participants in the educational structure—the students, teachers, administrators, parents, community members, and the profession. Each participant may respond according to the relevancy he or she sees in the goal. A matrix of responses for the objectives can give rank order significance to the objectives, or the specification of an objective can be valuable just for one student who desires to pursue it.

Modern school management is involving the lay community to help frame curricular and instructional goals. It is foolish to set up learning programs isolated and insulated from the society which the student is preparing to enter. A committee of parents, students, and business people who could give input into formulating program objectives should be established. Surveys of alumni, parents, and students can yield a wealth of data regarding the value each places on the various aspects of the intended program. Misconceptions can be corrected through communication. Professional input could be obtained from physical education associations or other professional organizations. After categories of objectives are determined, the objectives must be analyzed in the light of the constraints within which you must work: class size, time allotted, the equipment available, facility size, past achievement levels of the students, and the degree to which they have had to be responsible for their learning.

Terminal behavioral objectives should be assessed by reliable and reasonably determined criteria. Systematic gathering of achievement data should occur which can correlate with time allowed for mastery and levels of entry. For example, if you teach beginning basketball, consider the range of consistency attained in free-throw shooting in a 15-lesson unit versus a unit of 30 lessons, or consider the quality and quantity progress of students entering the unit who cannot make two out of ten free throws versus those who can make five out of ten. Longitudinal records will help to base specific learning objectives on measurement data. In a track and field unit, if a time is specified for a 50-yard dash, you could be more precise in identifying a reasonable time if you kept records on how long it would take one to establish the endurance to sustain the efforts, as well as how long it took to learn the necessary techniques.

The objectives to be accomplished would fall into categories of psychomotor, cognitive, affective, and process skills. The first two are relatively easy to evaluate. However, why they are or are not attained may have something to do with the affective environment. It is as important for students to understand the process by which they are to be taught, as it is for them to have the learning skills needed to proceed. The emphasis in individualized humanistic instruction is on the understanding of the actions; hence, any failure to accomplish results must be viewed in the light of how well you led the students to this understanding. Did you give them too much freedom? No one can be turned loose without an understanding of the constraints and rules. No game we play can be called by a name unless the conduct of the activity conforms to the limitations and specifications of that game. So it is with learning. As no one is free to use any size ball, run with the ball, disregard boundaries, or score as he pleases and call the game basketball, so he cannot take liberties with the rules of instruction and call it learning. And just as one may be creative and invent a new game for which innovative conditions may be devised, one could be creative in the learning process, but the results must meet the criteria established. The objective established must also be valued by the student. Sometimes students do not seriously pursue a goal because it does not fall within their expectancy of success level or they just don't see it as important to self-enhancement.

Thus, when judging the degree to which the objectives were met, you must consider the statistical validity of the specified objective, the value placed on the objectives by various populations, the understanding the student has concerning how to proceed to master the objective, and the value the student sees in the objective in relation to the time and energy investment. Any one or a combination of these factors may influence the outcome. The evaluation of *why* gives rise to *how* to improve future objectives and the process for learning them.

JUDGING THE PLAN OF ACTION

The formative evaluation embedded in the transactions allows for immediate and critical judgments to be made. You must develop standards for judging the feedback regarding the properties of the material. Brownell[2] suggests that these properties are the learnability, clarity, difficulty level, approach, sequence, organization, feasibility in the setting, students' and teacher's attitudes toward the material, and suggestions for improvement. These properties are interdependent. Learnability may be affected by the organization of the material, which in turn may be affected by the lack of feasibility of the settings. Decisions have to be made regarding the logical relationships between what is occurring and what is causing it to occur.

[2]Brownell, "Planning and Evaluating," p. 20.

An analysis should be made of the delivery system and media. Were they adequate? Did the information clearly identify what the student was to do? Were the quality and quantity of pictures, loop films, audio-tapes, and other forms of media adequate? Were they durable and easily operated? How much did the students use the media? If they were not used very much, was it because they were inaccessible or awkward to use?

An objective measure of the activity generated in the room can be obtained by using a critical incident instrument. An observer can be asked to come into the room to record, at regular intervals, what is occurring. Focus can be directed to the facilitator's activity or to one or several students. This tells you the degree of direct and indirect interaction that is taking place. If a video-tape recorder is available to record a day's lesson, you could review the video-tape and record the incidents yourself after the class. If this procedure is unwieldy for the gymnasium setting, you could set up a microteaching lesson (small segments of instruction with fewer students and shorter periods of time). In the *Quest* Monograph of January 1971, Neil Dougherty explains the development and use of this instrument. Figures 12–1 and 12–2 are examples of the critical incident and score sheet used for facilitator interaction. Figures 12–3 and 12–4 are examples of a form and score sheet upon which student activity can be recorded.

Your attention here is directed not at assessing individual students, but rather at judging the process as a whole and giving data to revise subsequent programs. As the plan of action unfolds, judgments regarding the schedule of events become critical.

JUDGMENTS OF THE SCHEDULE OF EVENTS

The plan of action may be short term or long term. The implementation of the program may have several target dates. Time must be allowed to gather input from a variety of sources for establishing objectives, to determine resources available, to develop transactions and delivery system materials, to orient students, to teach students skill for involvement, and to develop a plan for organization and evaluation. Realistic dates should be set for each of these steps. Trying to accomplish too much too soon can be a pitfall. Time agendas help to alert you to what still needs to be accomplished.

The schedule may have two frames of reference: one directed toward the pacing of the instruction for the student, the other toward pacing the events for yourself. In the former you may gather data as to whether you or students paced the learning too fast, too slow, or just right. One answer to this question may not suffice. It will have to be

CATEGORIES FOR INTERACTION ANALYSIS*

Teacher Talk	**Indirect**	1. ACCEPTS FEELING: Accepts and clarifies the feeling tones of the students in a nonthreatening manner. Feelings may be positive or negative; predicting or recording feelings included.
		2. PRAISES OR ENCOURAGES: Praises or encourages student action or behavior, jokes that release tensions, but not at the expense of another individual; nodding head or saying "um hum?" or "go on" are included.
		3. ACCEPTS OR USES IDEAS OF STUDENTS: Clarifying, building, or developing ideas suggested by a student; as teacher brings more of his own ideas into play, shift to category 5.
		4. ASKS QUESTIONS: Asking a question about content or procedure with the intent that a student answer.
	Direct	5. LECTURING: Giving facts or opinions about content or procedures; expressing his own ideas, asking rhetorical questions.
		6. GIVING DIRECTIONS: Directions, commands, or orders with which a student is expected to comply.
		7. CRITICIZING OR JUSTIFYING AUTHORITY: Statements intended to change student behavior from nonacceptable to acceptable pattern; bawling someone out; stating why the teacher is doing what he is doing; extreme self-reference.
Student Talk		8. STUDENT TALK-RESPONSE: Talk by students in response to teacher. Teacher initiates contact or solicits student statement.
		9. STUDENT TALK-INITIATION: Talk by students which they initiate. If "calling on" student is only to indicate who may talk next, observer must decide whether student wanted to talk. If he did, use this category.
		10. SILENCE OR CONFUSION: Pauses, short periods of silence, and periods of confusion in which communication cannot be understood by the observer.
		11. MEANINGFUL NONVERBAL ACTIVITY: Periods of silence in which the student is engaged in meaningful productive activity.†
		i. Place an *i* behind any of the teacher talk category numbers when the teacher is addressing his statements to an individual rather than to the entire group.†

*Neil Dougherty IV. By permission of the author.
†These items were added by the author and are not included in the original reference.

Figure 12–1

269

INTERACTION ANALYSIS MATRIX SCORE SHEET

Class _____ Date _____ Length of Observation _____

<u>Directions:</u> Every three seconds record the category number of the interaction observed. Record these numbers sequentially at the rate of one every three seconds on a <u>separate</u> paper. If more than one type of activity is occurring within the three seconds, record all types.

After recording the numbers, place the numbers in the matrix below by pairs. Add a 10 above the first number recorded and after the last number recorded in your list. Place numbers in matrix by overlapping pairs. Examples: If your numbers were (8,7,5,3,2), record (10,8) (8.7) (7.5) (5,3) (3,2) (2,10). Total each column. Divide the number of tallies in each row or column by the total number of tallies. Record the percentage.

		1	2	3	4	5	6	7	8	9	10	11	Total
ACCEPTS FEELINGS	1												
PRAISES	2												
ACCEPTS IDEAS	3												
ASKS QUESTIONS	4												
LECTURES	5												
GIVES DIRECTIONS	6												
CRITICIZES	7												
STUDENT RESPONSE	8												
STUDENT TALK INITIATION	9												
SILENCE OR CONFUSION	10												
NONVERBAL	11												
TOTAL													
%													

i: Place an *i* behind any of the teacher talk category numbers when the teacher is addressing statements to an individual rather than the entire group. Use ROW TOTAL COLUMN for initial record of interaction.

Comments:

Recorder _____

Figure 12–2

CATEGORIES FOR STUDENT INVOLVEMENT ANALYSIS

1. SELF-CONTAINED TRANSACTION: Working alone on tasks

2. INTERACTION TRANSACTION: Working with one or more students on tasks

3. DISCOVERY TRANSACTION: Working on guided discovery, problem solving, or creative tasks

4. INDEPENDENT TRANSACTION: Utilizing programmed learning packets or workbooks

5. MEDIA UTILIZATION: Watching films, loop films, slides, transparencies
    Reading books or handouts
    Observing pictures and drawings
    Listening to tapes

6. RECORD KEEPING: Recording data
    Securing file
    Checking prescription or learning program

7. ASSISTING OTHERS: Helping classmates by practicing, demonstrating, or explaining

8. SUPPORT WORK: Getting equipment, media, or supplies
    Preparing practicing area

9. GAME PLAYING: Enjoying the integration of the various skills and knowledges
    Attempting to implement skill and knowledge in game situation

10. NO ACTIVITY OR CONFUSION: Sitting or standing around in apparently no related learning activity

11. COUNTERACTIVITY: Displaying disruptive behavior or behavior not congruent with learning program or class procedures

Record observed activity here:

Figure 12–3

broken down for individuals or for categories of students. For pacing yourself, you might ask: "Did I feel the students were moving too fast for me?" or "Did I overwhelm them with too much before they had become accustomed to the process?" Perhaps you moved into the program without time to gather enough resources or to orient students, admin-

INVOLVEMENT ANALYSIS MATRIX SCORE SHEET

Student Activity

Class _____ Date _____ Length of Observation _____

Directions: Every three seconds record the category number of the interaction observed. Record these numbers sequentially at the rate of one every three seconds on a separate paper. If more than one type of activity is occurring within the three seconds, record all types.

After recording the numbers, place the numbers in the matrix below by pairs. Add a 10 above the first number recorded and after the last number recorded in your list. Place numbers in matrix by overlapping pairs. Examples: If your numbers were (8,7,5,3,2), record (10,8) (8.7) (7,5) (5,3) (3,2) (2,10). Total each column. Divide the number of tallies in each row or column by the total number of tallies. Record the percentage.

Item		1	2	3	4	5	6	7	8	9	10	11	TOTAL
SELF-CONTAINED TRANSACTION	1												
INTERACTION TRANSACTION	2												
DISCOVERY TRANSACTION	3												
INDEPENDENT TRANSACTION	4												
MEDIA USE	5												
RECORD KEEPING	6												
ASSISTING	7												
SUPPORT WORK	8												
GAME PLAYING	9												
NO ACTIVITY	10												
COUNTERACTIVITY	11												
TOTAL													

PERCENTAGE

Comments:

Recorder _____

Figure 12–4

istrators, or parents sufficiently. Maybe the goals you established were hastily drawn and were not indicative of the realistic capabilities of the students.

Schedule agendas may define what you wish to accomplish the first year. Data gathered would give direction for the next year. But it is helpful to identify what you wish to accomplish immediately, a year or two hence, and over a longer period of time.

REPORTING THE EVALUATION

Periodic assessments should occur which will report quantitatively and qualitatively what has occurred. The concurrent evaluation can give you direction as to how to set about improving the conditions for learning. Will it take more funds? If this is the case, the school administration must be advised as to what would be needed. A complete analysis of the utilization of existing funds by a breakdown per pupil per activity would be helpful. How do these costs compare to funds spent in other subjects? What benefits will accrue to the students if more funds are allocated? Similar analyses can be made for the amount of time and the number of students per class.

After each unit a debriefing should take place when all the facts and feelings are still fresh in your mind. The final assessment after the unit should be an analysis of students' scores, attitude scales, and process inventories. Pre-instruction interest inventories can be compared with post-instruction interest inventories. Figures 12–5 and 12–6 are examples of interest inventories. If the student's interest was low before instruction and remained low after the instruction, then you didn't affect the student in any positive way and probably wasted everyone's time. Conversely, how wonderful the student and you will feel if a new interest is opened for the student.

Reporting the findings is important. This is the closing of the cycle of communication. Students are interested in how well you put it all together, and post-communication on how well the goals were achieved is flattering to them. There is no disgrace in saying to the student: "We set out to this; however, I guess I (or we) missed here. What can I (or you) do to improve the process for future units or for those who will follow you in this unit?" This is engaging the student in the most trusting of relationships. For you, the facilitator, to admit errors shows the student that errors are human. Owning up to them is the first step toward correcting them. Obviously, we all want to minimize errors and everyone wants to be on the "winning team." But the students sense when you are shutting your eyes to your errors, and no one is fooled.

PRE-INSTRUCTION OPINIONNAIRE FOR STUDENTS

Read the directions before answering the questions.

You are about to begin to receive instruction in Basketball. Your teacher is interested in how you feel about this sport, how much skill you have in it, and how well you expect to do. With this information your teacher can plan your lessons better to meet your interests. This is not a test.

Directions: Please read each question carefully. Then read all the answers offered as possible answers to that question. After doing so, select one answer which best describes your answer to the question.

With the special pencil blacken the circle on the answer sheet in the column which corresponds to the number before the answer you selected. There are no right or wrong answers.

Be sure that the number of the question matches the line upon which you are placing the answer.

1. How much do you look forward to your unit in basketball?
   (1) not at all   (2) somewhat   (3) enthusiastically

2. If the opportunities were present, to what degree would you seek to play this sport in your leisure time?
   (1) never   (2) occasionally   (3) often

3. How much value do you place on learning basketball skills?
   (1) very little   (2) some   (3) a great deal

4. How much interest do you have in learning basketball
   (1) very little   (2) average   (3) a great deal

5. How much skill do you feel you now have in basketball?
   (1) very little   (2) average   (3) above average

6. How satisfied are you with the amount of skill you have in basketball?
   (1) not at all   (2) somewhat   (3) very satisfied

7. How much skill improvement are you hoping to acquire by the end of this unit?
   (1) very little   (2) some improvement   (3) a great deal

Figure 12–5

Pre-instruction Interest Inventory

Communication of your successes and failures to your principal and community helps them to see that you care. The community which has "paid the bill" for your efforts has a right to know what they got for their money. What is important is, if you didn't have total success, what will you improve? We have the example in athletics. The community knows

---

POST-INSTRUCTION OPINIONNAIRE FOR STUDENTS

Read the <u>directions</u> before answering the questions.

You have just finished receiving instruction in Basketball. In order for your teacher to evaluate how much you learned and how much you enjoyed the unit she would like you to answer the questions listed below accurately.

Your answers will not in any way affect your grade in this unit. Your answers to this opinionnaire will be tabulated by someone other than your teacher. Only the total class results will be given to her.

Directions: Please read each question carefully. Then read all the answers offered as possible answers to that question. After doing so, select one answer which best describes your answer to the question.

With the special pencil blacken the dotted lines on the answer sheet in the column which corresponds to the number before the answer you selected.

1. How much did you enjoy this unit?
   (1) not at all   (2) somewhat   (3) a great deal

2. If opportunities were present, to what extent would you seek to play basketball in your leisure time?
   (1) never   (2) occasionally   (3) often

3. How much value do you now place on learning basketball skills?
   (1) very little   (2) some   (3) a great deal

4. How much interest do you have in learning more basketball?
   (1) very little   (2) some   (3) a great deal

5. How much skill do you feel you now have in basketball?
   (1) very little   (2) average   (3) a lot

6. How satisfied are you with the amount of skill you have acquired in basketball as a result of this unit?
   (1) not at all   (2) somewhat   (3) very satisfied

7. How much skill improvement did you acquire from this unit?
   (1) very little   (2) some improvement   (3) a great deal

Figure 12–6

Post-instruction Interest Inventory

the win and loss record of the teams, the injury tally, and the individual player's records. Usually the athletic department has a Boosters Club where the coaches are available to answer questions, get suggestions, and tell what plans they have to improve the next year's season. Why should it be different for those who are in physical education classes?

DID I?

You will know the answer to this question only if you systematically gather data from which judgments can be made. How much data you gather depends upon the time and resources you have. Minimally, you should sample student achievement against the entry point. This achievement should extend from the skill and knowledge scores to attitude about the process and product. Some of the data will be objective and some may be subjective or intuitive on your part and the student's.

You need to report what criteria you are using as your measuring rod. Are these criteria consistent with the general educational aims of the school and community? Criteria that seem trivial or out of the educational context will not serve to impress anyone.

With time permitting, retesting or giving interest and attitude inventories and other surveys to determine how useful the skills, knowledge, and process were after several months or years can give you a longitudinal assessment of the permanency of the learning. After all, you should be interested not only in how well the students do immediately after instruction, but how much the instruction has become a part of their lives.

Now review the purposes and premises of individualized humanistic instruction as related in Chapter 1. Have you accomplished this as well as the personal goals of the students? It is hoped that you have. But in any case, do you know why you were successful or nearly so? Remember, education is affecting behavior. Are your students nearer self-actualization for having you as their facilitator?

CASE STUDY

SETTING:	Suburban elementary school
CIRCUMSTANCE:	Presentation to the Board of Education
PROGRAM:	700 students in the school, physical education taught twice a week for thirty minutes
STAFF:	One physical education teacher

The facilitator requested of the principal that more funds be allocated to physical education for the purpose of increasing instruction time, reducing the pupil-teacher ratio, and improving the learning program. The principal came to the gymnasium on several days to observe the program. She noted the students were interested in learning and the individualized tasks the facilitator had developed were helping the students learn. She further noted that students were reluctant to return to their classrooms particularly when they would not have physical education again for several days. The physical education teacher outlined his plans for what would be included if more time and resources were available. In addition he gave her a study he made of other teachers' appraisals of student behavior in class which revealed that on days when the students didn't have physical education they were more prone to fidgeting and discipline problems. In addition a study was conducted which indicated that students with learning problems also had low perceptual motor scores.

The principal suggested that he prepare a proposal and present it to the Board of Education. His preparation included student achievement, instructional effectiveness, and financial analyses.

The students' test scores in classroom subjects indicated that they were on a par with the national average. However, 65 percent of these same students were 4 to 20 percentiles below the average on national physical fitness and achievement norms. In addition, they were 6 to 35 percentiles below students in another suburban community where the pupil-teacher ratio in physical education was lower than at this school.

Diagnostic tests showed an average 67-point range in the abilities of the students in most fundamental skills. Individualized instruction had helped to significantly increase achievement scores for 45 percent of the students. However, time for student practice, teacher preparation, and interaction with each student was too short to substantially affect the other 55 percent of the students.

The facilitator outlined the instructional material which would be prepared to augment learning if he had more planning time, and indicated the activities which would be included if the instructional time were increased. In addition he gave the Board of Education members the AAHPER Position Papers on elementary physical education, as well as material summarizing the physiological, neuromuscular, perceptual-motor, and social benefits to be gained from appropriate physical education experiences.

At the present time $1.50 was spent per pupil in each of the other subjects while $.67 was spent for physical education. Increasing this by $.50 per pupil would help to improve the student ratio to equipment and augment the present variety available.

If one other teacher at $10,000 were added to the staff, the pupil-teacher ratio would be reduced to 350 students at an additional per pupil cost of approximately $15. At the present time $500 per pupil is being spent for the other classroom teachers' salaries. Thus, the physical well-being, coordination, and perceptual-motor abilities of the student could be significantly enhanced and be more comparable to average national norms by an expenditure of $16.17 per pupil.

The Board of Education granted the request and thanked the teacher for the interest he had shown in the welfare of their children. They admitted they had not realized the vital necessity for physical education or the changes made toward improving the instructional program since they were children. They had viewed physical education as a recreational adjunct to cognitive education rather than a vital need for child growth and development.

They invited the facilitator to report back to them one year later on the effects the additional funds had on the capabilities of their children.

SUMMARY

Facilitators must assume with the students the burden of accountability for the learning that transpired during the instructional program. Evaluation should be applied to all phases of the learning program in order to diagnose those aspects that were successful and those that were unsuccessful. However, merely assessing the outcomes of a unit on the basis of a statistical analysis is doing only half the task. You should be able to make causal relationships between what occurred and why it occurred.

A management plan can be established to help guide the evaluation process. This plan includes gathering input data and making an assessment of the environment and purposes of instruction, determining and communicating objectives, developing a plan of action, setting up a schedule of events and an evaluation of the instructional process. After judgments are made these can give new input to succeeding units.

Input for the objectives could come from students, citizens committees, alumni, and administrators. The objectives suggested by these groups could be checked against those forwarded by professional groups.

Quantifying and qualifying of specific terminal behavioral objectives must have some foundation in fact. Longitudinal records can assist in obtaining validity of those you have developed. The instructional objectives that you set up for yourself in the area of affective and process growth should be assessed as well as the product. Don't forget to evaluate the delivery system!

Formative evaluation can lead to immediate adjustments, but after the unit, an overall assessment regarding how many corrections were needed and the reasons for them can help you to construct better transactions. This evaluation will be directed to the learnability, clarity, difficulty level, approach, sequence, organization, feasibility, students' and teachers' attitudes toward the material, and suggestions for improvement of the material. The success of each of these factors may be interrelated.

As your plan of action for the events is drawn up, target dates for their completion should be determined. A one-, three-, and five-year plan with enlarging goals may be determined.

Reporting the findings of the evaluation is important. These findings should include the statistical data as to how well the students and you accomplished the goals. It should also indicate what the facilitating and inhibiting factors were. Decisions as to what was accomplished and what will be changed should be communicated to parents, students, and administrators. This is completing the communication cycle. Sharing the results of your cooperative effort is a trusting act and gives believability to the humanization emphasis.

The extent to which you can evaluate the product and process depends upon the resources, time, assistance, and amount of administrative support. But certainly you should attempt to evaluate in some detail each aspect of the program. Your growth as a facilitator and, thus, the growth of your students toward their self-actualization through physical education is dependent upon your knowing where you have been and where you are going.

REFERENCES

American Alliance for Health, Physical Education and Recreation. *Curriculum Improvement in Secondary School Physical Education.* Washington, D.C.: AAHPER, 1973.

Association of California School Administrators. "Thrust for Leadership: Assessment/Evaluation." Burlingame, Calif.: *ACSA*, Vol. I, no. 6 (May 1972).

Association of School Business Officials. International Inventory of Educational Research Management System (ERMS-PPBES) Committee Project. *ASBO* Research Library, Chicago, Illinois 60625.

AVEDISIAN, C. "Planning Programming Budget Systems," *Journal of Health, Physical Education and Recreation.* 43; 8 (October 1972), 37–39.

DOUGHERTY, IV, N. "A Plan for the Analysis of Teacher-Pupil Interaction in Physical Education Classes," *Quest.* Monograph XV (January 1971), 39–49.

FIELD, D. "Accountability for the Physical Educator," *Journal of Health, Physical Education and Recreation.* 44; 2 (February 1973), 37–38.

FRANKS, D., AND H. DEUTSCH. *Evaluating Performance in Physical Education.* New York: Academic Press, 1973.

GLASS, G. V. "The Many Faces of Educational Accountability," *Phi Delta Kappan*, June 1972, pp. 636–39.

GOLDER, P. "A New Physical Education Report Card," *The Physical Educator.* 26 (December 1969), 162–64.

GUSTAFSON, W. F. "A Look at Evaluative Criteria in Physical Education," *The Physical Educator.* 20 (December 1963), 172–73.

Illinois Office of the Superintendent of Public Instruction. *Action Goals for the Seventies: An Agenda for Illinois Education* (2nd ed.) Springfield, Ill.: OSPI, November 1973.

JEWETT, A. E., ed. *Curriculum Design: Purposes and Processes of Physical Education Teaching-Learning.* Washington, D.C.: American Alliance for Health, Physical Education and Recreation, 1974.

KAUFMAN, R. *Educational System Planning,* Englewood Cliffs, N.J.: Prentice-Hall, Inc., 1972.

MAGER, R. F. *Developing Attitude Toward Learning.* Palo Alto, Calif.: Fearon Publishers, 1968.

MAGER, R. F., AND P. PIPE. *Analyzing Performance Problems.* Belmont, Calif.: Fearon Publishers, 1970.

ROSENSHINE, B., AND B. MCGAW. "Issues in Assessing Teacher Accountability in Public Education," *Phi Delta Kappan*, 53 (June 1972), 640–43.

RUSSELL, J. D. *Modular Instruction.* Minneapolis, Minn.: Burgess Publishing Co., 1974.

STAKE, R. E. "The Countenance of Educational Evaluation," *Teachers College Record.* 68 (1967), 523–40.

STUFFLEBEAM, D. "Evaluation as Enlightenment for Decision Making," *Improving Educational Assessment and an Inventory of Measures of Affective Behavior.* Association for Supervision and Curriculum Development, NEA, 1969.

13

Changing:
Making
It Happen

Learner's Diagnosis

Directions: Read the questions below. Write out, discuss, or mentally review the answers. If you believe that you know the information, check the "yes" column. If you are not sure of the answer, check the "no" column. After reading the questions and deciding your knowledge, check the accuracy of your answers by reading the summary at the end of this chapter. If you answer a question incorrectly, change your answer to the appropriate column.

Can you

Yes	No	Questions
		1. Explain three ways change is initiated?
		2. List four roadblocks to change?
		3. List three change models or perspectives?
		4. Explain five strategies to activate a change model?
		5. Explain the model best suited for changing on a small scale?
		6. List at least five decisions needed to plan for a change?
		7. Explain the role of students in planning for change?
		8. Give the two major components to bring about change?
		9. Explain the extent to which change should be initiated?
		10. List the progression for gradually preparing students to be responsible for their learning?

Suggested Prescription

Directions: Count the number of checks you have placed in the "yes" column. When the percentages are determined, you may increase your knowledge and skill by using the suggested Learning Program activities recommended in the Input and Practice columns.

Results	Input	Practice
More than 80%	#1, 6	#4
60% to 80%	#1, 4 or 5	#1, 4
40% to 60%	#1, 2, 4 or 5	#1, 2 or 3, 4
Less than 40%	#1, 2, 3, 4	#1, 2, 3, 4

Learning Program

Directions: It is suggested that the reader attempt to follow any or all suggestions in this learning program. These are designed to improve knowledge and understanding of planned change to assist in implementing individualized instruction.

Proposed Learning Objective: The learner will be able to change from class-centered traditional teaching to individualized humanistic instruction.

Input:
*1. Read Chapter 13 of this book.
2. Read Van Dalen, "The Anatomy of Change," *Physical Educator*, XXIV, (March 1967), 3–6.
3. Read selected references at the end of this chapter.
4. Prepare a list of questions about your concerns and problems anticipated in changing from traditional teaching to an innovative approach. Discuss these questions with a teacher.
5. Observe a class or school utilizing an innovative educational instructional approach. Identify changes and problems. Discuss with a staff member of that school.
6. Plan an input of your own.

Practice:
1. Develop and implement a plan to effect a procedural change presently being used by a peer, teacher, or parent. Discuss results with a peer.

*Highly recommended.

2. Select a school of your choice. Identify the decisions needed to change from a traditional teaching approach to individualization.

3. Draw up a brief questionnaire designed to determine student concerns and feelings about class-centered traditional teaching and individualized instruction.

4. Plan a practice of your own.

Evaluation: You will be able to plan for implementing a change to individualized humanistic instruction. The plan should identify and provide for the following:

1. Change model
2. Change strategy
3. Preparation of students, school, facilities, and self for change
4. Procedures for remedying possible failures

Implementing a humanistic individualized instructional approach for facilitating the learning of physical education may seem like a monumental task. Any change is filled with uncertainty and requires a great deal of effort to prepare the materials and involve personnel, as well as to convince those whose support is needed to effect the change. However, change is inevitable; the only question is, "how soon!" Hellison states:

> Both the physical education profession and the world of sports are bending to the winds of progressive thought. In physical education, scholarship has taken a firm hold, and everything from traditional approaches to physical training to locker room slogans are under scrutiny. The newer textbooks in the field demonstrate that physical education has arrived in academic circles, not only in exercise physiology but in sport sociology, psychology, philosophy, and history as well.[1]

Researchers who assess and develop new approaches often are bitter that practitioners fail to implement what they develop. In turn, practitioners lament that what is "developed" can't be implemented for a myriad of reasons ranging from finances, administrative support, facilities, time, and the ability of the students to learn under different conditions.

Indeed, there are many impediments standing in the way of change. For the facilitator, personal rewards will not come before the change is

---

[1]Donald R. Hellison, *Humanistic Physical Education* (Englewood Cliffs, N.J.: Prentice-Hall, Inc., 1973), pp. 74–75.

effected. Student learning and satisfaction will be the only sustaining force. Any suggestion for change implies that something can be done better. The immediate reaction is one of mistrust; the power structure would like to believe that what exists is satisfactory! Furthermore, the magnitude of the educational system dictates a bureaucratic structure which, of course, requires approval for decisions by several agencies; a rejection by any one department or committee usually defeats the idea or plan. Another deterrent is the lack of funds to support a change, although this is often a convenient "cop-out." As the old axiom holds, "Where there's a will, there's a way." And finally, many innovations fail because the school, students, and teachers are not properly prepared to conduct, receive, or support a change. Changing is work. It must be recognized that the status quo is comfortable and is especially easy when no threat to excel is forthcoming from within the system.

Change occurs in one of three ways: (1) nondirect, (2) reactive, and (3) planned. The *nondirected* change is often fomented by noneducators. An example of nondirected change may be the support and encouragement by the business community for schools to utilize the management by objectives systems. *Reactive* change is responding to outside pressures. Physical educators often respond to the pressure applied by legislators to delete and to withdraw support of programs. Although pressure from outside may bring meaningful change, often the preparation and planning is not sufficient to ensure successful application of the change, and therefore many good ideas fail. Furthermore, the failure of a change plan often serves as an excuse for many practitioners to avoid any attempt at change. Thus, the only sure way to bring about change is to *plan* for it. Few would argue about the need for wise and sufficient planning; but unfortunately, few teachers or school systems arrange for adequate time and proper procedures to plan for change. Horvat and Clark lament:

> Most students of change do not view teachers as creators and developers of change programs or innovations. Rather teachers are seen as relatively passive consumers of, or targets for, change and innovation. If teachers are to be more than just consumers, they will need to improve their competency enormously in the area of change, while at the same time increasing their power, as professionals, within the educational establishment.[2]

PROCESS FOR CHANGE

The motivation for change may be generated within or outside the educational community. The initial thrust begins with an awareness of

2John J. Horvat and David L. Clark, "Educational Change," in *Teacher's Handbook*, eds. Dwight W. Allen and Eli Seifman (Glenview, Illinois: Scott, Foresman and Company, 1971), p. 616.

the need to alter a process or to solve a problem. If that awareness does not resolve the problem, then dissatisfaction develops and continues as social pressure on those responsible to "do something!" When the problem becomes a serious threat to culture and society, a crisis results which often brings to bear enough power to force a change. The final source of power usually brings massive changes in which both desirable as well as undesirable practices may result.

Although many models or perspectives exist for pursuing change, three processes are most plausible: (1) social interaction, (2) research, and (3) problem-solving. *Social interaction* perspectives hold that force for change occurs outside the educational community. The procedures followed are similar to those used in advertising. An awareness of an innovation is created. Merits of the change proposal are expressed, and encouragement is given to try out the product or procedure. A social interaction model relies on legislation and organizational forces to be exerted to bring about change. The *research* perspective rests upon the scientific process of problem identification, investigation of remedies, development and experimentation of solutions, and dissemination of the change. The expense involved in this process for change usually forces the change effort to be widespread and fairly universal. Research efforts usually receive impetus and support from external agencies. The *problem-solving* model has been developed and promoted by Ron Lippett and Associates. The effort and thrust come from within the agency. Little need for global acceptance is sought; therefore, the problem solving is well suited for autonomous units. Procedural steps begin with recognition of a need to change, development of a relevant solution, clarification of the problem, weighing of alternative plans, development of action plans, and stabilization of the change.

Any of the three processes for change may be followed, but all depend upon some strategy that will force action. The pressure applied may have economic, political, organizational, educational, and cognitive sources. Horvat and Clark[3] claim that the change system to be selected depends somewhat upon the goal of the change. For example, social interaction processes may work best when laws are invoked and widespread social acceptance is sought. The research, development, and diffusion model is best utilized by large agencies such as government, big organizations, and universities when new knowledge is being sought. Organizational and training strategy may be most useful for problem-solving processes. Regardless of the process employed, power is needed to bring about any sizable change effort.

[3]Horvat and Clark, p. 616.

GETTING STARTED

Implementing an individualized instructional approach does not require tremendous power or change on a massive scale. What is implied is that change from a traditional group-oriented system will require a problem-solving process with the energy being generated from within the physical education department or from a single instructor. Little economic, political, organizational or research strategy will be needed. What will be required is knowledge and skill in utilizing the process. This book is designed to provide that kind of assistance.

If you are convinced that the humanistic individualized instructional approach for teaching physical education has merit, then 50 percent of what is needed to change has been accomplished. Unfortunately, the other half of the task involves a tremendous amount of personal commitment. You may act on this commitment if administrative approval is obtained. However, approval may not be necessary since traditionally teaching methodology is the prerogative of the instructor. A number of decisions will be needed to guide planning. These decisions are dependent upon the amount of space, facilities, equipment, time, student ability and uniqueness, personal preparation time, appropriate subject matter, available media, and the extent of the change sought.

Students need to be involved in the change process if they are to be partners in the teaching-learning encounter. They need to be aware of the value, the issues, goals, and alternatives. Their help in evaluating the initial effort during and after the change is crucial to planning for improved results. Hellison[4] suggests the following progression to prepare students to take responsibility for their learning:

1. Begin with the method that students are accustomed to. This will probably be the command method.
2. Vary the pace requirements. The teacher decides the activity and amount; the student decides the time needed to perform.
3. Vary pace and quantity of activity. Teacher decides the activity and the student decides the time and amount of activity needed.
4. Provide optional practice procedures for the goals decided by the teacher.
5. Provide optional practice procedures to achieve optional instructional goals.
6. Provide optional practice procedures to achieve optional terminal objectices within the global goal framework.
7. Give student freedom to plan, execute, and evaluate learning the activity.

[4]Hellison, *Humanistic Physical Education*, pp. 91–92.

Figure 13–1 illustrates the recommended procedures to gradually release more responsibility and freedom to the student. However, remember that not all students are at the same stage of readiness for responsibility. It cannot be assumed that the pace at which progression to the final stage is reached will be similar for all. It is suggested that teachers utilize these procedures within a few units of instruction prior to instituting the change to individualization. This preparation time not only will serve to ready the students, but will assist the facilitator to learn more about the students, the teaching-learning environment, and structure of the change to individualization.

Since preparing an individualized instruction unit is time-consuming, it is not wise to become too heavily burdened at the onset. Perhaps one to three units may be developed each year until all courses normally taught are developed on an individualized basis. If your schedule is so demanding that insufficient preparation time is available, it may be

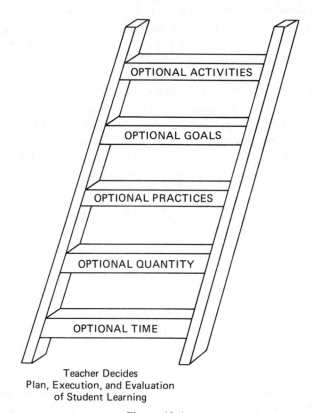

Teacher Decides
Plan, Execution, and Evaluation
of Student Learning

Figure 13–1

Student Freedom to Plan, Execute, and Evaluate Learning

worth seeking some released time or summer employment to develop the needed plans.

The change to a more contemporary approach need not be system-wide. If a singular attempt is successful, some colleagues may wish to follow your lead; others may rationalize their need to adhere to their present institutional processes or they may attempt to undermine your success. Seldom is change completely successful. As the initiator of change, you must keep in mind that you and your students are inexperienced with the approach. Every attempt must be made to determine the causes of failure and to develop plans to correct them. No inventor or innovator has ever been able to go from the drawing board to immediate success.

It is hoped that the process outlined in this book will serve as a guide to the development of plans and learning programs best suited for your specific teaching-learning situation.

To change is a challenge—it is like treading upon thin ice with many uncertain spots that are filled with insecurity and occasionally failure. The profession of physical education needs to have an image that provides the values of the product to all students. It cannot solely cater to those who have ready aptitude for acquiring a product that only the teacher wishes to "sell"! Only when the professional practitioner recognizes that students, products, and processes can and should vary will the professional be more secure.

CASE STUDY

SETTING:	Small community high school of 2,000 students
CLASSES:	1,000 girls, four classes per hour, daily physical education, class-centered teaching
COMMUNITY:	Industrial and conservative
FACULTY:	Five teachers (one with fifteen years' experience, two with seven years' experience, and two with three years')

An instructor with three years' experience desired to individualize instruction. She discussed her plans with her department head, who was convinced that the plan would not work, but permitted the teacher to attempt it. The new "facilitator" spent a great deal of personal time developing learning modules, finding media, and preparing the gymnasium. The program model was completely individualized. Students were diagnosed, conferenced, and guided. Grades were to be determined by the total points earned through the various completed modules.

However, students were not well prepared for the freedom given to them. Many were confused about the process, and their questions required a great deal of the facilitator's time to answer. Often students practiced skills already learned and time was wasted by "fooling around." Halfway through the unit, the facilitator instituted a tournament and completed the unit with tests of skill and written exams. Students were admonished as lazy and not responsible.

The "innovative, frustrated facilitator" declared to colleagues that individualized instruction was "ivory-tower stuff" and could not work with "these kids." However, after re-examination she decided to try again with a less complete approach. Self-contained, interaction, and discovery tasks with varied achievement levels were developed. The facilitator was the chief source of information, although several media alternatives were available. Students were given guidance and coaching as needed. Grades were criterion-based. This approach was much more successful and satisfying to both the facilitator and students.

SUMMARY

Implementing change is a difficult task because of the effort and insecurity inherent in the process. In addition, bureaucracy, ignorance, fear, and insufficient time make change difficult. Change occurs in one of three ways: (1) nondirect, fomented by noneducators, (2) reactive, forced by outside groups, and (3) planned change from within the institution.

Motivation to change begins with an awareness of the need to change. The power of the thrust is in ratio to the degree of threat to culture and society. Three models are most prevalent as change processes: (1) social interaction, which utilizes outside pressures and relies upon legislation and organizational power; (2) development, research, and diffusion which is expensive and utilizes external agencies for implementation; and (3) problem-solving, which relies on intra-agency effort and can operate on a small scale. Any of the three processes may be followed, but each depends upon some strategy to bring about action. The pressure may involve political, economic, organizational, and educational strategies. The goals of the change usually dictate the source of pressure. The social interaction model is best implemented when laws are evoked and widespread acceptance is crucial. The development, research, diffusion model is utilized by large agencies and organizations when new information or innovations are sought. Small-scale changes generated from within the institution are served well by the problem-solving model utilizing organization and training strategy.

The problem-solving model is recommended as the vehicle for changing from group instruction to individualized instruction. The change can be accomplished by a single instructor and needs little if any economic, political, research, or organizational assistance. Awareness of the value and need to change and the commitment to accomplish the change are the major components needed.

Commitment to change is translated into deciding the nature of the planning based upon student and institutional resources. Students need to be prepared for the change by gradually being introduced to increasing responsibilities for learning. The progression may span the following: pace, quantity, practice, goals, and activity options. Students need to be partners with the teacher in the change. They need to be oriented to the process and consulted concerning the goals and dimensions of the plans.

It is not recommended that the complete program be instantly converted to the individualized humanistic instructional approach if the students are not used to the approach. Gradual induction will bring better plans and student and staff acceptance. Failures are to be expected and remedies sought. It is imperative that members of the profession seek a change process whereby all the students may be winners of the values of physical education.

REFERENCES

FRYMIER, J. *A School for Tomorrow*. Berkeley, Calif.: McCutchan Publishing Co., 1973.

GREER, M., AND B. RUBENSTEIN. *Will the Real Teacher Please Stand Up?* Pacific Palisades, Calif.: Goodyear Publishing Co., Inc., 1972.

HAVELOCK, R. "Planning for Innovation." Institute for Social Research, University of Michigan, Ann Arbor, 1973.

HEINRICH, J. *How to Bring About Change in a School System*. Chicago: Science Research Associates, Inc., 1966.

HELLISON, D. *Humanistic Physical Education*. Englewood Cliffs, N.J.: Prentice-Hall, Inc., 1973.

HORVAT, J., AND D. CLARK. "Educational Change," *Teacher's Handbook*, D. Allen and E. Seifman, eds. Glenview, Illinois: Scott, Foresman, and Company, 1971.

LIPPETT, R., J. WATSON AND B. WESTLEY. *The Dynamics of Planned Change*. New York: Harcourt Brace Jovanovich, Inc., 1958.

MILLER, R. *Respectives in Educational Change*. New York: Appleton-Century-Crofts, 1967.

POSTMAN, N., AND C. WEINGARTER. *The Soft Revolution; A Student Handbook for Turning Schools Around*. New York: The Delacorte Press, 1971.

——— *Teaching as a Subversive Activity*. The Delacorte Press, 1967.

REICH, C. *The Greening of America*. New York: Random House, Inc., 1970.

VAN DALEN, D. "The Anatomy of Change," *Physical Educator*. XXIV (March 1967), 3–6.

14

Sample Individualized Instructional Units and Modules

ELEMENTARY SCHOOL I*

SCHOOL: Mill Street Elementary School
                Naperville, Illinois
FACILITATOR: Ruth Hamm
PRINCIPAL: Robert Hillenbrand

Activity: Rope jumping (third grade)

Objectives:

1. Students will be able to extend their physical endurance to jump rope.
2. Students will be able to jump rope in a variety of ways.
3. Students will enjoy jumping rope.

Process:

The students engaged in physical education twice a week. The individualized unit in rope jumping was planned for four lessons. Students were diagnosed by being asked to count the number of consecutive jumps they could make without an error. They were assigned to one of three stations based on the following results:

*Since each educational situation is unique, variation in the procedures to process individualized learning will occur. On the following pages are samples of plans developed and utilized in activity and theory classes at all educational levels. Each program was implemented in the school indicated.

Less than 25 jumps	Flea
25–50 jumps	Jumping Beans
More than 50 jumps	Astro Jumpers

At each station, students received a program suited for their entry level. The program was printed on both sides of a single piece of paper which was folded in half. The front and back of fold for the Fleas appeared as follows:

FLEA

12 points

Activity chosen   Name _____

Number — Points   Class _____

_____ _____

_____ _____

_____ _____   *Show time — 2 points*
                         circle — yes   no

_____ _____

_____ _____

_____ _____

Signatures

Student _____

Teacher _____
                    When completed

Things to remember

1. Any activity may be chosen in any order.
2. For help, check with:
     a. charts on the wall
     b. ask a friend
     c. ask the teacher
3. When activity is achieved, put the number and the points on the front of this sheet, on the blanks provided.

The Fleas were expected to achieve 12 points or six different jumps; the Jumping Beans were expected to achieve 18 points or to complete nine different kinds of jumps; and the Astro Jumpers were expected to complete 24 points and twelve different kinds of jumps. Of the list below, only the first twelve jumps were included in the Flea program, jumps 1 to 18 for the Jumping Beans, and the entire list for the Astro Jumpers.

SINGLE JUMP ROPE

1.	2 pts.	Jump on toes of both feet	60X
2.	2 pts.	Jump on right foot and also jump on left foot	15X
3.	2 pts.	Jump on toes of both feet	50X
4.	2 pts.	Jump on right foot and also jump on left foot	12X
5.	2 pts.	Left leg high, knee straight, toes pointed, jump on other foot	25X
6.	2 pts.	Rocker leap forward on left foot, leap backward on other foot	30X
7.	2 pts.	Rocker leap forward on left foot, backward on other foot	25X
8.	2 pts.	Figure 8, swing rope in front and side of body to form a figure 8 (alternate this with 2 jumps). This figure takes 4 counts.	Count of 32
9.	2 pts.	2 rope turns per jump (this necessitates very fast turning)	6X
10.	2 pts.	Move sideward right 4 steps, then left 4 steps	10X
11.	2 pts.	Work up a routine; use a combination of above, repeating each 4 times before starting another	Use 4 activities
12.	2 pts.	No. 1 turns rope forward; No. 2 runs in, faces partner, and both jump	10X
13.	2 pts.	Same as above but turn rope backward	10X
14.	2 pts.	No. 1 turns rope forward; No. 2 runs in, turns back to partner	10X
15.	2 pts.	Partners stand side by side inside hands joined and outside hands turning ropes	10X
16.	2 pts.	No. 1 turns rope forward; No. 2 runs in, faces No. 1, and executes quarter, half, and full turns on each jump	10X

17.	2 pts.	No. 1 turns rope forward; No. 2 runs in, turns back to No. 1, and bounces and catches a ball	10X
18.	2 pts.	Partners stand side by side, clasp left hands, face opposite directions, and each turns a rope in right hand (for one, the rope will be turning forward, for the other it will be turning backward)	5X
19.	2 pts.	Same as No. 18, but clasp right hands	5X
20.	2 pts.	Partners stand side by side and jump with inside knee raised	5X
21.	2 pts.	Work up routine using the ideas from above	Use at least 4 activities
22.	2 pts.	Alternate straight jump with cross-arm jump	12X

ELEMENTARY SCHOOL II

SCHOOL: Campanelle Elementary School
                 Schaumburg, Illinois
FACILITATOR: Donna White
PRINCIPAL: Susin McCann

Activity: Track and field (fifth grade)

Objectives:

Global Goal: To be able to participate in a track meet as a contestant and as a scorer
Students will be able to:

Perform one running event (50-yard dash, 75-yard dash, 440-yard run, 600-yard run, 440-yard relay)
Perform one throwing event (shot put, softball throw)
Perform one jumping event (high jump, standing long jump, running long jump)
Score for one running event
Score for one throwing event
Score for one jumping event

Equipment:

High jump: 2 high jump standards, 2 crossbars, 2 landing pits
Running long jump: 1 sand pit, 1 cloth tape, 1 rake
Standing long jump: 2 mats with starting line and measurements taped on
Softball throw: 9 softballs, 1 cloth tape, 6 cones to mark running area set at 10-foot intervals, 1 short rope to use as starting line
Shot put: 3 shots, 1 cloth tape, 1 rope to use as circle to help place small stakes to mark the distance of each put
Dashes: 3 lanes painted on blacktop drive
Runs and relay: area in grass marked with sawdust, 3 batons, 1 clock

Media:

The following equipment will be placed on a wagon to store and to move to activity area:

battery operated slide viewer and slides
transparency viewer and slides
books

Block Plan:

Monday	Wednesday	Friday
Orientation to unit and Method Presentation of: 1. High Jump, 2. Running long jump 3. Standing long jump 4. Use of equipment 5. Scoring and record-ing 6. Media	Presentation of: 1. Softball Throw 2. Shot 3. Running events 4. Use of equipment 5. Scoring and record-ing 6. Media	Pick up any of presenta-tion not covered in first two days. Experiment with events to find area of special-ization.
Monday	Wednesday	Friday
Experiment Conferences and agreement cards	Experiment Conferences and agreement cards	Carry out agreements Conferences and guidance
Monday	Wednesday	Friday
Carry out agreement Conferences and guidance	⟶	
Monday	Wednesday	Friday
	Sign up for events ⟶	Meet Two hours all fifth grades (with classroom teach-er's help)

Management:

Equipment: To be moved and set up with student help

Record Keeping: Each student will have a daily log to keep track of his or her progress; pencils will be kept in a box near each event area and will be returned after use.

Each student will have an agreement card to be filled out at the time of the first conference (sample below). On this card his goals will be stated, and the card will be kept on file in the library wagon. When a child reaches his or her goals, this will be recorded.

Goal Cards: These cards, describing basic rules for each event, tell-ing where to go for more information, will be kept near each event area. There will be three copies of each. Directions for scoring each event are on the back of each card.

Field Layout:

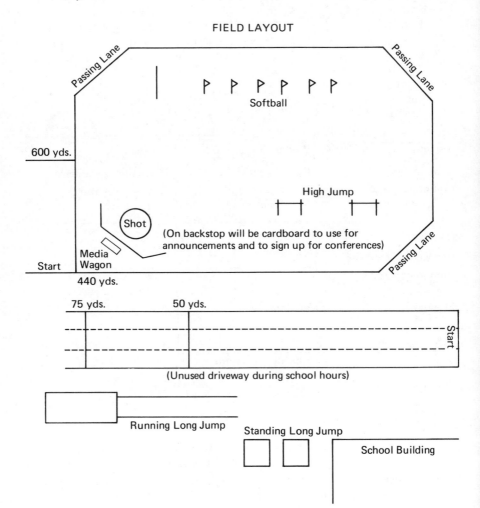

FIELD LAYOUT

Agreement:

TRACK AND FIELD AGREEMENT

Purpose: So that I may be able to participate in a track meet as a contestant and a scorer.

Teacher Goals: Every student will take part in one running event, one throwing event, and one jumping event. Every student will also score for a classmate in one running event, one throwing event, and one jumping event.

Student Goals: Recorded on chart on back.

Date Started   _____

Conferences   _____

_____

_____

Date Completed   _____

_____   _____

Student Signature   Teacher Signature

	Starting score	My goal	I did it!	I scored it!	I scored for:
Running Events					
50-yard dash					
75-yard dash					
220-yard dash					
600-yard run walk					
440-yard relay					
Jumping Events					
High jump					
Standing long jump					
Running long jump					
Throwing Events					
Softball throw					
Shot put					

JUNIOR HIGH SCHOOL I

SCHOOL: Simmons Junior High School
                 Aurora, Illinois

FACILITATOR: Tom Vida, Department Chairman

PRINCIPAL: Gordon Postlewaite

Activities: The following activities are presently offered:

1. Archery	17. Balance beam
2. Badminton	18. Modern dance
3. Basketball	19. Ping-pong
4. Bowling	20. Physical fitness
5. Boat safety	21. Shuffleboard
6. Cageball	22. Soccer
7. Camping and outdoor education	23. Softball
8. First aid	24. Tennis
9. Golf	25. Touch football
10. Side horse	26. Volleyball
11. Vaulting (boys & girls)	27. Weight lifting
12. Parallel bars	28. Wrestling
13. Uneven bars	29. Handball
14. Trampoline	30. Horsemanship
15. Floor exercise	31. Jogging
16. Tumbling	32. Paddleball
	33. Swimming

After completing sufficient skill and cognitive concepts, students form their own teams.

Objectives:

1. To improve students' reading ability and understanding of the English language.
2. To teach game strategies and techniques.
3. To provide activities that will improve student knowledge of leisure-time experiences.
4. To develop self-discipline through self-directed learning.
5. To provide neuromuscular development that will be measured by grade, skills, sense of rhythm, and improved reaction time.
6. To create situations that encourage self-confidence, sociability, initiative, and a feeling of belonging.

7. To provide challenges that give students the opportunity to overcome difficulties, experience thrills out of teamwork, and develop an increased appreciation of athletic experience.

8. To meet the inner needs of the individual by means of self-directed activities.

9. To provide immediate and positive reinforcement, which will improve the student's self-image.

10. To involve parents to foster a better understanding of the physical education program.

Process:

The following are the students' responsibilities:

1. All students must work on physical fitness, at their own level, every day, all year.

2. All students must work on tumbling and must pass nineteen lessons.

3. All students must complete or make reasonable progress in two team sport units.

4. All students must complete or make reasonable progress in three different individual sports.

5. All students must complete first aid course.

The computer-monitored program offers both familiar and new experiences. Students may fulfill the objectives of the course through a variety of instructional techniques such as: listening to and looking at a sound page, viewing a wall chart, viewing a transparency, listening to a cassette, signing out and using equipment within the school facilities, using appropriate off-campus facilities such as bowling alley, reading a book, and receiving instructions from a teacher, student teacher, or even a student assistant.

Every task is clearly defined by a performance objective. Within each performance objective the who, what, where, why, and how are described to the learner. Most physical skills are supplemented by cognitive concepts. Students learn while an activity is performed. There are no letter grades given. Each student has individual conferences with the teacher and is given a computer print-out sheet that indicates the progress the student is making. There are no group calisthenics. All students are required to work eight minutes a day on their own physical fitness. Equipment is handled through a central distribution system, and an equipment manager distributes and collects all equipment. The student's progress or history is kept by the computer. All students begin work on the fourth level and may work up as high as the twelfth level. The following year, instead of repeating the same schedule, students simply review what they have accomplished and then start up where they left off.

Boys and girls work together in the various activities.

Students come into the gym, change clothes, turn their tags to indicate that they are present, and immediately begin eight minutes of a physical fitness circuit. As each student finishes the exercises, he or she works on the individual program of study that has been selected. If the teaching-learning unit (TLU) calls for reading a book, listening to a tape or a sound page, the student leaves the gym, enters the resource center across the hall, and completes the tasks listed. A typical TLU is as follows:

FORWARD ROLL

You will be able to do 2 forward rolls correctly and with good form.

Use:	Physical Education Handbook	*Do*:	Read pages 1–4.
Use:	Sound Page	*Do*:	Listen and view.
Use:	Classmate	*Do*:	Ask a classmate to help judge your form.
Use:	Teacher	*Do*:	Demonstrate to your teacher

The student checks a daily computer print-out to see which TLU's have been passed. If a TLU is not passed, next to the student's name will read something like "not mastered, repeat TLU #3409." This takes the student back to the previous TLU for review and then another attempt at the noncompleted TLU. After determining what is to be done that day, the students are on their own, and the teacher is there for advice, assistance, and evaluation.

JUNIOR HIGH SCHOOL II

SCHOOL: Edgewood Junior High School
                St. Paul, Minnesota
FACILITATOR: James B. Danner
PRINCIPAL: Philip Leonard

TITLE: Flag football—Holding the ball
LEVEL: (S)
WRITTEN BY: J. Danner
LEARNING PACKAGE NO.   C-102
DEPARTMENT: H.F.R.

---

1. You will hold a football the proper way with the hand over the far end and the near end tucked under the upper arms for your Post-test.
2. Do at least 2 of the things listed:
   A. In the resource center see the picture of holding the ball.
   B. Practice holding the football.
   C. Ask a fellow student for a demonstration.
3. Self-test: Tell the aide of work done.
4. Post-test: See a school aide.
   A. If you do this skill, go on to another.
   B. If you are <u>not</u> able to do this skill, repeat the things listed.

HIGH SCHOOL I

SCHOOL: Regina High School
                 Minneapolis, Minnesota
FACILITATOR: K. Cash Luck
PRINCIPAL: Sister Mary Eileen

Activities: (35 possible, sample below)

Ice skating	Fishing	Outward bound
Karate	Horseback riding	Weight control
Snowmobiling	Teaching swimming	Coaching softball team
Camp counseling	Canoe trip	

Process:

In order to be approved for participating in the individualized study program, a girl must:

1. Demonstrate her ability to handle freedom responsibly.
2. Possess enough self-motivation and drive to follow through in order to complete a successful learning experience.
3. Show she has the ability to organize, execute, and evaluate her project.
4. Research, write, and submit her contract for approval. The study must be completed before a student is excused from a quarter of on-campus physical education.

The application lists the student's objectives along with those of her parents and an off-campus facilitator who is an expert in the area of the study being undertaken. Previous experience, time needed to achieve objectives, and support for feasibility of the project are included.

HIGH SCHOOL II

SCHOOL: Omaha Public Schools
                 Omaha, Nebraska
FACILITATOR: Robert Schrader, Supervisor of Physical Education
SUPERINTENDENT: Dr. Owen Knutzen

Activity: Basketball

Objectives: (Global)

    1. To improve self-concept
    2. To learn how to learn
    3. To improve physical fitness
    4. To develop helping, caring behavior
    5. To increase knowledge of physical self
    6. To maintain good health
    7. To improve psychomotor skills
    8. To enjoy physical activity

Process:

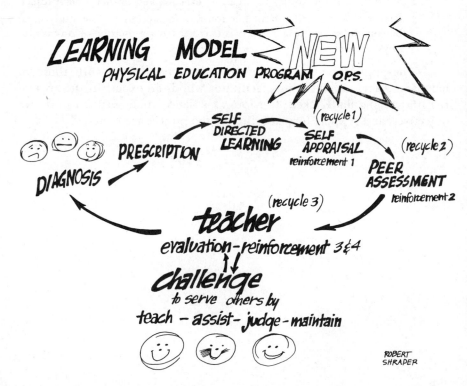

OMAHA PUBLIC SCHOOLS
BUILDING BLOCKS TO BASKETBALL SUCCESS

Girl

Name _____ Age _____ Boy _____ Grade _____

School _____ Height _____ Weight _____

Starting date _____ Completion date _____

Box Score			
Psycho-Motor	Cognitive	Challenge	
Begin	Begin	Teach	Assist
Finish	Finish		
Success	Success		

1. Cognitive 1–2 Orientation	8. Psycho- 1–3–4 Motor Dribbling	15. Psycho- 1–4 Motor Rebounding
2. Psycho-Motor 4 Stopping	9. Psycho- 1–4–5 Motor Set shot	16. Cognitive 1–2 Rules Girls A, Boys B
3. Psycho-Motor 4 Pivot	10. Psycho- 1–4–5 Motor Lay-up shot	17. Cognitive 1–2–4 Offensive tactics Girls A, Boys B
4. Psycho-Motor 1–4 Vertical jumping	11. Psycho- 1–4–5 Motor Hook shot	18. Cognitive 1–2–4 Defensive tactics Girls A, Boys B
5. Psycho- 1–5 Motor Push pass and catch	12. Psycho- 1–4–5 Motor Reverse lay-up	19. Psycho-Motor 5 Team play
6. Psycho- 1–4–5 Motor Overhead pass and catch	13. Psycho- 1–4–5 Motor Jump shot	20. Cognitive 1–2–4 Officiating Girls A, Boys B
7. Psycho- 1–4–5 Motor Baseball pass and catch	14. Psycho- 1–5 Motor Ball manipulation	21. Psycho-Motor 5 Officiating

PHY-PAK BASKETBALL 2

1. *Content Classification*

   Basketball stopping

2. *Purpose*

   To provide you with learning activities that will enable you to demonstrate correct stopping procedures.

3. *Learning Objective*

   You will be able to demonstrate correct stopping form for the stride stop and the scoot stop.

4. *Diagnostic Test*

   Run at full speed for 15 feet, then stop abruptly demonstrating, first, correct stride stops form, and second, correct scoot stops form.

5. *Taxonomy Category*

   Psycho-Motor 2–4

6. *Learning Activities*

   Choose any or all of the listed learning activities that you believe will help you accomplish your learning objective. (3)

   _____A. View the basketball loop film, then practice.

   _____B. Read page 23, "Stopping," *Physical Education Activities for College Men and Women.*

   _____C. Ask a classmate who has mastered stopping techniques to help you learn the skill.

   _____D. Consult with your teacher.

   _____E. View the wall chart.

7. *Self-Test*

   Ask a classmate to watch you demonstrate the two stops. If he believes you have mastered the skill, go to the teacher for the final test.

8. *Final Test*

   Ask your teacher to judge your demonstration of the stride stop and the scoot stop.

9. *Challenge Activities*

   A. Volunteer to teach a classmate the stride stop and the scoot stop.

   B. Judge a classmate's self-test.

HIGH SCHOOL III

SCHOOL: Inner City High School
                    Chicago, Illinois

FACILITATOR: Marian E. Kneer

Activity: Badminton

Description:

The course was taught by a university professor with extensive public school experience to a class of 35 senior girls with no previous badminton experience. The school is in a deprived neighborhood with meager facilities and equipment (three singles-width courts with 3 feet of space between wall and end line, 17 racquets, and 12 shuttlecocks). The course consisted of fifteen lessons of 40-minute periods.

Objectives:

1. Students will be able to play a doubles game in badminton.
2. Students will be able to execute all major badminton strokes with 50 percent accuracy and consistency.
3. Students will be able to pass rules test with 70 percent or better accuracy.
4. Students will be able to share equipment and help each other as evidenced by class conduct.
5. Students will enjoy badminton as evidenced by their eagerness to play and reluctance not to participate.

Diagnosis:

Students were asked to respond to a questionnaire concerning their ability. No skill or knowledge tests were given as summative evaluation.

Prescription:

A schedule for all fifteen lessons was posted, along with directions.

Schedule:

Day 1 .... Explain plans and diagnose.

Day 2 .... Conferences, play, and begin work on skills.

Days 3–7 .... Each student spent one-third time playing, one-third practicing, and one-third securing information from pictures on learning module.

Days 8–15 .... One-third of time was spent playing in tournament and two thirds working on learning modules.

Guidance:

Ten learning modules were developed, placed on posters, and taped on the wall. A module was developed for each of the following topics:

Equipment, lines, courts	Smashes
Clears	Defensive play
Drives	Offensive play
Net shots	Game play
Service	Rules

Evaluation:

Each learning program was valued at 5 points. Attendance was rewarded by granting a point each day the student was present. The maximum number of points possible was 65. Grades were based as follows:

A = 45+
B = 38+
C = 31+
D = 24+

Sample Module:

---

2 BADMINTON SERVES

Low, short serve

Learn by:

1. Study pictures below, and/or
2. Check chart to find a student who has completed serves, and ask him or her to help you, and/or
3. Ask instructor for help, and/or
4. Watch demonstration and explanation on May 8 (Friday).

Practice by:
Find a classmate in your group to help you. Hit ten low short serves over the net, under the rope, and land on the target.

Prove your skill by:
Hitting five out of ten low short serves which go over the net, under the rope, and land on the target.
(Check off #2 after your name when you can do the above.)

This system was kept simple since the students had never experienced the process before, had never learned to share equipment, and had low reading ability.

HIGH SCHOOL OR COLLEGE

SCHOOL: Purdue University
                    West LaFayette, Indiana
FACILITATOR: Dr. Anthony Annarino

Activity: Archery

Process:

Students are informed of the values of individualized instruction and, if unfamiliar with independent learning, are given experience in practicing more on their own before attempting the program. Each skill lesson is accompanied by a statement of the purpose, the behavioral objective, proposals for practice, and evaluation. The course is preceded by a written and skill pre-test to diagnose and to provide students with norms for determination of their status. Instruction is guided by an I.I.P. (Individualized Instructional Packet).

Sample Instructional Core (Abstracted from Archery I.I.P.*)

LESSON FOUR

Skill: Shooting and Error Analysis

Student information:

If you can overcome your errors, your shooting ability and scoring will improve. It is important to know what causes an error. It may be due to your stance, grip, nocking, drawing, anchor point, aiming and holding, releasing, or follow-through. Shoot with a partner and analyze each other's shooting errors.

Purpose:

You should know what causes a shooting error and be able to make the proper corrections for scoring consistency.

INDEPENDENT WRITTEN ASSIGNMENT

Resource Materials:
    Text _____Pages _____

Matching: Match the error column to the cause column.

---

*Anthony Annarino, *Individualized Instructional Programs: Archery, Badminton, Bowling, Golf, Tennis* (Englewood Cliffs, N.J.: Prentice-Hall, Inc., 1973).

	Cause		*Error*
___ 1.	Hips and shoulders open to the target	a.	Left
___ 2.	Anchoring high on the cheek	b.	Right
___ 3.	Squeezing the arrow nock	c.	Low
___ 4.	Raised forefinger of bow hand	d.	High
___ 5.	Closing the right eye	e.	Arrow falling off the bow hand
___ 6.	Creeping		
___ 7.	Peeking		
___ 8.	Moving the bow hand toward the target		
___ 9.	Jerking the drawing hand away from the face		
___10.	Bow grip elbow bent too much		
___11.	Arrow nocked less than 90 degrees between the arrow and string.		
___12.	Dropping the bow arm		
___13.	A high elbow with the drawing arm		

INDEPENDENT SKILL ASSIGNMENT

Instructional cues:

1. Check your shooting form errors before shooting.
2. Make your corrections after each arrow is shot.
3. Don't overcompensate for a shooting error.

Partner skills:	*Error*	*Cause*
1. Shoot six arrows at 20 yards		
Arrow #1	_____	_____
#2	_____	_____
#3	_____	_____
#4	_____	_____
#5	_____	_____
#6	_____	_____
2. Shoot six arrows at 30 yards		
Arrow #1	_____	_____
#2	_____	_____
#3	_____	_____
#4	_____	_____
#5	_____	_____
#6	_____	_____

3. Shoot six arrows at 40 yards
   Arrow #1   _____   _____
         #2   _____   _____
         #3   _____   _____
         #4   _____   _____
         #5   _____   _____
         #6   _____   _____

COLLEGE

SCHOOL: University of Illinois, Chicago Circle
                   Chicago, Illinois
FACILITATOR: Marian E. Kneer

Activity: Co-ed basketball

Objectives:

1. The learner will be able to perform with good form basic basketball handling, passing, dribbling, driving and shooting skills as evidenced by his or her ability to complete pertinent tasks.
2. The learner will possess sufficient knowledge to teach basketball rules, techniques, and strategy as evidenced by playing performance and written tests.
3. The learner will be able to coach and officiate basketball at a minimal level of ability if he or she so desires, as evidenced by the playing performance and written tests of those coached.
4. The learner will be able to structure a basketball learning experience to meet the needs of future students as evidenced by pertinent projects.
5. The learner will be able to analyze the various basketball skills and prescribe corrections as evidenced by instructor and peer assessments.
6. The learner will be able to pursue personal basketball goals.
7. The learner will experience joy in performing and learning as evidenced by observation of class behavior and personal assessments.

Process:

This course will be taught basically on an individualized basis. Students will be diagnosed initially and will determine their objectives. Students may pursue their course objectives essentially at their own pace and through a variety of learning experiences which they can select.

Pace:

Each class will have a few structured experiences in which the entire class will be requested to participate. Most of the time, the student may select the skills and experience which he/she wishes to develop as well as the process by which to learn.

Learning Resources:

Instructor	Transparencies
Colleagues	Tasks
Books	Video tape
Loop films	Charts
Recorded tapes	Movies

Learning Environment:

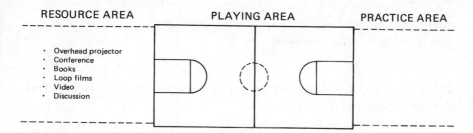

RESOURCE AREA   PLAYING AREA   PRACTICE AREA

- Overhead projector
- Conference
- Books
- Loop films
- Video
- Discussion

Class Procedures:

Lesson 1   Students will be oriented to the course, diagnosed as to their knowledge and skill, decide on goals for course

Lesson 2–20 Students will decide their learning experiences with the assistance of the instructor. Students will sign up for group skill practices, play, coaching, and officiating experiences.

Evaluation:

Assessment will be a continuous process and will be engaged in whenever the student is ready.

Grades will be determined on the basis of goal achievement of the learner. Each student will decide what his or her goals for the class will be after diagnosis. The instructor will discuss and approve these plans. Each plan must include the following:

75% attendance or approved alternatives

Evidence of knowledge of rules and strategy

Teaching experience: 1 large group, 2 small group, 3 individual

In addition, students will select appropriate learning tasks. Grades will be based upon the following contract or task totals:

A = 65+ points
B = 58+
C = 50+
D = 42+

TASK-CONTRACT #12 OFFENSIVE PATTERNS
(4 points)

Student _____Starting date _____

Do not attempt this contract until you complete #9.
List learning aids that you need.

Perform each task as proposed in the program below and place a check next to the task when completed.

	Attempted	Completed
A. *Single Post* 　1. Read page 51 in *Women's Basketball* by Athletic Institute.		
2. Secure four teammates and practice setting up the single post for 5 minutes.		
3. Play 10–15 minutes using the single post exclusively.		
B. *Tandem or Double Post* 　1. Read about either one of these offenses.		
2. Secure four teammates and practice one of these two offenses for 5 minutes.		
3. Play 10–15 minutes using your choice of one of these two offensives.		
C. *Pattern Observation* Arrange to have observation by instructor, by classmate working on coaching or video-taping of your group using one of these offensive patterns. Observers must sign below if they observed at least two successful executions of the pattern. (Successful means that a shot was attempted from the pattern.)		

Task completion testimonial _____

Completion date _____

TASK-CONTRACT #15 DEFENSE
(2 points)

Student _____Starting date _____

List learning aids that you need.

Perform each task as proposed in the program below and place a check next to the task when completed.

Man-to-man	Attempted	Completed
1. Read pages 58, 59, and 61 in *Women's Basketball* by Athletic Institute.		
2. Play 10 minutes of man-to-man defense in a practice game.		
3. Obtain an observer of your play for 5 minutes. Have the following points checked: a. Defensive stance, knees flexed, balance		
b. Use of sliding steps		
c. Loose guarding below dribble complete		
d. In closely after dribble complete		
e. Sag when ball is thrown		
f. Play in front of man in close to goal		
4. Play 10 minutes of man-to-man defense and limit "man" to 3 points.		

Task completion testimonial _____
(Opponent in man-to-man and observer)

Completion date _____

TASK-CONTRACT #20 COACHING (out of class)
(4 points)

Student _____ Starting date _____

List learning aids that you need.

Perform each task as proposed in the program below and place a check next to the task when completed.

	Attempted	Completed
A. *Background* Read pages 226–32 in Elbert and Cheatum, *Five Player Basketball*.		
B. *Teaching* 1. Get team to play: a. One offensive play in a game.		
b. One defensive play in a game.		
2. Help at least one team member to improve the following skills: a. Screening		
b. Pick		
C. *Game Management* a. Arrange for substitutes in 5 games.		1 2 3 4 5
b. Arrange for timeouts in 5 games.		1 2 3 4 5
c. Arrange for defensive plans in 5 games.		1 2 3 4 5

D. *Record*
 Your team must win at least 40% of its games.
 Record scores below:
 	
     Game one _____
     Game two _____
     Game three _____
     Game four _____
     Game five _____		

Comments:

Task completion testimonial _____
(Team member)

Completion date _____

COLLEGE

SCHOOL: University of Illinois, Chicago Circle
                 Chicago, Illinois
FACILITATOR: Marian E. Kneer

Activity: Theory course in Instructional Techniques in Physical Education

Objectives:

PE 278, Instructional Techniques, is designed to assist you to learn how to teach Physical Education. The process of teaching should be based on proven techniques which result in learning. It is the instructor's philosophy that if learning does not take place, it is the responsibility of the teacher, *not* the student. Research in learning theory indicates that learning is a "change in behavior" and that such a change results when two situations occur:

1.   The student is motivated—that is, some internal idea, need, emotion, or organic state prompts action.
2.   The learner is active.

The instructor desires that the students have a major voice in the content and conduct of the course. This is of paramount importance if condition number 1 above is to occur. Therefore, the following objectives are proposed:

1.   Students will be able to diagnose their weaknesses, determine their needs, set their goals, and develop a plan for goal attainment in PE 278 as evidenced by their assessment, plans, and by the kind, quality, and quantity of learning experiences that they select.
2.   Students will be able to utilize a variety of teaching methods and solve problems in teaching various forms of sport activities as evidenced by discussion, actions, and projects.
3.   Students will be able to develop solutions to their problems as evidenced by their contracts as well as by the nature of their class work.
4.   Students will be able to determine the content and appropriate progression of various forms of sport activities as evidenced by their written work and class work.
5.   The teacher will learn more about "student-centered" teaching as evidenced by his/her willingness to listen and to be flexible.
6.   The teacher will be sensitive to the needs and interests of the student as evidenced by his/her teaching behavior and interaction with students.

Course Content:

Activities and information related to the teaching of sports will be based on stated needs of the students. Examples of possible topics are as follows:

Learning process	Lesson planning
Communication	Teaching strategies:
Progression and unit planning	command
Motor learning techniques:	class-centered
knowledge of results	self-contained
feedback, practice conditions,	interaction—small group, partner
mental practice	independent
Concept teaching	discovery—problem-solving,
Conditioning techniques	guided discovery, creative
Human Relations	Coaching
Interaction analysis	Motivation—discipline
Class management	

Course Development:

The course will be based on the individual student appraisal, goals, and plans.

Course Procedures:

1. Students will be attired in apparel during lab sessions which will not harm the floor or themselves and which will provide freedom of movement and a minimum of fellow student distractions.

2. Regular attendance is encouraged and recommended, since emphasis will be on learning through involvement. If the course is not stimulating, the student should arrange an appraisal of the content and conduct of the student goals and plans.

3. The learner is responsible for the planning and conduct of the learning experiences.

4. The teacher is responsible for the motivation, facilitation, and enablement of the student learning experiences.

5. Grades will be based on the quantity of points gained from student selected contract values.

Process:

This course will be conducted with a variety of teaching methods: lecture, command, interaction, self-contained, independent, guided discovery, problem-solving, and creative. The course conduct is always open to modification by students and the instructor urges that inconsistent and ineffective methods be called to the attention of the instructor so that more congruent methods can be selected. Individualization techniques will be used as the delivery system to achieve the goals of this course. Specifically the components of the process will be as follows:

Diagnosis: Each student will be given learning experiences to help determine his or her goals for this course. In addition, the instructor will provide some tasks to further diagnose the student's knowledge and skill in Instructional Techniques.

Week 1   Orientation, Objectives
Human relations, Communication, Interaction analysis

Week 2   Students to take the POI (personal orientation inventory)
Class Management

Prescription: Each student will have an individual conference with the instructor to decide appropriate learning experiences and to agree upon learning goals.

Guidance: Each student will be involved in learning experiences to permit self-learning to flourish. The instructor will facilitate and guide the learning experiences. Tentative plans are as follows:

Week 3   Writing objectives progressions
Unit plans and lesson plans

Week 4   Teaching strategies
Lab: Instructor demonstration of teaching strategies to accommodate learning needs

Week 5   Techniques for teaching
Lab: Micro teaching—emphasis on techniques for teaching

Week 6   Quiz
Lab: Student practice of teaching strategies

Week 7   Task construction
Lab: Tricks of trade—Kneer

Week 8   Conceptual learning
Individualization
Media/Coaching

Week 9   Motivation
Discipline

Week 10   No school (holiday)
Lab: Teaching an unfamiliar skill

Evaluation: Students will demonstrate their learning through written work, demonstrations, projects, and commitment to operationalize plans as required in task-contracts.

Week 11   Final exam
All contracts due.

Grades:

Learning experiences are provided through task-contracts. Each task-contract is designed to help students achieve their goals and the course objectives. Each contract is assigned varying point values. Students may select task-contracts that they believe will assist them most to acquire knowledge and skill in Instructional Techniques. The students are *encouraged* to shape *their own* experiences and propose task-contracts to the instructor that may be more meaningful to them.

Conditions:

All students must:

1. Complete contracts 1–5.
2. Complete task-contracts totaling as follows for earning grades:
   A = 100 +
   B = 90–99
   C = 80–89
   D = 70–79

Instructor must:

1. Reject, for resubmission, contracts that fail to meet stated terminal objectives.
2. Reward exceptional performance with additional points.
3. Penalize rejected contracts.

Learning Laboratory:

The learning activities will be carried on in a variety of places. The initial meeting room will be used most often as a meeting place for lectures, discussion and as a center for resources. However, students may pursue their work at home, in the library, gymnasium or any other place that may provide meaningful and appropriate learning experiences to assist the students to meet their goals for this course.

PE 278 INSTRUCTIONAL TECHNIQUES
Assessment and Prescription Form

Name _____Instructor _____

Summary of Accomplishment

_____Planned Points   Requirements: ___1. Orientation
___2. Theoretical
     considerations
___3. Unknown skill
___4. Motor learning
___5. Teaching behaviors
___6. Practical ideas
___7. Self-awareness

_____Grade

Diagnosis	Beginning	Some work	No further work
Writing Objectives			
Communication			
Self-awareness			
Teaching Interaction			
Motor Learning Techniques			
Teaching Behaviors			
Planning			
Environmental Management			
Student Management			

Comments:

Prescription:

Using the test results, students are to cross off skills which they can perform or in which they have mastery, knowledge, and skill. (Use a series of vertical lines.) Draw a diagonal line through tasks listed below which are to be pursued as learning goals. Draw a diagonal line from the opposite direction when the task has been completed. (This should form an X.) *Each task or contract listed below has a corresponding task sheet to assist you to acquire that knowledge and/or skill.* Place the task sheet in your folder as a reference or when completed.

Orientation R* 1	*Theoretical* R 2 *Considerations*	*Unknown Skill* R 3
Goals Diagnosis 3 points	Objectives Readings 3 points	Video-taping Lab 7 points
Motor Learning R 4	*Teaching* R 5 *Behaviors*	*Practical Ideas* R 6
Lecture Text: Robb Quiz/Lab 5–10 points	Lecture Text: Heitmann, Kneer Lab/paper 5–10 points	Tricks of trade Text: Walker 5–10 points
Self-awareness 7	*Interaction* 8 *Analysis*	*Teaching* 9 *Experiences*
Personal orientation inventory Values 5 points	Lecture Practice 5 points	Lesson plans and agendas Teaching 5–10 points
Readings 10	*Unit Plan–Class* 11	*Unit Plan–* 12 *Individual*
Selective articles or chapters from reading list 1 point each	Sport of choice Follows outline 10 points	Sport of choice Follows outline and individualized instruction procedures 10 points

*Required.

Transactions 13 *Construction* 6 Task sheets 10 points	*Class Management* 14 Micro and macro assignments 3 points	*Attendance* 15 Extra credit for attendance in connection with planned contract 1 point each
Media 16 Produce media to support teaching 2–5 points	*Workshop/* 17 *Conference* Attend and write up 2 pts. per hour	*Final Exam* 18 Covers lectures and readings (R) 15–25 points
Motivation 19 Lecture Strategy 5 points	*Discipline* 20 Lecture Practice 3 points	*Coaching* 21 Lecture Practice 5 points
Student Proposal 22 _____Points	*Instructor* 23 *Proposal* _____Points	*Extra* 24 _____Points

ORIENTATION
(3 points)

Name _____ Starting date _____

Behavioral Objective: All of the students will understand the class procedures and objectives.
All of the students will be able to identify needs and plan a meaningful program.

	Attempted	Completed
A. *Input*: 1. Listen to lecture by instructor.		
2. Read: *The New Learning Model in Physical Education.* Collection of articles from *JOHPER*, September, 1971. *The Five Traditional Objectives of P.E.* Collection of articles from *JOHPER*, June, 1970. *Traditional Methodology: Prospects for Change.* Shirl Hoffman, *Quest*, January, 1971. *Performance-Based Instruction, Today's Education*, 1972.		
3. Browse through the three textbooks. Pay particular attention to the section noted in the reading list. This should help you think in terms of your needs, understanding, etc.		
4. Talk to a former student in PE 281 or a student teacher to get a feeling of appropriateness of their preparation for teaching. Compare with your competencies.		

	Attempted	Completed

B. *Practice*:
  1. *Self-appraisal*
    Write out *for yourself only* answers to the following questions:
    Who am I? How do I look? How do I want to look?
    What are my fears? What can I do about them?
    What do I need: physically, emotionally, professionally?
    Where do I stand in relation to my confidence as a future teacher?		

2. *Needs*
    What kind of teaching has been best for me? Can I teach like that? What do I need to know?
    What do I value in teaching? Achievement? Friends? Students? Pleasure? Autonomy?
    Can I make lesson plans? Unit plans?
    What should Physical Education be trying to do for you in your opinion? How well do you know how to do it?
    What do you believe about coercion?
    What kind of a person can best operate in a democracy? Why?
    What worries you the most in anticipating teaching?
    Why? What worries you the least? Why?
    What are you going to do about your needs?		

C. *Assessment*:
  The student will be able to:
  1. Complete the Diagnosis section on the Assessment Sheet.		

2. Plan prescription with assistance from instructor.		

TASK-CONTRACT #4 MOTOR LEARNING
(5–10 Points)

Student _____ Starting date _____

Behavioral Objective: All of the students will be able to utilize motor learning knowledge as evidenced by their teaching and/or quiz results.

	Attempted	Completed
A. *Input*: (#2 Required) 1. Listen to lecture by instructor.		
2. Read: Robb, *Motor Skill Acquisition.*		
B. *Practice*: 1. Practice application of these techniques with classmates: mental practice, practice schedules, knowledge of results, manual assistance, whole-part-whole, part-whole.		
*2. Draw up a 5-minute lesson plan or agenda and execute in lab based on an assigned motor learning technique (further instructions will be given). Lesson plan or agenda must follow prescribed format and show provision for technique.		
C. *Assessment*: The student will be able to demonstrate knowledge of motor learning techniques by: 1. Answering 70% of the questions correctly on a quiz based on Robb.		
2. Teaching a 5-minute lesson to peers utilizing a selected motor-learning technique, and having the students learn.		
Comments:		

Task completion testimonial:
  1. Attach quiz.
  2. Attach lesson plan and evaluation.

*Required. This contract is worth 5 points without C2, 10 points with C2.

Appendixes

Included in this section are Input and Practice experiences referred to in Chapter 9.

NEUMANN PHYSICAL EDUCATION
LIKE/DISLIKE INVENTORY*

Likes

Directions: Listed below are aspects of a physical education class that students like. How do you think that high school students would rank these items? Place a (1) by the aspect that you think they like most, a (2) by the next most liked, and so on until you reach the final item which would be ranked (15).

_____Praise or recognition for achievement

_____Responsibilities you had

_____The activity itself

_____Good personal relationship with teacher

_____Teacher's manner of teaching

_____Good personal relationships with classmates

_____Level of personal skill achieved

_____Amount of basic knowledge and understanding you attained

_____Method of grading

_____Policies and routines

_____Good basis for out-of-school activities

_____Feeling of accomplishment

_____Adequate safety precautions

_____Challenge

_____Amount of activity in class

Dislikes

Directions: Listed below are aspects of a physical education class that students *dislike*. How do you think that high school students would rank these items? Place a (1) by the aspect that you think that they most dislike, a (2) by the next most disliked, and so on until you reach the final item which would be ranked (15).

_____Lack of praise or recognition

_____Lack of responsibilities

_____The activity itself

_____Poor personal relationships with teacher

_____Lack of personal skill achieved

_____Amount of activity (too little or too much)

_____Teacher's manner of teaching

_____Inadequate safety measures

_____Little basic knowledge and understanding of the activity attained

_____Method of grading

_____Policies and routines

_____No relationship to out-of-school activities

_____No feeling of accomplishment

_____Poor personal relationship with classmates

_____No challenge

*Study conducted by Anna Neumann, University of Illinois, Chicago Circle, Master's thesis at George Williams College.

COMPARISON OF TEACHERS' PERCEPTION
WITH STUDENT PERCEPTIONS
OF STUDENTS' LIKES AND DISLIKES
FOR PHYSICAL EDUCATION

Listed below are the rankings given for "liked" items and "disliked" items. Place your ranking in the appropriate column and compare your perception with those reported in the study.

Like			Dislike		
Student Ranking	Item	Your Ranking	Student Ranking	Item	Your Ranking
1.	Activity itself		1.	Teaching manner	
2.	Relation with classmates		2.	Activity itself	
3.	Amount of activity		3.	Amount of activity	
4.	Challenge		4.	Grading	
5.	Teaching manner		5.	No feeling of accomplishment	
6.	Relation with Teacher		6.	Policies	
7.	Feeling of accomplishment		7.	Relation with teacher	
8.	Skill		8.	Little knowledge	
9.	Knowledge		9.	Lack of skill	
10.	Out-of-school Activity		10.	No challenge	

	Like			Dislike	
Student Ranking	Item	Your Ranking	Student Ranking	Item	Your Ranking
11.	Praise		11.	No out-of-school activity	
12.	Grading		12.	Relation with classmates	
13.	Responsibilities		13.	Praise	
14.	Policies		14.	No responsibilities	
15.	Safety		15.	Safety	

A VALUES EXERCISE

*Lost at Sea**

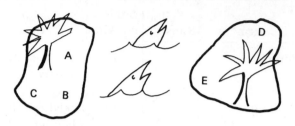

Once upon a time there was a plane crash. The crash separated the people on two islands. "A" was the lover of "D." She missed "D" so much that she finally tried to obtain the assistance of the other two survivors on her island. She asked "B" to help her get to "D." "B" said he was too busy trying to build a radio to signal for help. "C" said, "I'll help you if you will favor me." Seeing no other way, "A" complied. Thereupon "C" built a raft and took "A" to "D." "D" at first was overjoyed until he became suspicious of "C's" motives. "A" explained the bargain. "D" became very angry and abandoned "A." "E" comforted "A" and won her love.

Directions: List the letter of the person you can most identify with or admire in rank order below in Column A. Descriptions of these personalities are given in Column B. (inverted)

Column A	Column B
1.	A. Loyal, affectionate
2.	B. Futurist, creative
3.	C. Opportunist
4.	D. Egotist, moralist
5.	E. Humanist, realist

*There are many versions of this story. The original was attributed to the David Frost Show.

CHALLENGE TASK

This game is designed to help you understand about motivation. *Directions*: Select a task below. You must spend five minutes pursuing the task even if you are successful prior to the completion of the five minutes.

Task	Reward
Shoot layup shots from a stationary position under the basket on your dominant-hand side.	None
Make at least five out of ten free-throw tries	Candy bar
Stand in the middle of the floor and make at least one long shot.	Twenty-five cents

Questions:

1. Which task did you pick? Why? If there are others in your group, find out their reasons.
2. Would changing the rewards change your selection? Why?

Glossary

BEHAVIORAL OBJECTIVES The specification of an observable measurable behavior which verifies learning resulting from the educative process.

CREATIVE TRANSACTION. A practice experience that permits the learner complete freedom to reach a learning objective.

DELIVERY SYSTEM. Multi-media resource alternatives designed to give information in multiple ways to match the learning modes and needs of learners.

DISCOVERY TRANSACTION. A practice experience that generated out of the student's inquiry desires.

FACILITATOR. A person responsible for fostering learning environments which will enable students to participate in learning programs to maximize the attainment of their desired goals.

FORMATIVE EVALUATION. Evaluation incorporated in the transactions to measure the degree of mastery of small segments of the learning program for the purpose of identifying inhibiting or facilitating learning factors.

GLOBAL GOAL.   General purpose of the course or unit of instruction.

GUIDED DISCOVERY TRANSACTION.   A practice experience by which the discovery of the intended end product is guided by cue questions offered by the facilitator or incorporated into the transaction.

INDEPENDENT PROGRAM.   Complete learning packet such as programmed instruction which permits the learner to proceed independently of the teacher's surveillance.

INDIVIDUALIZED INSTRUCTION.   Instruction based on a functional theory of learning which provides delivery systems, transactions, and terminal objectives consistent with the needs, abilities, and interest of each learner.

INPUT.   Information needed to help the learner grasp the idea, framework or information needed to direct the acquisition of new knowledge or skill.

INSTRUCTIONAL OBJECTIVE.   Aim or intention that specifies how the facilitator will reach the desired outcome.

INTERACTION TRANSACTION.   A practice experience that permits instruction, or evaluation with peers or other persons.

LARGE-GROUP INSTRUCTION.   Skill or knowledge instruction given simultaneously to many students. This type of instruction should require little student-to-student or student-to-teacher interaction for understanding or performing.

LEARNER OBJECTIVE.   Behavior desired by the learner after instruction.

LEARNING MODULE.   Small learning segment, individually prescribed, which specifies a learning objective, delivery system and transaction options, and terminal behavioral objectives.

LEARNING PROGRAM.   The bridge between learner objectives and terminal objectives, consisting of input and practice alternatives.

LESSON AGENDAS.   Designation of the sequence of activities available during each instructional session to accommodate the varied needs of students.

PRACTICE.   Involvement in tasks or transactions designed to fix the learning.

PROBLEM-SOLVING TRANSACTION.   A practice experience that encourages the student to seek out the answers to predetermined cognitive or psychomotor problems, generally relying upon synthesizing of previous knowledge that the learner possesses.

SELF-CONTAINED TRANSACTION.   An experience that permits the learner to practice the skill or activity on his own.

SMALL-GROUP INSTRUCTION.   Skill or knowledge instruction which requires student-to-student or teacher ⟵⟶ student interaction for clarity of information or procedure, social intercourse development, and competition. The group should be small enough to enable all members to have sufficient opportunities to interact verbally or physically to have their needs fulfilled.

SUMMATIVE EVALUATION.   A general assessment of the degree of mastery of the intended objectives at the conclusion of instruction, for the purpose of grading, certifying, ranking, predicting future success, and/or evaluating the unit.

TERMINAL BEHAVIORAL OBJECTIVE.   An aim that specifies the degree of proficiency to be attained for successful mastery of the intended behavior.

TRANSACTION.   Experiences stating conditions for practice, feedback cues, and alternatives of choice that are congruent with the learner's needs.

UNIT PLANS.   Static learning conditions which specify objectives, subject matter, learning sequence, evaluation, and operational procedure for a unit of instruction.

Index